SHREE SWAMI SAMARTH
AKKALKOT MAHARAJ

(AS THE ETERNAL SAGE)

SHREE SWAMI SAMARTH AKKALKOT MAHARAJ

(AS THE ETERNAL SAGE)

Edited & Revised
by
Dr. V.R. PRABHU

JAICO PUBLISHING HOUSE

Mumbai Delhi Bangalore Kolkata
Hyderabad Chennai Ahmedabad Bhopal

Published by Jaico Publishing House
121 Mahatma Gandhi Road
Mumbai - 400 001
jaicopub@vsnl.com
www.jaicobooks.com

© Dr. V.R. Prabhu

SHREE SWAMI SAMARTH AKKALKOT MAHARAJ
(AS THE ETERNAL SAGE)
ISBN 81-7224-591-2

First Jaico Impression: 1997
Third Jaico Impression: 2007

Printed by
Sanman & Co.
113, Shivshakti Indl. Estate, Marol Naka
Andheri (E), Mumbai - 400 059.

FOREWORD

by Param Poojya
P. B. (Nana) Paranjpe

Whenever Dharma has been threatened in Bharatvarsha, God has come in the form of an Avataar, everytime to save each and every devotee and protect them. It is for this purpose that Sri Swami Samarth Akkalkot Maharaj manifested Himself. He is the most famous Datta Avataar in the Sri Datta Sampradaya, therefore, however much one may write about Him, it will be inadequate to express His magnificence and glory.

On April 3rd, 1878, He completed His mission on earth and took Mahasamadhi. Even though He is no longer in bodily manifestation, He still guides His true devotees and manifests Himself even now.

Through this English biography of Sri Swami Samarth, people all over the world will come to know of His divine work and by practising His sacred precepts, they will be able to achieve the purpose of life viz., to attain Moksha. This is my deep conviction.

Yours in the service of Sri Swami Samarth,
Pandurang Balkrishna (Nana) Paranjpe

284, "KUBER"
Lonavala, Dist. Pune 410 401
Maharashtra. India

7.9.96

INDEX

Swami leaves Mangalvedha - Earn
merit first - Swami goes to Solapur -
Mahatma or Mad man?

Chapter 5
Sri Swami Samarth at Akkalkot -
Auliya's Test - All kinds of devotees -
No distinction - Some miracles of
Akkalkot Maharaj - Are Miracles
necessary? - Feeding the multitude -
Averting Death - Feeding fire with
water - Restoring Eyesight - Look for
animals - The loving Mother - Greed
and its control - Tasty chilly - Who
can defy Scientific progress?

Chapter 6
Raja Dhiraja Yogiraj Akkalkot Swami
Maharaj - Emperor of the Soul - Gift
of an Heir - Humanity and Piousness
attracts Blessings - Pomp and Glory
gets short shrift - Saints not
recognised - HE knows what is best -
Come...come...come - His Creation -
Fixing a Royal Alliance - Crossing the
Ocean of Samsara - Kaal Buva -
Footprints engraved - Con man -
What a Yogi ! - Divine Grace -
Vedantic States & Intellect -
Wavering Faith - Feeding 1000
Brahmins - Arrogance cured - Time
has not come - Ineffective Hair -
Sceptical mind - True Healer -
Making of an Ustaad

Chapter 7
Swami Samarth, the Sadguru -
Swamiji's Spiritual Heirs - Gupta

Shishya - Sri Ramakrishna Paramhamsa - Sri Shirdi Sai Baba - Vasudevanand Saraswati - Sri Krishna Saraswati - Sri Namdev Maharaj - Vithal Swami - Bidkar Maharaj - Bramhanistha Wamanbuva - Balappa Maharaj - Tat Maharaj - Gondavlekar Maharaj - Anandnath Maharaj - Anand Bharathi - Peer Saheb - Swami Soota - Gopal Buva - Sitaram Maharaj - Shankaracharya of Sankeshwar Peetha - Swami Swaroopananda - Pawas Vishnudas Mahurkar

Chapter 8
The Blessed ones:

Cholappa - Sunderabai - Thakurdas - Raje Rayan - Moreshwar Joshi - Abaji Ramdasi - Govindji & Khanoji - Bapu Kulkarni - Narendra Sawkar - Radha - Sayyed - Nana Rekhi Joshi - Gajanan Borkar - Tatya Puranik - Srinivas Kadgaonkar - Umabai Raste

Chapter 9
Mahaniryan

Approaching Departure - The Sun sets - Samadhi Muth - Resurrection of Swami Samarth

Chapter 10

Swami Samarth's manifestation even now - Devotees' experience - Memories and anecdotes

PREFACE

OM SHRI GANESHAYA NAMAH

Mere words cannot adequately express the glory and the magnificence of an avataar. Who knows their origin? Who can authoritatively say what the purpose for their manifestation is?

This difficult task was attempted in the first edition of the biography of Sri Akkalkot Swami, also known as Sri Swami Samarth, in English, by Mr. Karandikar and Mr. K.V.R. Rao, both now deceased*. They did a very good job, considering the difficulty in writing about an avataar of the magnificence and immensity of Sri Akkalkot Swami. This first edition was responsible for triggering my interest in the spiritual world and acquiring knowledge about Indian philosophy. Many of the questions, that a "sadhaka" faces, were answered in a comprehensive yet succinct manner, throughout the delineation of the manifestation of Sri Akkalkot Swami. I owe a great deal to both the authors.

The first edition was sold out within a short time. There has been persistent demand for reprinting the biography. It was thought that we could take advantage of this opportunity, and rewrite the biography. This edition has been rewritten, keeping in mind the fact that many of our readers may not

---

* They were helped by Mr.S.R.Tikekar, Mr.D.M.Pandit & Mr.B.N.Sibal. The main source books in Marathi were written by Mr. V.K.Phadke & Mr. B.N.Mokashi.

know Sanskrit, nor be able to read Devanagari script, especially children of devotees who have grown up abroad, or have been educated in the English medium in school.

The delineation has also been altered to present the 'life' of Sri Swami Samarth, in a much smoother fashion. The flow of the narrative is also historically more accurate. New material has been added on the life of Sri Krishna Saraswati, who was the "first generation" disciple of Sri Akkalkot Maharaj. An entirely new biography of Sri Namdev Maharaj, who was the chief disciple of Sri Krishna Saraswati, has also been incorporated.

Apart from these additions, an effort has been made to explain the spiritual significance of some of the events that took place, which may seem inexplicable to our mundane mind. The concept of OMNISCIENCE and "Gupta Shishya" has also been explored. An English translation of "Nana" Paranjpe's discourse has been included. Pointers have been given on how to recognise a "guru."

Poojya Nana Paranjpe, the publisher of the first edition, recounted to us the miraculous way in which assistance and money would always turn up, whether in the building of our Muth in Apta or in publishing the first edition of the biography of Sri Akkalkot Swami. In the present venture too, the guiding hand of Sri Swami Samarth was experienced throughout. HE removed all obstacles and ensured successful completion.

A British secretary agreed to type the manuscript, in spite of the pressure of work in her regular job. In response to my plea, she also used to type the manuscript at home, in spite of being a mother with demanding children; and she did all this work FREE. May Mary Mouldes always enjoy Maharaj's grace and blessings, for typing half the manuscript.

In order to expedite the publication of this much awaited second edition, it was decided to send the balance manuscript to Mr. A.B.Borkar, Life Trustee of our trust in Bombay, who arranged for it to be typed. Since I was residing in London at that time, the manuscript had to be sent from London to Bombay and back again, I was worried about its safe delivery and return in the normal course. By the grace of Sri Swami Samarth, relatives, whether flying to Bombay or returning to London, came forward to carry the manuscripts! And their travel plans would materialise, as soon as it was time for the manuscript or typed copy to be sent or returned, without a single day being lost!

The direct experience of Swamiji's grace by devotees continues, some of these later experiences have been incorporated. While the previous work has been rigorously edited and some parts abridged, my contribution is very limited.

The author of the first edition wrote "If this book can awaken interest to the divine mystery of Sri Swami Samarth, HE HIMSELF would help and guide them further. HE is the ever existing divinity responding readily to the call of the earnest and yearning seekers. The Master will reveal HIMSELF, as HE has been doing to so many people so far. The Master is not far off, HE is in our own heart: HE is the transcendental and immanent reality of this universe. May HIS grace be showered on all! It is hoped that this edition will help the readers experience the supreme Grace and blessings of Sri Swami Samarth, that many readers of the first edition have had.

I have endeavoured to present this revised edition in a compact yet more informative way. All errors are solely my responsibility and readers may forgive me for them. Isaac Newton said that he could see further, because he stood on the shoulders of the great scientists before him. Similarly no credit accrues to me as I could rely on the works of spiritual giants, a few of whom are listed in the bibliography.

My deepest respect and thanks to "Nana" Paranjpe who has been the spiritual moving force behind this revision. The efforts of Mr. Swapan Dey and Mr. Borkar can never be adequately expressed in words.

May the blessings of SRI SWAMI SAMARTH be on all of us!!

Dr.V.R.Prabhu (Editor)
Sri Swami Samarth Vishwa Kalyan Kendra
Apta Phata
Panvel, Maharashtra
India

22/8/96

CHAPTER 1

Introduction

We live in a spiritually dark age, where extra-ordinary greed for power and money reigns supreme. The social responsibilities are forgotten and qualities like compassion, caring and sharing have become mere words in the dictionary.

Greed and Selfishness are honoured by the new philosophy of "Market driven economy" and massive social suffering is being unleashed on people all over the world. Traditions and cultures which made men and women behave like "human beings" have all been discarded in the name of "rational thinking" and self interest.

For most people born and bred in this *age of science*, the knowledge our ancestors had is fit only for libraries, where research scholars could write exotic theses and get Ph. D's -- knowledge of the past is considered to be of no value for coping with the problems of the present.

According to such rationale or "scientific" people, our ancestors could not help being backward - they did not have technology. Their pre-occupation with religion was one of the many signs of under-development. In India, we still see thousands of apparently sane men and women subjecting themselves to utterly meaningless restrictions like tormenting themselves by celibacy and fasting, wasting time on pilgrimages, fantastic rituals, repetitive prayers and so on - in this enlightened age! All for nothing, all out of ignorance and stupidity; none of it to be taken seriously today - they are ignorant, backward looking *fundamentalists.* They are turning their backs on reality! It is still permissible to refer to God sometimes, although every educated person knew there was no God! Our ancestors did not know about evolution and so they invented these rituals and myths.

E. F. Schumacher, who studied Gandhi's work and presented it in "SMALL IS BEAUTIFUL", writes "the result of the last 300 years is that Western man is rich in means and poor in ethos. The hierarchy of his knowledge is lopsided and decapitated; his will is paralysed because he has lost the grounds on which to base a hierarchy of values. What are his highest values? Modern society prides itself on *pluralism,* which means that things which are 'good' in themselves *as ends rather than "means to an end."* Not only are power and wealth treated as good in themselves *provided that they are mine* and not somebody else's but also knowledge for its own sake, speed of movement, rapidity of change, quantity of education, number of hospitals, are treated as good. In truth none of these *sacred cows is a genuine end,* they are all means to an end[1].

He quotes: Etienne Gilson who writes "a world which has lost (the Christian) god cannot but resemble a world which had not yet found him" - it is a relapse into mythology, like blind Evolution, Orthogenesis etc.

---

[1] E.F.Schumacher, "A guide For The Perplexed", Pp. 10-11

3

It is important for us to realise that mankind is doomed to live more and more under the spell of a new scientific, social and political mythology" unless we relentlessly exorcise these befuddled notions whose influence on modern life is becoming appalling...".

When there are so many modern gods, all competing with one another and claiming first priority and there is no supreme God, no supreme value, no supreme good, society cannot but drift into chaos.

The modern world is full of people whom Gilson describes as *pseudo-agnostic who combine scientific knowledge and social generosity with a complete lack of philosophical culture.* The modern world tends to be sceptical about everything that -- demands man's higher faculties and wisdom, but it is not sceptical about "scepticism," which demands hardly any intellect!

The pathways produced by modem materialistic science leave all the questions that really matter, unanswered. They do not show a way to a possible answer. They deny the validity of the question!

Questions like *what am I to do with my life?* is today answered in an individualistic, *selfish way - make yourself as comfortable as possible.* Mankind were after all only animals!!

Paramahamsa Yogananda writes, (about science)[2], "In her (nature's) domain, she is eternal and inexhaustible; future scientists can do no more than probe one aspect after another of her varied infinitude. Science thus remains in a perpetual flux, unable to reach finality; fit indeed to discover the laws of an "already existing" and functioning cosmos, but powerless to detect the Law Framer and Sole Operator. The majestic manifestations of gravity and electricity have become known, but what gravitation and electricity "are", no mortal knows."

He further quotes Marconi, the great inventor, who said "The inability of science to solve life is absolute. The mystery of life is certainly the most persistent problem ever placed before the thought of man. This fact would be truly frightening were it not for faith."

Traditional wisdom had a reassuringly plain answer - move higher, develop your highest faculties, gain knowledge of God. Unselfishness was considered the highest value and working for the greatest happiness of the greatest number, the highest principle.

Human Birth - An Opportunity

The human race has been in a continuing process of spiritual evolution from the beginning of creation. Human beings occupy the supreme position in the entire creation, because they alone have been gifted with intellect, the power of discrimination and

---

[2] "Autobiography of a Yogi" by Paramhansa Yogananda, Jaico

reasoning, which faculty has been denied to the other species, sentient or insentient.

Human birth is the most precious and sacred opportunity for spiritual evolution and self-realisation. One should realise this and strive to use this life to release oneself from the cycle of birth and death. If we miss this opportunity what guarantee is there that we may get another human birth? We might slide down and be born as a subhuman species in the next birth and be doomed to the unending misery of repeated births and deaths.

Utilising the faculty of discrimination, one should discover and become aware of one's inner divinity. GOD has created us in HIS own image as our scriptures proclaim: *Jivo brahmaiva naparaha* - the Jiva is not different from Brahman.

We should strive hard for spiritual evolution. When there is earnest effort, Divine Grace would be forthcoming to lead and guide us towards the fulfillment of our life mission. We have to first rid ourselves of the animal traits and cultivate and foster higher human values. Cleansing our mind and heart, we should discharge all our duties in a spirit of dedication and altruism. Cultivating love of God and fellow beings, we should seek *satsanga* (company of saintly people). *Satsanga* works out a spiritual alchemy accelerating our march on the Godward path. This brings God Himself nearer to us. Pray for and attain a guru, for without the grace of God we cannot find a guru. Divine grace comes in the form of a guru - *Gu* means darkness and *ru* means dispeller - thus guru means 'dispeller of darkness'. The guru brings about a complete metamorphosis in the disciple. A guru enlightens the disciple and helps one attain truth and *Jnana.*

The guru is not different from God:

"Gurur Bramha Gurur Vishnu, Gurur devo mahesvara; Gurur sakshat parabramha, Tasmai Shree Gurave Namaha" means: Guru is Bramha, Vishnu and Mahesvara, guru is verily the para Bramha; I bow unto that guru.

Unreserved and wholehearted surrender earns the grace of the guru. Once the guru's grace is earned, blessed indeed is the life of that disciple! Guru is the mother, father, teacher, friend - indeed God for you! The guru leads the disciple from darkness to light, from untruth to truth and from death to immortality. Through the guru only is the attainment of *Moksha** or *Mukti** possible. (See Appendix I on How to identify a Potential Guru).

The chosen land of the Lord

India-is the most blessed land indeed. It is *Punya Bhumi,* the sacred land of the Lord. Through the ages Maharishis have expressed only one desire - if rebirth is necessary, then let it be only in India! India is the only *tapo bhumi*[3]; all other lands are *bhoga bhumis*[4].

---

* Complete cessation of Rebirths and Deaths.
[3] Land where "Tapasya" has been performed for a long time.

The Lord has taken several incarnations in India (known as *maha avatars*) from time to time. Besides the Maha avatars, there have been numerous avatars and a continuous line of Paramahamsas, mahapurushas (Supermen of God), saints and *yogis* keeping the spiritual torch continuously alight in India. (The saint is not different from God: *Bramha vid Bramhaiv bhavati* - the one who has intuited Bramha becomes Bramha himself.)

Indeed after Pope Paul VI returned from his visit to India in 1965, in his X'mas message he said "India is not Catholic, but what a country, what opening of the spirit....... We saw in the crowds a humanity of great nobility....... They were not all Christians, but they were profoundly spiritual and in so many ways so good and winning." This from a person who declared before his trip "Honesty compels us to declare our conviction that there is but one true religion, that is Christianity"!

In India God is worshipped in many forms. There are several sects and various names and forms are attributed to their gods. But there is nothing to be baffled about by this diversity of faith and worship, because all of them have one common basis, the teachings of the Vedas: *Isavasyamidam sarvam* - All this (the world) is indwelt by God. God inheres in everything: in stone, plant, reptile, animal, human beings and in every bit of creation. HE is the inner reality, HE is all pervading. Cultivation of this vision is the sole objective of Indian philosophy and religion.

---

[4] Land of enjoyment and pleasure.

Thus in India, the objects of worship range from stones, trees, rivers, mountains, animals and the sun to idols, saints, deities with form and the formless Brahman. All these have their votaries and all receive devout worship. Paramahamsa Yogananda has related his initial reluctance to bow to a stone at Tarkeshwar shrine with amusing and somewhat painful consequences in His *Autobiography*[5].

When the *tulsi* plant is worshipped, kinship with all plant life is established. Similarly when a cow is worshipped, kinship with all animal life is established. The endeavour is to breakdown egoistic individuality, expand love and attain a cosmic vision of all creation. (India had a holistic approach to our planet and practised ecological principles thousands of years ago!).

Reason for different *Sampradayas*

Ekam sat, taadvipra bahuda vadanti -Truth is one, the realised ones call it by many names.

No two human beings are alike. Each differs from the other in temperament, aptitude, likes and dislikes, each is at different stages of intellectual and spiritual evolution. For this reason the same path or spiritual doctrine may not suit all.

In spiritual endeavours, each aspirant has to choose his or her own path. If this is understood, one will not be perplexed by the multiplicity of gods that are

[5] Ibid Pp 134-139

worshipped in India. This is why various *sampradayas* flourish in India. (The word *sampradaya* means at one and the same time discipline, tradition and cult). All forms and names are different facets of the same supreme being, the form one has chosen for worship being symbolic of the One Absolute Godhead.

All rivers flow into the same ocean and all *sampradayas* lead to that all pervading God.

Various *sampradayas* have evolved in India over the past thousands of years, within the fold of Vedic *Sanatana Dharma* - the Eternal Code. There is no discord between the different *sampradayas*. Each *sampradaya* has its own special feature and each is rich in its own traditions and beliefs. The *Vaishnava* and *Shaiva* sampradaya centre around Lord Vishnu and Lord Shiva respectively. The *Dattatreya sampradaya* is one of the important sampradayas in India, as all faiths are in harmony in this *samprada*. Votaries of Lord Vishnu and Lord Shiva. also revere Lord Dattatreya. All four spiritual disciplines - Bhakti yoga, Raja yoga, Jnana yoga and Karma yoga, are harmoniously blended and integrated in this samprada. This samprada has its origin with the *Datta avatar* - the Avatar of Lord Dattatreya - Guru of all gurus, the Trinity of the Godhead Bramha, Vishnu and Mahesvara in one form. To keep the sampradaya pure and to revitalise it, there are *Avatars** (Manifestations) of Sri Dattatreya from time to time. In the last millennium the *Datta avatars* have

---

* Avatar means coming down - Thus the Lord comes to earth for revitalising and guiding Humanity towards upholding Dharma

been Shripad Sri Vallabhaa, Sri Narasimha Saraswati, Sri Manik Prabhu and Sri Akkalkot Maharaj Swami Samarth. As will be seen later, Swami Samarth is actually Sri Narasimha Saraswati reappearing after a lapse of three centuries.

Lives of Paramahamsas, Mahapurushas and Avadhoots are like icebergs i.e. an iceberg may be as massive as a mountain, but only a tiny portion may be seen above the surface of the ocean. We live on an earthly plane of consciousness which prevents us from comprehending the divine plane and transcendental states of their consciousness. Behind their external worldly manifestation, there is a vast fathomless inner life which we can neither perceive nor understand.

Like an iceberg, only a tiny portion of Sri Swami Samarth's manifestation is known. To try and describe His glory is like attempting to grab the sky in one's hand!

This biography may have captured only an infinitesimal fraction of Sri Swami Samarth's true glory; it is hoped that like a few drops of holy *tirtha*[6] it will provide benefit to readers.

Sri Swami Samarth's Message

Sri Swami Samarth was Gurudev Datta in human form having come to give His divine message for the well

---

[6] Holy water

being of all humanity. Let us reflect upon His message.

1. You reap what you have sown. You cannot shirk off your responsibility for your past Karma[7]. Nevertheless, Divine Grace can ward off some bad effects of your karma. Take to His name, chanting of His name (*japa*) can destroy all sins, it consumes them like fire. Surrender unto Him unreservedly, there is no greater succour for you in this *kaliyuga* than the name of the lord.

2. Cultivate *viveka* (discrimination) and try to recognise the reality i.e. God behind all the pluralistic phenomena in the world. Just as the *param hamsa* (divine swan) separates milk from a mixture of milk and water[8], one should look within oneself and experience the eternal *atma* (spirit), which is the substratum and reality behind all the layers of matter which constitute this ephemeral cosmos.

3. Do not shirk work. Work is the means for both self sustenance and self perfection. Laziness destroys both the body and soul. Whatever work has come to your lot, take it up in all sincerity, devotion and earnestness as worship unto Him. No work is lowly

---

[7] The consequences of all past thoughts, words and actions, good or bad to be reaped in the current life.
[8] The "Param Hamsa" secretes an enzyme which curdles milk and thus seperates it out from from the milk-water mixture.

provided it accords with one's *"Swadharma* "* Efficiency and perfection in work is *Yoga.*

4. Only enunciation of principles or precepts will not help spiritual growth, it is sheer hypocrisy if they are not put into practice. What our *Dharma* requires is *Acharan* (practice or implementation) and *not prachar* (talk or preaching).

5. Seek *satsang,* the company of the pious and saintly people - *darshan* of these holy people sanctifies one.

6. Cultivate selfless devotion. Cultivate humility and egolessness. God loves the humble and pure hearted. God is in all - see God in all. Do not forget that all are alike in the eyes of God - all are His children.

Swami Samarth Assures us

"I am ever alive; I am everywhere, at all times. If you call my name, I shall certainly respond. All are dear to me. Call out *Swami Samarth and* I shall be with you instantly."

---

* Sri Krishna had said "Better one's own duty (work), though defectively performed, than the duty (work) of another, well-performed. One incurs no sin in doing the work ordained by one's own nature" Bhagvad Geeta Ch. 8.47.

For a discussion on "Swadharma" see 'Managerial Effectiveness & Quality of Work Life' by S.K.Chakraborty, Tata McGraw-Hill, 1987, pp137-140.

We have in Sri Swami Samarth the *kalpavriksha* (the wish fulfilling tree), He is the ever responding Almighty, which has been experienced by thousands of devotees in the past, as well as today.

CHAPTER 2

THE DATTATREYA SAMPRADAYA

Sri Dattatreya is a very ancient Avataar, highly venerated through the ages. He has been spoken of very highly in "Jabala Upanishad", "Narada Upanishad", "Yagnavalkya Upanishad" etc., according to Swami Harshananda[9].

The Dattatreya Sampradaya is one of the oldest in India and is the most revered too. It is popular because the welfare of all, whether at the individual or universal level, is the object of this Sampradaya. There is a synthesis of all that is good in Vaishnava and Shaiva Sampradaya (along with the now defunct Bramha Sampradaya). The Dattatreya Sampradaya began with the birth of Lord Dattatreya.

There are several anecdotes concerning Gurudev Datta in the "Mahabharata", "Bhagvatam", "Vishnu Purana" and the "Markandeya Purana".

The story about the origins of Lord Dattatreya is as follows:

After Lord Bramha created the universe, He used to manage its affairs Himself. After some time, as the universe grew in size He requested Lord Vishnu to help in the management of the universe, so that He could continue with the task of creation.

[9] Avadhoot Gita by Swami Harshananda, Advaita Ashrama, 1988.

Lord Vishnu agreed and looked after the task of maintenance. The population of the universe grew and Lord Vishnu realised that unless some reduction were brought about, the available resources would soon be exhausted. Thus He requested Lord Shiva to undertake the task of destruction. Lord Shiva agreed and controlled the task of destruction.

In order to co-ordinate their work they would meet every Thursday. This fact was revealed to the people on earth, in Satya Yuga, by Narada Muni. He told them that if they prayed on Thursday, they would receive the blessings of all three Gods.

The three Gods were pleased at the devotion of the people and gave a boon that they would manifest as Lord Dattatreya, combining in One Form the qualities of all three.

In order to make the boon come true on earth, they needed to take birth in a very pure family. They selected Atri Rishi and his wife Anusuya the semi divine couple as their "parents" for their earthly sojourn. This is how it came about :

There was a *brahmin* who was a leper. His wife was known far and wide for her devotion, steadfastness and chastity. One dark night, while she and her husband were going along a road, the husband's foot accidentally brushed the body of a meditating hermit. The hermit cursed "One who has disturbed my meditation shall die at sunrise tomorrow". The wife was upset and she declared "There shall be no sunrise from tomorrow". Her "shakti" caused these words to come true and the world was filled with darkness and chaos prevailed.

The gods went to Bramha for a solution. He said, "Only one with power of Tapasya can surmount the "shakti" of a chaste woman. Thus the gods sought out Anusuya, the pure and chaste wife of Atri Rishi. They told her the problem and asked for her help. Moved by their pleas, Anusuya approached the Brahmin's wife saying "If you ask the sun to rise again, I shall by my power restore life to your dead husband". The Brahmin's wife agreed and the sun rose and Anusuya kept her word.

The gods were extremely pleased and offered Anusuya a boon. In reply, she asked that "Brahma", "Vishnu" and "Mahesh" be born as her sons - a wish that was granted and Gurudev Datta was born to her later.

When the right day came, the three Gods, Bramha, Vishnu and Mahesh (Shiva) decided to manifest on earth, to fulfill the above boons given to the people and Anusuya. They played the Divine "Leela" as follows:

Following the boon gained by Anusuya, she had grown in spiritual stature and had attained the highest level of spiritual purity. She had no envy or malice and had overwhelming love for all beings. She was the embodiment of chastity and worshipped her husband like a God. This pure woman induced jealousy and envy in others however and the three

Gods decided to prove to these doubting Thomas's how wrong they were.

They transformed themselves into mendicants, approached the hermitage of Atri Rishi and begged for alms. At that time Maharishi Atri was away at the river offering his daily oblations. Anusuya came out and offered food to the three mendicants. They made a strange request; the food be prepared and served to them by Anusuya, in the nude. In the Indian tradition any *atithi* (guest) cannot be turned away, as they are considered to be an aspect of God. Hence, Anusuya was placed in a dilemma. She thought for a while and decided she must agree to the request. As she pondered, she found the solution. If the guest were babies - her babies and she, their mother - Oh yes! She could then feed them naked. Her thoughts - the thoughts of a pure and chaste person - instantly became reality; the elderly guests became babies! When Atri Rishi returned home, to his amazement, he found Anusuya fondling three babies! Anusuya said "These children are the gift of God to us who have been childless so far". Atri Rishi was overjoyed and named them Datta which means "given". At this, the three Gods reverted to their real forms and disclosed the truth. They extolled the power of the chastity and purity of Anusuya which vanquished the combined and colossal power of all three of them. Both Atri Rishi and his wife prayed that they should remain as their sons. They consented and the three Gods merged into one body. This is how Lord Dattatreya incarnated in the world and is known as Gurudev Datta - the Guru of all Gurus.

SRI DATTA PRABHU*, was an incarnation, who came to light the lamp of wisdom among the people. Sri Datta Prabhu is a splendorous form. His face radiates all wisdom and draws us away from the lures of the world. Though He is the supreme Lord of the Universe, yet He is a total ... nd supreme recluse. Though He is a *Parivrajaka*, ever moving from place to place, His favourite abode is the Holy Banyan Tree (Audambar). He has matted hair on his head. He holds the conch in one hand and the Sudarsana Chakra in another hand. His body is ever smeared with holy ashes and He wears tiger-skin for his garment. A cow and four dogs are always with Him as His constant companions. He is an Avadhoot, ever anchored in Spirit, but always over-flowing with compassion for all the beings and the entire creation. His three faces are symbolic of Brahma (the Creator), Vishnu (the Sustainer) and 'Maheshwara (the Purifier) and who absorbs into Himself eventually all creation. Thus, He is the embodiment of the total Godhead. All the aspects of Godhead are fully manifest in Him. His faces and form are ever radiant with peace and divine charm.

The cow which is always near Him represents the Mother Earth and Dharma. The four dogs symbolise the four Vedas - the external repositories of Spiritual Wisdom. His trident indicates that He has transcended the *gunas* which constitute the *Prakriti* the elements and their conglomeration. The Sudarshan Chakra indicates that He is beyond the

---

* Another name of Lord Dattatreya.

Sri Swàmi Samarth Akkalkot Maharaj with His devotees.

Sri Swami Soota, the direct disciple of Akkalkot Swami. (Soota in Sanskrit means 'son'). He was called 'My son' by Akkalkot Swami. Hence the title.

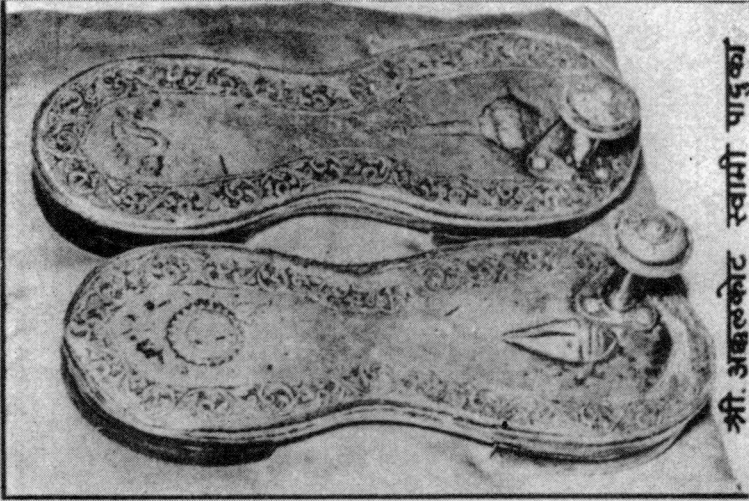

श्री. अक्कलकोट स्वामी पादुका

Sri Akkalkot Swami Padukas.

Sri Krishna Saraswati also known as Kumbhar Swami. He was one of the illustrious disciples of Sri Akkalkot Swami.

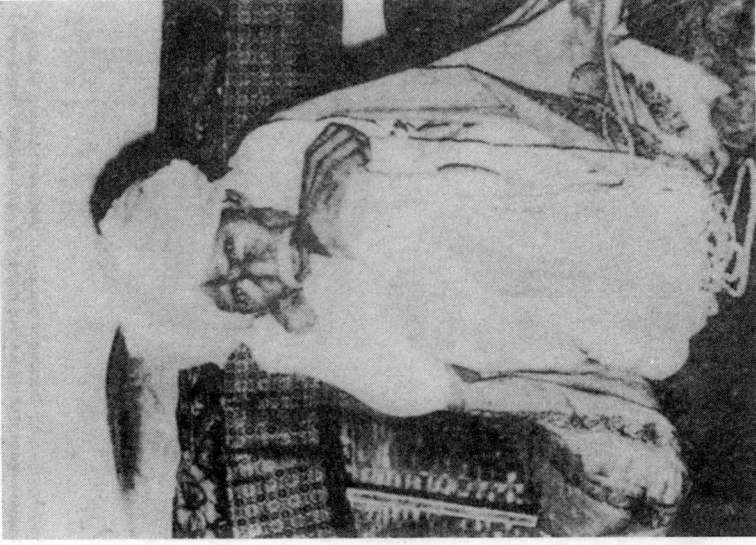

Sri Namdev Maharaj, the illustrious disciple of Sri Krishna Saraswati. This photograph was taken when he was 122 years old.

Sripad Sri Vallabha, the first Datta Avataar in this millennium.

Sri Narasimha Saraswati, the second Datta Avataar in this millennium. He wrote the Gurucharitra which is the prime source of knowledge regarding the Datta Sampradaya and various religious practices to be carried out by devotees.

Sri Swami Samarth Akkalkot Maharaj.

Sri Manik Prabhu who was a Datta Avataar and was in manifestation at the same time as Sri Akkalkot Swami.

This Dattatraya idol was given to Swami Niranjan Raghunath by Lord Dattatraya Himself. This idol has only one face and two arms unlike the conventional representation of Lord Dattatraya as having three heads and six arms. This idol is installed in Kashi (Varanasi).

bounds of time i.e., the past, present and future and His holding the Chakra means He is the controller of time. The conch represents the *Pranava* 'AUM', resounding in the hearts of all of us, as well as in the heart of the universe. It is the *Nada*, the sound manifestation of the Spirit. It is the life-principle in us and in the cosmos. The *bhasma* (the ashes smeared over His body) indicates His *vairagya* (dispassion) as well as His purity. Ashes indicate the evanescent nature of all created objects and the ultimate state of all matter.

Although Datta Prabhu is ever satiated, yet He always carries a begging-bowl so as to teach us the lesson that we will have to share our wealth and food with others. If we feed any, it is like feeding (or offering food to) God. It is Narayana-Seva. The Japa-mala He wears is to remind us that our primary *dharma*, i.e. our duty is chanting of the sacred name of the Lord (Japa) and doing of meditation (Dhyana), meditation on the Feet of the Lord, and that our redemption depends upon this discipline alone. Japa provides the foothold and Dhyana provides the scaffolding for us to be able to ascend to the Divine Awareness and Supernal Consciousness. If we but attach ourselves to His Lotus Feet, we are sure to be ferried across the ocean of samsara safely and can for ever be secure and happy.

Dattatreya had taught Avadhuta Gita to Lord Subrahmanya (Lord Kartikeya). Avadhuta Gita contains the highest Vedantic (Advaitic) philosophy, and is a most valuable treatise expounding the science and non-duality of the spirit. it propounds Advaita - the absolute oneness of the Jiva, ISWARA AND PRAKRITI (the individual-being, God and Nature).

God's creation itself was His Guru - He had twenty-four gurus: the Earth, the Sky, the Sun, the Moon etc. Unlike Vishnu "Avataars" like Sri Ram or Krishna, who came to defeat evil and restore "*Dharma*" on earth, Lord Dattatreya is the only "Avataar" to have manifested solely for the redemption of mankind.

HE is the Guru of all Gurus on earth. Among His 1001 notable disciples in primeval eras were Sahastrarjun, Kartavirya, Bhargava, Parshuram, Yadu, Alark, Ayu and Prahlad. The last millenium saw the manifestation of Four Datta Avataars - the most recent and magnificent being Sri Swami Samarth Akkalkot Maharaj, who is the subject of this book.

While Lord Dattatreya is often represented with 3 heads and 6 hands, great saints like Sri Niranjan Swami who have had "darshan" of Dattaguru, i.e. the direct vision of Lord Dattatreya, have affirmed the fact that HE has one head and two arms and hands. In fact he has installed an idol of Sri Dattaguru at Kashi, having one head and two arms (see plate -). At Nasik, too, the Dattatreya temple has an idol with one head and two arms. The traditional representation may be meant for illiterate disciples who would otherwise not realise the presence of three Gods in one body.

Lord Dattatreya gave Astanga Yoga to the world thousands of years ago. Patanjali codified this knowledge in "Sootra" Form. Gurudev Datta taught the Astanga Yoga i.e. the eight fold path of yoga comprising:

(1) Yama - Moral discipline

(2) Niyama - Spiritual discipline

(3) Asana - posture

(4) Pranayama - breath control

(5) Prayahara - withdrawal of senses from sense objects

(6) Dharana - concentration

(7) Dhyana - meditation and

(8) Samadhi - the transcendental or super conscious state of being one with God.

Yoga is described as "Chitta Vritti Nirodhah" i.e. cessation of all modifications of the mind. We are slaves of Chitta Vrittis i.e. all types of thought eruptions and movements of the mind.

These Vrittis are represented by the five states of human consciousness, as under :

(1) Pramana - the state of mind in which we see things as they are.

(2) Viparyasa - the state of mind in which our vision is perverted like seeing silver in nacre shell or a snake instead of a rope.

(3) Vikalpa - is the state of mind in which we see a thing which does not exist e.g. mirage in the desert.

(4) Nidra - is the state of mind in deep sleep.

(5) Smriti - is the state of mind in which we remember or recollect things from the past.

When the human mind through the practise of yoga can transcend all 5 states, then mastery of the mind is attained. A purified mind is a tranquil mind, free from thought agitations and disturbances and remains absorbed in the self. In this peace and quiet, when the consciousness is centred in the self, the supreme state of Self-Realisation or "kaivalya" is attained.

For a proper practise of yoga *Viveka* (discrimination) and *Vairagya* (detachment) are necessary. An average person obsessed with the problems of life and living would find it difficult to practise yoga without Viveka and Vairagya. Renunciation is advocated; mental as well as physical renunciation. The renunciation should primarily be of one's ego reflected in external action and thoughts.

The principle tenets of the Dattatreya Sampradaya, are briefly as follows :

1. Everyone should know oneself first and should know one's own reality, which is but God.

2. One should realise the relationship between God, man and creation - the underlying kinship, unity and oneness of these three entities, the truth is all beings in essence are Bramhan. Bramhan is the immanent and all pervading reality in all matter - it is the origin, the support and sustenance of all.

3. To attain this vision and discern this truth, one should conquer one's ego through yoga and renunciation.

4. Guru's grace is indispensable. One has to surrender oneself totally and unreservedly at the feet of the guru. His grace awakens *jnana* by which we can recognise the Reality of Bramhan, which is the real self of all. Apart from this, disciples should:

   a) Have purity of thought, word and deed.

   b) Do *nama smaran* - remembrance of the Lords name and meditation on it.

   c) Have compassion and love for all beings.

   d) Render selfless service at the feet of the guru and surrender completely.

The Datta Avatars - Incarnations of Sri Gurudev Dutta

While Lord Dattatraya was the primal manifestation in the "Datta Sampradaya", the incarnations in this millennium were:

(1) Sripad Sri Vallabhaa

(2) Sri Narasimha Saraswati

(3) Sri Manik Prabhu and

(4) Sri Swami Samarth Akkalkot Maharaj.

These divine incarnations by their spiritual splendour and eminence, as well as by their guidance to the people have made India a glorious place. A brief account of the first three incarnations will be given in this chapter. The Divine life of Sri Swami Samarth, which is the main theme of this book, will follow from the next chapter onwards.

SRIPAD SRI VALLABHAA

Sripad Sri Vallabhaa was born in a brahmin family at Pithapur, probably a town near Kakinada, in Andhra Pradesh. On the new Moon day (Amavasya) a religious ceremony was being performed. While the rituals were on, a Sanyasi (renunciant) arrived and asked for food. Although the meals were ready, tradition demanded that the priests be fed first. Thus Sumata (Shripad's mother) was in a dilemma, because she felt that the Sanyasi was no ordinary being. Trusting her intuition, she broke with tradition and rushed to serve the *Sanyasi*. Lo! the renunciant was Lord Dattatraya Himself. Gurudev Dutta said "Mother, I am very pleased, you may ask any boon". Sumata was overjoyed and in ecstasy she spoke "Maharaj! You addressed me as *mother*, please let your word be converted to reality". The Lord replied *Tatastu* (so be it) and vanished.

In course of time, she became a mother of Shripad Sri Vallabhaa, the incarnation of Lord Dattatraya. There was no birth in the normal sense, the Lord just manifested Himself as a child in the house. One of the 1001 names of the Lord[10] is *Om Ayoni Sambhavaya Namah* signifying that HE is not born through the *Yoni* or vagina, HE manifests at HIS sweet will! Great saints like Ramakrishna Paramahamsa also known to have come down to earth in this way, as did Jesus Christ.

Shripad had mastered all the Vedic scriptures by the age of sixteen and shone like a *Jnana Bhaskar*. The significance of this can be understood by the fact that it takes at least 48 years for an average person to master all the Vedas and Vedic Scriptures!

When Shripad attained marriageable age, he was asked his opinion, "All women in this world are like my mother. I am married to *Sanyasa* (renunciation). My mission is to give initiation and guidance to *sadhus* (holy men)". Speaking thus he sought permission from his parents to become a *sanyasi* and to leave

---

[10] Sahasra Namavali

the house. The parents were loathe to forgo such a son. Apart from this the other two children were dumb, deaf and blind. If Shripad forsook them, who would look after his brothers in their old age?

Shripad understood their anxiety. He called His brothers to Him, cast a divine glance full of benevolence and love and Lo! Their physical and mental disabilities suddenly disappeared. They instantly gained knowledge of all Vedas and scriptures and exhibited normal health. Everybody was overjoyed. Shripad blessed them with a healthy and prosperous life and enjoined upon them to serve their parents with love and dedication and assured them of Moksha, in that birth itself.

Guru Shripad then decided to set out on his mission and bade good-bye to His parents. To His mother He said "I have to redeem this world from the ignorance in which it is immersed. I have to instill faith in God and reveal the Divine Glory to the people." He consoled His relatives with kindly words and loving advice and went out of sight in a trice! By His yogic power He travelled at the speed of light and reached Benaras instantly. He then went to Badrikashram,, worshipped the deity there and moved to the south of India. Subsequently He visited Gokarn-Mahabaleshwar in Western India, remained there for three years and finally settled down at Kurvapur.

One day a widow, Ambika came to the river to end her life due to her unbearable poverty. Miraculously Shripad Sri Vallabhaa also came there at that moment. Ambika's heart thrilled at the Divine radiance emanating from the face and body of the saint. She ran to Him and fell at His feet and said plaintively "Guru Maharaj! At least in my next life let me have a son like you." Shri Guru blessed her and said "Worship Lord Shiva every day early in the morning and your desire will be fulfilled." It was perhaps Shri Guru's own *Sankalpa* to reincarnate again as Sri Narasimha Saraswati. Therefore he had pre-arranged this *Leela* so as to meet and bless His next incarnation's mother-to-be!

Shripad Sri Vallabhaa disappeared one day after entering the Ganges river. Though he is physically no more, His presence and grace are ever felt by devotees. His divine spirit is ever manifest as the following event shows: An apparently normal delivery in a maternity hospital, in Bombay, went awry - the new-born was not breathing in spite of all emergency procedures. His grandmother, an ardent devotee of Sri Swami Samarth phoned "Nana* " and told him the situation. "Nana" prayed to Swami Samarth who told him the child would be fine. She asked the doctors and nurses to continue attempts to resuscitate the child, which they did four hours after birth they gave up all hope and asked the family to remove the child's body. Again the grandmother phoned Nana and was told by him that the child would be fine and under no circumstances was it to be moved from the hospital. He also advised her to read the *Guru Charitra* - one of the most sacred books of the Datta

---

* means grandfather

Sampradaya, recounting the miracles performed by *Datta Avatars* Sripad Sri Vallabhaa and Sri Narasimha Saraswati. When the grandmother reached the section about Shripad Sri Vallabhaa* , indeed as she enunciated His name, the child started bawling! The total time the child was supposedly "dead" was almost 8 hours!

The doctors and nurses were profusely apologetic and stated that they had never witnessed anything like this in their entire professional career. Most of them became devotees of Sripad Sri Vallabhaa and Swami Samarth from that day. The child is now over ten years old and is named "Shripad" in commemoration of the miracle. Over a dozen people apart from the doctors and nurses involved have knowledge of this miracle.

SRI NARASIMHA SARASWATI

Narahari was born in Karanja a town near Akola (Central India). The year of His manifestation is not known exactly and scholars are not unanimous about the date.

From His birth, instead of crying as infants normally do, He uttered only the sacred word "OM". This caused wonder in the whole town and people rushed to see this wonder child. Other than saying "OM" the child appeared to be dumb and the parents were upset. Narahari tried to convey by signs and gestures

---

* In the "Guru Charitra", chapters V, VIII & IX deal with Shri Sri Vallabhaa's life and miracles.

that He would be normal after His thread ceremony. The parents could not understand these signs and gestures and continued to feel anxious. To convince and comfort them Narahari once took an iron article and turned it into gold by merely touching it!

When he was seven years old, the thread ceremony was performed and a miracle happened! To the wonder of all the priests and people assembled there, Narahari chanted *Vedic Mantras*. The formerly "dumb" child chanted them perfectly[+]. The parents were overjoyed but their joy did not last. According to tradition after the thread ceremony, the initiate is a *Sanyasi* and has to beg alms from his mother and leave for pilgrimage afterwards. Thus the mother asked Him to beg alms and young Narahari, taking it as her *Adesha* (command) sought permissionto take *Sanyasa*, renounce worldly life and leave for pilgrimage. The mother bewailed her plight and pleaded with him to give up such an idea.

Narahari placed His hand on her forehead and revived her memory of her previous life as Ambika and the boon she had obtained from Shripad Sri Vallabhaa. The mother nevertheless pleaded with Him to stay for a few more years. Sri Guru agreed and stayed till two brothers were born. Thereafter He left to fulfill His mission which was to revive faith and uplift the people morally and spiritually.

[+] Vedic Mantras are complex sounds and very difficult for a lay person to pronounce properly.

Narahari went to Benaras and came in contact with Sri Krishna Saraswati. After bathing in the Ganga, He used to worship *Kashi Visweshwar*, (Lord Shiva) thrice daily. Sri Krishna Saraswati was much impressed by this Divine boy and readily agreed to His request for initiation into *Sanyasa*. The *Sanyasa Ashrama* is normally the 4th stage after *Bramhacharya* (student), *Grihasthashrama* (Family life), *Vana Prastha* (Retirement to Forest). Only highly spiritually evolved people can proceed directly to *Sanyasa*, as it requires strong detachment, great self-restraint and strong will-power.

One may wonder why an *Avatar* requires initiation from a Guru. Lord Krishna had also been initiated by Sandipani, who was HIS Guru. The purpose of this Divine *Leela* (drama) is to demonstrate the need for a Guru. They are knowledge incarnate and complete in all respects. Since they manifest when the world is steeped in ignorance, they undergo these rituals to set an example for us to emulate. By asking Sri Krishna Saraswati to be His Guru the importance of having a Guru was emphasized.

After His Initiation ceremony He was renamed Sri Narasimha Saraswati. To his new name, a swami adds a word that indicates his connection with one of the ten sub-divisions of the Swami order. Some of these are:

Saraswati (wisdom of nature), *Giri* (mountain), *Sagar* (sea), *Bharati* (land), *Puri* (tract), *Aranya* (forest), and *Tirth* (place of pilgrimage).

Sri Narasimha Saraswati conducted a number of *Jnana Yagnas** for enlightening the common people. Hundreds of people were guided on the spiritual path by Him.

From Benaras He went to Badrikashram with his disciples. Then moving from place to place for the welfare of the common people, he arrived at Ganga Sagar, near Calcutta. Some twenty years passed by in this way. Sri Narasimha Saraswati reappeared at His home to the wonder and joy of his family and town people. He blessed them all.

In the *Guru Charitra** the miracles performed by Him are described. These miracles were meant to increase faith among people in a higher power and start them on the path of seeking spiritual truth.

Sri Narasimha Saraswati then went to Trimbakeshwar, Nasik and Parli Vaijnath. At Parli Vaijnath He did *Tapasya* for one year and remained in seclusion. Afterwards He went to Audumbar and Amarapur near the confluence of the rivers Krishna and the Panchganga, At Amarapur He stayed for 12 years. This place-was called "Narsimhawadi" and later "Narsoba Wadi" by His affectionate disciples and devotees. From Amarapur He went to Ganagapur and remained there for 24 years. During his stay there many astonishing incidents and miracles took place.

---

* Discourses and sermons
* An English translation by the late Mr. K.V.R.Rao is available.

Sri Narasimha Saraswati was now considered a *Siddha Purusha* (perfect, almost Godlike being) with Divine powers of healing physical ailments and alleviating worries of His devotees. Hindus and Muslims used to come to Him considering Him their *Sadguru* (greatest Guru).

He went to Trimbakeshwar for the *Simhastak* and afterwards returned to Ganagapur. He knew that His mission was coming to an end. One day He bade good-bye to the people of Ganagapur and with His 7 select disciples went to the confluence of the Bhima and Amraja rivers and stood for a while under an *Aswatha* tree. He stated "worship this tree and practise penance, your wish will be fulfilled and your life will be blessed". He announced His departure from this world and His disciples were plunged in grief.

A float was prepared on banana leaves and was adorned with flowers. This float was then placed in the river and Sri Guru sat on it. All the disciples offered worship although their hearts were weighed down by grief. Sri Guru cheered them up and told then He was going to *Kadali-vana* (grove of banana trees), near Sri Sailam* and upon reaching there, as a mark of His safe arrival, clusters of flowers would come back floating "against" the current. After He left on the float to the wonder and joy of His disciples, clusters of flowers did come against the current. The disciples took them as *Prasad* (sacred gift) extolling the omnipotence of Sri Narasimha Saraswati.

---

* One of the 12 "Jyotir Linga" is located here and is called "Mallikarjuna".

His mission was especially to guide the Brahmins (priestly class), who are supposed to be the custodians of *Sanatana Dharma* and put them on the right path and spread the *Dharma* of the *Datta Sampradaya*. As a result of His teaching the "Sampradaya" has taken deep roots all over what are now the states of Maharashtra and Karnataka, especially at a time when Islam had tried to destroy Hindu faith and religion through savage repression.

When people were in utter despair, Sri Narasimha Saraswati brought about a religious and spiritual renaissance and restored their morale. The places where He stayed, have become centres of pilgrimage viz., Narsobawadi, Audumbar and Ganagapur[#] . Ganagapur is believed to be the *Dattasthan* - abode of Lord Dattatraya. There is a holy hillock of *Vibhuti* (holy ash) from which devotees pick up the ash as (Prasad) to take home. This hillock has not been depleted, even though devotees have been taking away Vibhuti for centuries.

The atmosphere in all three pilgrimage centres is sublime and devotees feel peaceful and spiritually uplifted. Miracles take place at Ganagapur specially, even now.

The message of Sri Narasimha Saraswati is summarised as under:

(1) In our short fleeting span of human life, we should attempt to realise God through devotion.

[#] See Appendix for their location.

(2) Use *Buddhi* (intellect) and *Viveka* (discrimination) to purify your minds.

(3) Never think of hurting others in thought, word, or deed.

(4) Consider yourself blessed, if you secure the grace of a Guru.

(5) Strive to realise God who is inhering in your own heart.

SRI MANIK PRABHU (1817 - 1865 AD)

Maniknagar is a town named after this *Dattavatar*, in Gulbarga district of' Karnataka.

Sri Manik Prabhu was born in 1817 on *Datta Jayanti* i.e. the same lunar day that Gurudev Datta manifested HIMSELF on earth for our welfare and spiritual evolution. This day is very auspicious and of great spiritual significance.

Sri Manik Prabhu had two brothers and their father died when they were quite young. They were brought up by their maternal uncle. As a child, Manik evinced no interest at all in study and was disliked by His uncle because of this. He used to run away to the nearby forests and search parties had to be sent to locate Him. He was at ease with the animals and snakes, in the forest and this often surprised the search parties and His uncle. By the age of 16, Manik had no education at all. One day His uncle scolded Him severely with the result that Manik decided to leave the house. He threw away His clothes, wore only a loin-cloth and walked out saying "the Supreme Protector of the world who sustains and nourishes all of creation is my succour. All is HIS will."

He began to wander in the dense forests of Manthal. He would sometimes come on a horse, talk and mix with the villagers and disappear as suddenly as he came.

In the meanwhile Manik had performed many miracles and had become well known.

Manik's mother was pining to see Him and went to Manthal in search but could not find Him. She was exhausted and disappointed, when Manik suddenly appeared and there was an emotional reunion of mother with son. As the news spread, people began to flock for the *Darshan* of Manik. Manthal village turned into a holy pilgrimage centre.

Like previous *Avatars* Manik too was a celibate and would beg and go from place to place. His face radiated Divine lustre and every word He spoke was full of spiritual significance and wisdom. He knew Marathi., Urdu, Persian and Kannada. In debates, He was like Adi Shankara[11] and used to convince even the most learned people with His irrefutable logic and supreme wisdom.

---

[11] The first Shankaracharya, who set up 4 Muths at Puri, Sringeri, Dwarka and Badri.

As His fame spread, devotees came from all over India for solution of their spiritual and secular problems. He would relieve their distress and fulfill their desires through miracles which caused astonishment. He used to say "It is all God's grace" and never claimed credit for Himself. Wealth came to Him unsought, but Sri Manik Prabhu distributed it freely among the needy. Nothing was hoarded or kept for personal use. Sri Manik Prabhu went all over the country and visited holy places, making them holier by His visit. Wherever He went, that place became a place of pilgrimage. He was considered a "Yogi Raj Maharaj" - emperor among Yogis, There was a regal splendour about Him, with abundant wealth and riches.

Once when He was going from Bidar to Kalyani in a palanquin, they came across dense impenetrable jungle. Sri Manik Prabhu decided to stay at a spot where two brooks met and Maniknagar was born. In due course it became a pilgrimage centre and began to flourish. All relatives, friends and devotees came and settled down there.

Thousands of visitors from all castes and communities including Christians, Muslims and Parsees thronged for His Darshan. Many of them chose to reside there in the company of the great saint. Practising Bhakti Yoga (path of devotion) they achieved peace and happiness. Even highway robbers from the nearby forests came for His Darshan and were turned into pious devotees.

Scholars and Pundits, artists, singers, dancers, *Kirtankars* and Sadhus displayed their art, knowledge and skills before their Guru, He used to bestow gifts as token of His grace. This heavenly *Darbar* used to last for 3 - 7 days at a time. Everyone had access to their Guru's *Darbar* and received *Prasad* (sacred food) as Guru's grace. He used to project love which was intensely individual, yet equally universal.

Sri Manik Prabhu had knowledge of all Vedic scriptures and shastras. He was omniscient and could gauge intentions and read thoughts of others. Once meat was offered to Him by some sceptics as food. The meat turned into jasmine flowers to the utter discomfiture of the mischief mongers.

Sri Manik Prabhu used to ask for food[12] from door to door in spite of the fact that there was no dearth of food, clothes or money.

The mission of Sri Manik Prabhu was drawing to a close and He selected a place for His *Samadhi* (final resting place) keeping it secret from His devotees as He did not want to upset them. He made arrangements for the administration of Maniknagar and selected a day for giving up His body.

Before the end He called His nephew Manohar, gave him a sacred cloth and *Japa Mala* (prayer beads). On the 11th lunar day (*Ekadashi*), in 1865 at the age of 48, He entered the place pre-selected for His *Maha-Samadhi*. As bidden by the Master the

---

[12.] This is known as "Madhukari Vritti".

Samadhi entrance was sealed by the disciples. Like Jnaneshwar Maharaj, Sri Manik Prabhu too had *Sanjeevan Samadhi*[13] and by His Yogic power merged himself into the Supreme. This news spread in no time and thousands of devotees, even from far off places of all religions and creeds congregated there to pay their last homage and returned with a heavy heart.

The *Dattatraya Sampradaya* had spread widely due to Sri Manik Prabhu. His mission and message were unique; He composed hundreds of songs in different languages, which are rich in devotion and wisdom and are popular even today. Each composition concludes with the line "Manik Prabhu says ....".

Sri Manik Prabhu was a contemporary of Sadguru Sri Swami Samarth and an admirer of the latter's spiritual eminence and power. It is the same spiritual stream, assuming wider and more magnificent dimensions in the immortal Akkalkot Maharaj.

One need not be surprised at the fact that two incarnations of Lord Dattatraya could be contemporaneous, It is not an uncommon occurrence with *Vishnu Avatars*, Sri Parashurama and Rama, Krishna and Balarama, Buddha and Mahavira being in manifestation at the same time.

What is not possible for the Omnipotent Lord?

---

[13] The body is intact and does not decay, while their Atma is merged with The Supreme.

CHAPTER 3

GLORY OF SRI SWAMI SAMARTH

Lord Dattatraya was an *Avadhoot* as were HIS incarnations Sripad Sri Vallabha Sri Narasimha Saraswati and Sri Swami Samarth. Though they assumed human form and lived in this world, they were beyond both the body and the world. They were beyond the states of life or death, beyond limitations of time and space.

Degenerate humans mostly live a physical existence totally oblivious to their *Atman*. Their understanding of life is faulty and their values are erroneous. They are tyrannised by their senses and their control of senses are imperfect and superficial. Only one who controls one's senses and mind awakens to soul consciousness and can be called a Master.

CHARACTERISTICS OF AN AVADHOOT

An *Avadhoot* has no *Deha Atma Buddhi* i.e. detached from body consciousness or the belief that "I am the body". An *Avadhoot* is established in the Self and the world and surroundings have no importance. HE is not worried whether HE is in a forest or town. HE seldom speaks to others, paying no heed to past, present or future. HE treads on thorns or stones, silent, ever joyous, seeking neither comfort nor shelter. HE does not seek food or a place to sleep, because an *Avadhoot* requires neither. HE is beyond the bondage of *Sansara* (mundane world) and revels in *Sat - Chit - Ananda*.

The "Avadhoot Gita" says that the syllable "A' of "*Avadhoot*" indicates He is free from expectations. The next syllable "VA" indicates He has uprooted all desires. His speech is purifying. The syllable "DHOO" indicates that His body is smeared with ash, but His mind is pure and healthy. He no longer needs to practise meditation. The syllable "TA" indicates He is absorbed in "Bramhan". His life is pure from its beginning, through its middle and to its end.

Thus the *Avadhoot* state of Sri Swami Samarth is beyond our comprehension. Others had to feed Him like a child - whether it was crude stale bread or a royal feast made no difference to Him. A palace or stony ground, a cushioned sofa or hard rock, made no difference to Him. Others had to bathe Him too - sometimes He would have a bath twice a day or He would go without a bath for days on end. He was ever asleep to the needs of the body.

Sometimes He was approachable and His love was like a mother's love. At other times He was remote and stern. Sometimes He would talk sweetly, at other times He would keep quiet for days on end. Such behaviour is beyond our comprehension because even though He manifests in a body on earth, He is not of it.

One of the 1001 names of Sri Swami Samarth is *Om Atulyaya Namah* - immeasurable - cannot be appraised and therefore non-comprehensible for ordinary human being like us. Other *Mahapurushas* reveal similar behaviour and characteristics. It is mentioned in the Gospel that once Jesus Christ cursed a barren fig tree. When an onlooker asked a disciple why he had done so, the reply was "Become a Christ, then you will know why He did it."

Sri Swami Samarth was above all distinctions of castes, creed or status. All had place at His feet and in His heart. His love was all encompassing, universal. At the same time every individual felt intense love as many devotees can testify even today!

YOGIRAJ SRI SWAMI SAMARTH

Sri Swami Samarth was unsurpassed in His spiritual powers and a supreme *Yogi*. Once, one Baba Sabnis a devotee of Manik Prabhu, saw Swamiji occupy the seat of Sri Manik Prabhu. Sabnis felt annoyed that his Guru's sacred seat was occupied, but Sri Manik Prabhu told Sabnis to fall at the feet of Sri Swami Samarth and seek Him as His Saviour and Sadguru. Sabnis was later directed by Swami Samarth to come to Akkalkot and in due course he became highly evolved spiritually, by His grace and blessings.

Only the Divine can measure the Divine! Sri Manik Prabhu and Sri Swami Samarth were two facets of the same Divinity. Sri Manik Prabhu chose to live in regal splendour like Lord Vishnu while Sri Swami Samarth chose to live like the ascetic Lord Shiva. Sri Swami Samarth was the Supreme Renunciate - an ascetic God, an Avadhoot in the truest sense. He was *Jeevan Mukta* - ever free from the shackles of space and time. He was the supreme example of *Stita Prajnya* - the perfect Sage glorified in the Geeta.

Sri Swami Samarth is Omnipresent - He manifests Himself to devotees, answers their prayers, fulfills their desires and provides them with constant protection. His presence is felt and experienced by devotees even now in all corners of the world. (See chapter X).

Sri Swami Samarth is "Omniscient" - All knowing. There was no necessity for any devotee to express his/her problems or worries. Everyone's mind was an open book to Him, even if they were in far off places. No event ever escaped His cosmic vision.

Ordinary human beings like us cannot even begin to understand what "Omniscience" is. Ordinary Yogis can demonstrate *Asthavadhana* - the capacity to monitor eight simultaneous events. This can be observed in some temples in Andhra Pradesh. The yogi sits in the centre surrounded by eight people in a circle. For 20 minutes each of these 8 people will simultaneously perform certain tasks - one will throw flowers at the yogi's back, another will say certain *Shlokas* erroneously, another may say poems in a certain metre and then switch to another poem in a different metre, another person will state the time at 30 second intervals etc. At the and of 20 minutes the yogi will tell exactly how many flowers were thrown at his back, which *Shloka* was wrongly enunciated, the metre in which various poems were sung, with the correct time intervals when all these activities were done.

More advanced yogis can perform *Shat Vadhana* - the perception of 100 events simultaneously.

Ganpathi Sastry, one of the eminent disciples of Sri Ramanna Maharshi could perform *Sahasra Vadhana* sometimes - simultaneous knowledge of 1000 events! Swami Bramhananda who succeeded Swami Vivekananda, stated that at all times he had knowledge of all the swamis and trainees of the Ramakrishna Order!

If yogis or ascetics can perform these mind-boggling feats; what can we say of the "omniscience" of *Avataars* like Sri Swami Samarth? He is known as *Anant Koti Brahmand Nayak* - the Omnipotent and Omniscient Lord of several millions of universes!

There is nothing beyond His power. He revealed supreme mastery over nature, over all the five elements. He revived the dead. His mere *Sankalpa* was enough to make the impossible possible. His power transcended all human understanding. He is "Omnipotent".

Sri Swami Samarth loved all alike. His was the religion of love. None was beyond the circle of His love. People of all social classes of all religions, of all communities came to Him for solace and peace.

Great saints *Maharishis* Yogis, *Siddhas*, Sannyasis scholars, pandits, professors, doctors, engineers, the poor, the illiterates and the diseased all found shelter at His feet, without the least distinction. No one ever returned disappointed and unfulfilled. His *Darshan* itself filled their hearts with an abundance of peace and happiness. Devotees would feel new caurage, strength and confidence in life. They would feel a sense of fulfillment in life by His mere *Darshan*.

He was like the *Pareez* stone (Philosopher's stone) which transforms base metal into gold. There were countless people who were totally transformed, sinners metamorphosed into saints. While He relieved the physical ailments and solved worldly problems by His grace. He was at the same time putting everyone on the Godward path.

He always taught His devotees that they should try and overcome the twin demons of "ego" and "anger", which tyrannize them without their being aware of it. One's ego estranged one from God, while humility takes one nearer to God. He advised total surrender, selfless love and devotion to the Master, as the best means to the discovery of the "Self". Surrender to the Guru is like passing on the responsibility about oneself into the safe and competent hands of the Master. He will undertake all the responsibility for our welfare here and beyond as well.

Countless were the miracles Sri Swami Samarth performed in the past and even today continues to do, as large number of devotees testify in Chapter X. His miracles are not the result of *Siddhis* attained through *Sadhana* (spiritual discipline). They are innate and natural to Him who is Self Manifest Divinity. They are His very nature.

PURPOSE OF MIRACLES

These miracles had a purpose: They were meant to instill faith in sceptical minds; to restore wavering faith and to proclaim the divine power beyond comprehension of our human senses and mind. Through miracles He saved many devotees, relieved their sufferings and conferred His grace - the ultimate purpose of all of them was the reinforcing of their devotion and faith in Divine powers, taking them on the path to God.

Sri Swami Samarth was Lord Dattatraya in human form, having come to give us guidance and ensuring the welfare and protection of His devotees. Great saints received His guidance and many of His direct disciples rose to olympian spiritual heights and took thousands of people on the path to God. Swami Samarth is called, *Om Devabhrit Gurave Namah* - He is the Divine preceptor and Sadguru of great saints like Shirdi Sai Baba, Gajanan Maharaj of Akola, Sri Krishna Saraswati of Kolhapur, as well as being Upaguru to others. He gave *Darshan* to Ramakrishna Paramahamsa.

Other disciples of Sri Swami Samarth who rose to great spiritual heights were Sri Bidkar Maharaj, Sri Balappa Maharaj, Brahmanista Wamanbuva Bramhachari, Sri Gondavlekar Maharaj, Sri Anand Nath Maharaj, Sri Tat Maharaj, etc.. There were many *Gupta Shishya* (secret disciples) as well. Their biographical details are given in Chapter VII.

THE MYSTERIOUS ORIGIN OF SWAMI SAMARTH

Sri Swami Samarth is *Ayoni Sambhava* - one who manifests of His own will and not through the agency of a woman's womb. He is the reincarnation of Sri Narasimha Saraswati. After spending some time in Kadalivana near Sri Sailya Sri Narasimha Saraswati moved to the Himalayas where He remained in *Samadhi* for over 300 years. A huge ant-hill grew around the body of Sri Narasimha Saraswati and the site completely merged with its environment. Many years later a wood cutter's axe accidentally hit the ant hill and he was aghast to find his axe stained with blood. Curiosity led him to excavate the ant-hill and he was surprised to find a majestic yogi in deep *Samadhi*! The yogi slowly opened His eyes and rose from the ant-hill and looked at the wood cutter who was trembling with fear and remorse. To his great surprise, the yogi beaming with love spoke kindly "My child, do not feel sorry for what has happened. The time has come for me to resume my spiritual mission and reappear in the world[14] - this is the Divine Will."

The 'yogi' was Sri Swami Samarth. The axe wound left a scar on His thigh and was seen by those who attended on Him.

The manifestation of many a *Mahapurusha* in this world has been mysterious. While both Jesus Christ and Sri Ramakrishna Paramahamsa manifested as babies without undergoing "natural" birth, Sri

---

[14] His 'active' phase lasted for 400 years till 1878, in His physical body. Of course, He manifests HIMSELF even now to His devotees.

Sadasivendra Saraswati (the great saint of Nerur, in southern India) first appeared as an adult, out of a mound of mud, on the Cauvery river banks. Who can trace the birth of the birthless?

THE APPEARANCE OF SRI SWAMI SAMARTH

Who can adequately describe the glorious appearance of Sri Swami Samarth? All human faculties fail in this attempt, at best one may give a superficial account. Our mortal eyes can seldom hope to even see His glory - Swami appeared like a glorious sun.

One of His disciples Madhav Shastri describes Him in poetic terms:

> "Birthless and emerging from nowhere,
> Glorious like the sun, extolled by Gods
> Beautiful body with glittering eyes,
> Full of compassion, face like the full moon,
> Long arms reaching below the knee,
> Loin cloth round His waist
> With tender lotus feet......."

His face always radiated bliss, there was a halo behind His lustrous face. There was divine splendour in His appearance. He looked young, even though His first appearance was in an apparently advanced age. There were no wrinkles. He was tall, more than six feet in height. An *Ajana-Bahu*, His long arms extended below His knees. His shoulders were broad. His complexion was wheat coloured. His ears were large, with large thin lobes; like Lord Ganesha. His belly was large. His forehead was broad, His eyebrows grey and His eyes looked as if they were probing one's inner-most soul. There was omniscience in those lustrous eyes and the minds of all were an open book to Him. His appearance was august, majestic and awe-inspiring.

One of his 1001 names is *Om Mahavegaya Namah* - one supremely fast, moving with high speed. While walking His stride was big and fast, so that few could keep pace with him. He looked like a *Purana Purusha* - a *Rishi* from ancient times. There was always a "Tilak" on His forehead and His body would be smeared with sandal paste. He used to wear only a *Kaupin* (cod piece). He had a fine set of teeth and He wore "Tulsi" (necklace) and ear rings inset with gems.

Sri Swami Samarth was an *Avadhoot* - A *Maha Yogi* possessing great spiritual powers. He was always muttering mystic 'Mantras' or something few could understand. He was a *Jnana-Murthi* - exemplar of wisdom and knowledge. He expressed oneness and kinship with all creation. His mere glance could bless, His presence sanctify and His silence a sermon. His touch could trigger spiritual change and transformation would begin.

Other characteristics of an *Avadhoot* were displayed by Swami, queer actions, strange speech so that many thought He was mad. He would often swear at people, but His abuse had the effect of blessing, The vision of *Avadhoots* is on a transcendental plane and on cosmic scale, whereas we are glued to an earthly plane with mundane vision.

People of all religions - Muslims, Parsees, Christians and Jews used to come for His *Darshan*. He used to visit mosques and dargas, just as He would visit temples and "Muths" (places of spiritual authority). Devotees often found Him in various postures and poses; at times sitting under a tree, lying by the river bank, yet His appearance always commanded respect. Even those who saw Him for the first time, could recognise His towering spiritual stature. While His face was full of compassion, love and kindness, occasionally He also looked like a fierce lion; the *Narasimha* Avatar of Lord Vishnu.

LEELA AVATAR - THE FIRST PHASE

After the emergence of Sri Swami Samarth from the ant-hill, He travelled all over the country. Little is known about His movements, as there was none with Him to record these events. His 'active' manifestation was for 400 years. Whatever is known is based on what He revealed to His earliest disciples. The following incidents over the years, were recorded by His disciples, from His statements: they are not in chronological order.

In the thick forests of the Himalayan foothills, Swami Samarth came upon a Chinese couple who were indulging in sexual foreplay. The couple had come to collect herbs. They saw Him and made fun of Maharaj, as He was wearing only a *Kaupin* (cod piece). Then in spite of His presence, they continued their sexual antics, jeering at Him. Swami Samarth looked sternly at them and they found their sex had changed from male to female and vice versa. Realising that they were in the presence of a great sage, they apologized for their behaviour and were pardoned. They became their normal selves again.

OM AMITA VIKRAMAYA NAMAH[15] (Infinite power and strength)

Swami was sitting under a mango tree when a deer dashed towards Him in panic, seeking protection, Swami Samarth fondled the deer. The hunters who were chasing the deer came and demanded He release it, threatening Him with guns. The hunters found themselves immobilised and their guns inoperative. Wisdom dawned on them that they were stupid to threaten a Divine Personality and apologized for their behaviour. Swami pardoned them and told them to be kind to animals in future.

OM MUKTANAM PARAM AGATAYE NAMAH (Supreme abode of those seeking "Mukti")

On another occasion a pair of deer searching for their young ones, came upon Akkalkot Swami. Sri Swami Samarth said to the female dear "You were a pious lady in your previous birth, but showed disrespect to saints and in consequence you are born thus in this life. You are lucky to have met me, you will be born as a human being in your next life."

---

[15] One of the 1001 names of Sri Swami Samarth

Meanwhile the missing fawn came and there was a joyous reunion.

Wherever He went in the Himalayas, yogis came out of their caves to receive Him with great reverence and respect. They sought His guidance in their spiritual pursuits. He visited almost all the holy places like Badrinath, Kedarnath, Gangotri, Yamnotri, Hardwar and Rishikesh.

After this, He travelled to the east and visited Jagannath Puri. One Alwanibuva with 4 companions from Baroda had come on pilgrimage there. Unfortunately they were laid up with high fever. With nobody to render aid, they lost hope of survival and were praying to be saved. Just then the majestic towering figure of Swami Samarth appeared before them. Like the Divine mother He stroked their bodies and soon their fever subsided. They became well again and they enquired who their benefactor was. Swami Samarth said "Every place in the world is mine, I travel all over but my favourite places are Girnar, Sahyadri and Kashi (Varanasi). I also visit other places, specially Matapur, Karvir, Kuruvpur, Audumbar, Karanja, Narsobawadi and Ganagapur. Alwanibuva immediately prostrated at Maharaj's feet knowing Him to be Sri Narasimha Saraswati. Then Swami distributed *Prasad* to them.

From there, Swami Samarth travelled to Hardwar, on the banks of the Ganga. Here He performed many miracles. The blind got their sight; the deaf their hearing. His Grace alleviated disease of many by His mere glance or touch.

Redemption of a Brahmin

There were two Brahmins who had degenerated into evil ways. One was well built and would bully and harass pilgrims. He approached Swami Samarth too, in his usual arrogant way and asked all sorts of questions. Instead of replying, Swami Samarth asked why he had killed a cow the previous day. The bully had done the foul act in great secrecy and at once realised the spiritual eminence of Swami Samarth. He fell at Swami's feet repenting his evil ways and sobbed in remorse. Swami Samarth went to the place where the dead cow lay. The evil Brahmin washed Akkalkot Maharaj's feet and sprinkled the holy water on the dead cow and a miracle took place. The dead cow got up and went on its way as if nothing had happened. All those present started extolling "Sri Swami Samarth, Jai, Jai, Sri Swami Samarth".

The Brahmin then prayed to Swamiji to visit his house and sanctify it by His grace. Sri Swami went there and in answer to the unasked question said "I am a Yajurvedi Brahmin and my name is Narasimha. My ancestor is the banyan tree and my native place is Dattanagar". Swami then taught the Brahmin some portions of Vedas and told the Brahmin to chant them regularly. He impressed upon him the value of human birth and the obligations and duties of a Brahmin, thus. "A Brahmin has to realise God inhering in his heart. He has to guide all on the pathway to God. He is like an elder brother to all and is responsible for their spiritual welfare. He is their spiritual guardian and sacred duty is assigned to Brahmins by God." The fame of Sri Swami Samarth as an incarnation of Lord Dattatraya spread everywhere.

In Kathiawad and Dwarka

From Hardwar, Sri Swami Samarth went to holy Narayan lake in Kathiawad. As He went to the holy lake for a bath He met some people who regularly harassed pilgrims and extracted money from them. They asked Him to pay money too! Swami refused and they said they would not allow Him to proceed. Swami Samarth rose in the air above their heads and walking in space, alighted near the lake and sat on the bank. The oppressors were trembling in fright and were afraid of being cursed by the *Maha Purush* (Superhuman person). The head priest interceded on their behalf begging that they be forgiven. Swamiji acceded to their request. Worship was offered to Him and there were celebrations in the town. *Bhajans* (songs in praise of the Lord) *Kirtans* (Bhajans interspersed with explanatory discourses) and mass feeding was carried out in honour of Sri Swami Samarth.

One of the townsmen a *Pandit* (scholar) was sceptical, and did not accept the miracle had taken place. Swami Samarth knew his thoughts and asked about his parents. The pandit replied that they had been dead over 35 years. Swami smiled and said

"Go home and see your father rocking your baby's cradle". The pandit emphatically restated that his father was long dead. Maharaj replied "Your father is reborn as a serpent and is rocking the baby's cradle". They went to the pandit's house and a big serpent came out and people wanted to kill it. Swamiji stopped them and lifting the serpent said "You did not show kindness to anyone in your past life. Your selfish attachment is so great that even now you come back to your son. Cast off your attachment and give up your venom!" Swamiji took the serpent to the lake. The serpent went into the lake and then He said "All his sins are now washed away and he will be reborn in a pious yogi's family."

Maharaj disappeared from Narayan lake and emerged in Dwarka. One Bhurya Buva was pining for *Darshan* of Lord Dattatraya. He met Swami there. He had seen Gurudev Datta in his dreams, now he saw HIM in person! He had some spiritual problems and Swami Samarth clearly explained the Upanishadic texts and blessed him by touch. The yogi went into *Samadhi* (transcendental trance) instantly and remained in that ecstatic state for some time. Swamiji also blessed a blind man who regained his sight!

At Girnar and Central India

Sri Swami then went to Girnar via Gautam "Tirth". Girnar (near Junagadh) is considered a very sacred place as Gurudev Datta is believed to visit and reside there. Many great sages have done their *Tapasya* there. Sri Swami Samarth stayed at the *Guru Datta Sikhar* and performed many miracles.

A devotee named Sevadas came for *Darshan*. Swamiji advised him *Chitta Shuddhi* (purification of consciousness) is essential. It is achieved by dedicated action. Duty should be discharged selflessly and as part of worship. Then the 'ego' slowly vanishes, spiritual vision broadens and the mind expands. Then one must surrender to God or a Guru. *Sravana* (listening), *Manana* (reflecting) and *Niddhidhyasana* (contemplation) on spiritual truths is the next step. Thus will erroneous notions and wrong beliefs disappear. Once ignorance is removed *Bramhan* is realised.

Then Swami Samarth gave Sevadas the vision of Lord Dattatraya in Himself!

From Girnar, Swami Samarth emerged in Ambe Jogai (in Maharashtra, in Central India). There Swami mixed freely with villagers and gave spiritual guidance to them and eliminated many bad social practices. Child marriage was common and traditionally the girl's parents received money for their daughter. One 5 year old girl displayed deep devotion to Sri Swami Samarth. Her parents were greedy and were planning to make money by marrying her off. Swami admonished them and made them give up their evil scheme and blessed the girl. Finally, she became a great devotee of Sri Swami Samarth.

At Rameshwaram and South India

Swami then arrived in the South at Rameshwaram, the holy place where Sri Ram made a *Shiva Linga* and consecrated it. Here He performed many miracles relieving the worries of people helping the distressed and blessing all those who sought His *Darshan*. He used to sit in *Turiya*[16] state (the 4th transcendental state), not caring for food, clothes or shelter.

A clerk in the temple office watching Him so utterly lost to the world, realised that He must be great divine person and pressed offerings of food on Him. The clerk who was childless was blessed with a son in due course, by the grace of Swami Samarth.

People started coming for His *Darshan* in large numbers. The lake known as *Koti Tirtha* (literally a place where 10 million sins would be washed away by a dip in it) had greedy and unscrupulous priests, harassing pilgrims demanding money and defiling the sanctity of the lake. Maharaj went there for a bath one day. The priests demanded money. Swamiji refused and told them money should not be charged for a bath in the holy waters provided by God. The dull and stupid priests not realising the spiritual glory of Maharaj did not allow Him to proceed. Maharaj declared "This *Tirth* has lost its sanctity and purificatory power - There's no point in taking a bath now." The priests ignored Him, but Lo! To their surprise, the water turned foul, dirty and worm

---

[16] The other three being 'Jagruti, 'Nidra' and 'Susupti'.

infested. They realised now that this calamity must have occurred due to the "man" they had turned away; He must be a great saint! They deeply repented their affront to Him and searched for Him, to beg His forgiveness. They found Him at the Rameshwar Shrine, near the *Shiva Linga* and fell at His feet. The ever compassionate Swami Samarth forgave them and reminded them of their holy responsibility to the pilgrims which they should discharge with devotion, without monetary considerations.

Swamiji then restored the sanctity of the *Tirth*, which regained its original purifying power.

We cannot recognise Divinity even when it is in front of us! Our mind and eyes are clouded by greed , power, status, etc. This is why the *Avataars* in their Infinite grace perform miracles and *Leelas* to awaken us from *Avidya* (ignorance or wrong knowledge) and *Maya* (illusion).

Shri Maharaj next went to Kanchi, near Madras. There were legal disputes and much hostility between *Shaivites* and *Vaishnavites*, as proof of their rights could not be traced. The *Vaishnavites* approached Sri Swami and prayed for help. He told them to search for the *Sanads* (original documents) in the river. Lo! A big stone was found on which was engraved the original claimant's name. This proof regained the *Vaishnavites* their rights. After this incident the disputes ceased and peace and harmony prevailed.

In Western India

From Kanchi, Swami arrived at Rajoor (Bhir District).

With His arrival spiritual activity started. A large number of people came for His *Darshan*, worshipping Him as an *Avataar* of Gurudev Datta.

A Muth was set up and Swami's holy *Padukas* (footwear) installed for worship. Even now His *Padukas* are well preserved and worshipped reverentially.

After this, Swami Samarth appeared on the banks of the Bhima river near Pandharpur. The river was in high flood at that time. The flood waters were no deterrent to Maharaj and He was seen walking on the waves. Seeing this the people of Pandharpur started extolling Him.

Thus did the first phase of Sri Swami Samarth's *Leelavatar* come to an end.

The various *Leelas* and miracles performed by Sri Swami Samarth were meant to shake us out of our slumber and apathy. They were a declaration of the Supreme Power's descent on Earth so that we can wake up, become aware and seek His grace and blessings.

CHAPTER 4

AT MANGALVEDHA AND OTHER PLACES

Mangalvedha is a town near Pandharpur (in Sholapur district) and is a spiritual centre hallowed by its association with saints like Damajipant, Kanhopatra, Chokhamela, Govindbaba, etc. all of whom hailed from this town. Sri Swami Samarth further heightened its glory by His stay there for 12 years.

From Pandharpur, Sri Swami Samarth came to Mangalvedha in 1838 and stayed till 1850. At first, few had heard of Him and very few recognised Him for the Divine manifestation He was. He stayed near the forest on the outskirts of the town, He did not beg for alms like most renunciants, but ate whatever little food was sometimes offered to Him.

One Balkrishna, instantly recognised His divinity by intuition. He saw Lord Dattatreya in Him and began to serve Him with devotion. His thoughts were always centred on Sri Swami Samarth and He became a spiritual infatuation for him; he was always thirsting to be in His presence and pining for His *Darshan*. By Maharaj's grace he developed spiritually and was called Balkrishna Buva later, in recognition of his saintly qualities. The people of Mangalvedha who had thought that Swamiji was a beggar, did not take long to recognize His spiritual glory.

Dry Cow?

One day, when Swamiji was at the *Samadhi* of Damajipant, a poor Brahmin, Krishnajipant arrived there and on seeing the glorious and divine personality of Maharaj, was wonderstruck. Swamiji did not take any notice of him, being totally absorbed in the "Self". Krishnajipant sat gazing upon the Divine visage, even though the day was through and the sun was about to set. After some time Swamiji slowly opened His eyes and smiled at him. Krishnajipant prayed to Swamiji and invited Him to his house. Pleased by his devotion Swamiji accepted and accompanied Krishnajipant whose joy knew no bounds.

When they reached his house, he asked his wife to offer some milk and fruits, whilst ensuring that Swamiji was comfortably seated. She was embarrassed as there was nothing in the house and she tried to attract her husband's attention by gestures and whispers.

The all-knowing Maharaj knew her predicament and suggested that a little milk from their cow grazing in the yard, would suffice. Stating that the cow was dry, she set out to fetch milk from her neighbour. Stopping her, Swamiji went to the cow and patted her on the back and said "The Brahmin is poor, unless you are gracious and kind to him, how can he look after his family?" He then asked the Brahmin to milk the cow and cook milk bread for Him, saying that he would come later to eat it and went away.

When Krishnaji milked the cow he found milk flowing profusely! The vessel was full in no time! The news of this miracle spread very quickly in the town. The milk bread was prepared and the couple was very happy when Maharaj appeared as promised. Swamiji ate the milk bread with gusto as if it were the tastiest food, reminded all those present of Lord Krishna who had similarly gulped parched rice, offered by his poor friend Sudama.

Mad Beggar!

Basappa, a poor resident of Mangalvedha came upon Swamiji lying on thorny shrubs. Basappa was wonder-struck at the serenity and lustre on His face and wondered who this mystic could be? Instantly Swamiji said "Why do you bother who I am?" From His Omniscience, Basappa realised His divinity and was overwhelmed by devotion. He became one of the most ardent devotees and followed Swamiji everywhere, to the eternal regret of his wife who thought that Swami Samarth was a mad beggar!

Inspite of his wife's disbelief, Basappa did not give up his devotion and attachment to Maharaj for over 2 years. One day Maharaj entered the deep forest and Basappa followed Him though he was very much afraid. In the deep jungle suddenly hundreds of serpents appeared, crawling towards them at great speed. Basappa froze with terror and tried to shield himself behind Swamiji. To his surprise, Maharaj said "Basappa, don't be afraid! Pick up as many serpents as you like and take them home." Basappa was still very frightened and did not understand. Once again Swamiji commanded "Be quick! Pick up as many serpents as you can!" Basappa with total faith in Swamiji, made bold to catch only one small serpent about 1½ times the size of his hand, wrapped it in his shoulder cloth and went home in great fright, as instructed by Swamiji. On his way home, the weight of his "burden" was increasing. When he reached home, he opened the cloth with great trepidation and found a solid 24 carat gold bar in place of the snake! His wife was deeply regretful of the negative thoughts she had entertained about Swami Samarth.

With such incidents, even those who scoffed at Sri Swami Samarth began to realise His spiritual prowess; many turned into His devotees and His name and fame began to spread far and wide.

Dry Well?

Once, during the hot summer, Swamiji entered the house of one Babaji Bhat and asked for cool water. Bhat's wife was thrilled to have Swamiji coming to their house and was rushing to the neighbour's house to get water, as the well in their compound was dry. Swami Samarth started laughing in His characteristic way and said "Why are you going there? Your well itself has sweet and cool water." Saying thus, Swamiji led her to the dry well and as soon as they reached the well, it was full of water, as if Mother Ganga herself had rushed to quench the Master's thirst!

Once a woman came to Swamiji with her son, who had lost his eye sight. She had tried many *Vaidyas* (doctors) for a cure, but to no avail. When she implored Swamiji to bless her child with eye-sight, He plucked the leaves from a nearby tree and rubbed and fastened them on the child's eyes with a bandage. He asked the mother to fast for 3 days, before removing the bandage. She did so and the child regained his lost sight by the grace of Maharaj.

Creation of an "Aulia"

Sri Swami Samarth used to stay mostly in the jungle. A Muslim mendicant would visit Him there for *Darshan*. Occasionally he would offer a "Hukka" to Swamiji, who would accept it to please him. Maharaj was pleased by his devotion and one day he was given the transcendental state of *Samadhi* just by His glance! What a blessed person! Later by the grace of Maharaj he became a Fakir, revered by all and many used to come for his *Darshan* on the banks of the Krishna river. He preferred to be left alone and did not like the crowd pestering him and to dissuade them he started throwing stones at them. He was careful not to hurt anybody; however those who were hit by the stones were blessed indeed and fortune used to smile on them. The Fakir was called an *Aulia* and became known in the locality as a "miracle man".

Other Miracles

Then there was a poor weaver in Mangalvedha. He came in contact with Maharaj and became His devotee. One night Swamiji appeared in his dream and told him "Your father has buried a huge treasure under the *Tulsi* copse in your back yard. Dig there." Next morning the weaver remembered the command given in the dream and dug up a heavy trunk full of treasure. Thus was his poverty eliminated by Maharaj's grace.

A childless couple narrated their unhappiness to Basappa Teli, who advised them to pray to Sri Swami Samarth. On knowing their problem, Swamiji told the woman to mix a little of the Sirsa tree resin with sugar and eat the mixture daily for some days. The woman who was 54 years did so and steadfastly went for *Darshan* of Swamiji daily. She would not eat unless she had His *Darshan*. In course of time she was blessed with a lovely child.

Such was the compassion and grace of Sri Swami Samarth. He fulfilled the yearnings of all. He relieved the sufferings of the afflicted, fulfilled the desires of His devotees. He performed many miracles spontaneously, but their sole purpose was to instill faith in people, to put them on the path to God and uplift them spiritually.

Sri Sai Baba, a great disciple of Swami, used to say "I confer on people what they desire (physical and material well-being) so that they will eventually desire what I desire to give them - their spiritual well-being."

Who can bind a "Muktatma?"

During His stay at Mangalvedha Sri Swami Samarth once went to Cholambee Muth, which was looked after by one Ramdasibuva. Swamiji went to the Muth and slept there, but did not wake when it was time for Buva to go out. He went away locking the doors from outside, thus locking Swamiji inside, thinking that he would let Maharaj rest for some more time. Whilst out in the town he heard some people saying that Sri Swami Samarth was in the town square and saw people rushing there for His *Darshan*. Ramdas idly thought that some *Mahatma* must have come to town and went too. He was surprised to see Swamiji there and, wondered who could have opened the locks. When he went back to the Muth, be found the locks intact! He was thunder-struck. Ramdasibuva immediately went in search of Swami Samarth and fell at His feet on finding Him. Who can bind a *Mukta-Atma* - a realised and ever-free soul?

Yogakshemam Vahamyaham

Another interesting incident took place in Mangalvedha. One day, one Yeshwant Mahadev, a revenue officer in the British revenue services, came for *Darshan* of Swami Samarth, who blessed him and gave him a *Shaligram* for worship at home,

Mahadev soon got promoted to Assistant Collector. In his spiritual quest too, he made good progress due to the Swamiji's blessings and grace. He became a popular and respected officer. When he was in charge of Bhiwandi, in Thane District, there was a severe famine, people and cattle perished and there was great suffering. He released grain stocks from the Government stores, for free distribution. The cost of the grain amounted to the then stupendous figure of Rupees Ten thousand, which should have been remitted to the Treasury. The Collector of Thana district came to know about the dues and arrived with the District Superintendent of Police, for inspection of accounts. Mahadev pleaded that thousands of lives would have been lost had he not released the grain - human life was more precious than money. The Collector was in no mood to listen. When he began an inspection of the accounts he found to his surprise that there was already a credit of the 'outstanding' amount against grain stocks!

It was a miracle by the grace of Sri Swami Samarth. The Lord's grace is ever protecting His devotees. Has He not said in the *Geeta* - *Yogakshemam Vahamyamam*[17] - I take upon myself the burden of looking after my devotees' welfare. The Lord will never allow HIS devotees to suffer.

After this incident, Mahadev could no longer resist his spiritual yearning; he resigned his job and left for Nasik. There he and his wife took to intensive *Sadhana* and *Tapasya*. They were a most pious and saintly couple - fully blossomed spiritually with the warm and nurturing rays of grace of Swamiji. Later both of them entered *Maha Samadhi*.

---

[17] Chapter IX . 22.

The Lord's mysterious intervention is recorded in two similar instances, about 100 and 150 years earlier than the one above, Damajipant was a great devotee of Lord "Vithal" and was a revenue officer in the kingdom of the Sultan of Bidar and had acted similarly to save lives. The Lord had appeared in the form of a "Vithu Mahar" to pay the dues at the court of the Sultan.

In the second instance another great devotee Ramdas, who was revenue officer of Bhadrachalam, in the kingdom of Golkonda, had acted similarly and was released from prison by the mysterious intervention of the Lord. Sri Swami Samarth's mysterious protection is experienced by many even today and it will continue to be so for ever! This is HIS assurance.

Swamiji leaves Mangalvedha

Maharaj had stayed in Mangalvedha from 1838 and in 1850, He decided to leave for Mohol via Pandharpur. When His intention to leave became known, the people were deeply distressed. He assured them of His continuing protection. Blessed indeed is Mangalvedha and its residents, that they had the *Darshan* of Sri Swami Samarth for 12 years.

On Swamiji's way to Mohol, He had to cross the river Bhima which was then in flood and no boats were plying across. Swamiji asked some boatmen to ferry Him across, but they were afraid to risk their life in that dangerous flood. Sri Swami Samarth laughed at them and stepped into the river and walked across, as though it was a small stream! The boatmen were convinced that this *Yogi* had command over nature!

While Swamiji was residing at Mohol, one Gavé*-Swami met Him. Gave-Swami was over 125 years old and had mastered some intricate and subtle yogic practices. He could levitate his body 2 - 3 feet above the ground and do other complicated *Hatha* yoga exercises. Swami Samarth brought home to him the futility of Hatha Yogic practices and asked him not to waste further time in its pursuit, but to take earnestly to the real Yoga - not mastery of the body but mastery of the "Self". Gavé-Swami, with Maharaj's blessings took to severe spiritual *Sadhana*, giving up his obsession with Hatha Yoga once and for all!

Swamiji stayed for some time at the residence of G.H. Sohoni, who was Assistant Collector of Mohol. Sohoni used to celebrate religious festivals on a grand scale. On one such occasion, Swamiji decided to leave, in spite of the rain and thunder storm outside. Sohoni begged Him to stay, but He left saying "You are morally not worthy and your house is not a pure place."

Sohoni suffered from series of troubles thereafter. He was dismissed from service and had to leave Mohol. He passed through very hard times. Later on, Swami Samarth taking pity on him, gave him *Darshan* and he progressed spiritually. By the grace of Maharaj he

---

* An accent is placed over the letter 'e' in Gavé to differentiate Marathi pronounciation from the normal English one.

went to Baroda, where he got a good job and prospered.

Earn Merit First

A weaver who was a little eccentric used to visit Swamiji quite frequently and pester Him to show him *Brahman*. Maharaj never used to reply. One day, when Sri Swami Samarth was in the Nagnath temple, the weaver approached and asked Him for the vision of *Brahman*. Swamiji pointed and said "Look there! See *Brahman*"! The weaver looked in that direction and was stunned to see a huge cobra. The weaver was seized with fright and ran away. Later he went insane. Gavé-Swami taking pity on the weaver, pleaded with Maharaj to forgive and cure him. The ever compassionate Swami Samarth made him well and he never asked for the vision of *Brahman* again.

Swami Samarth intended that one should understand one's limitation and not aspire for unmerited spiritual experience. One should first strive to earn the *Adhikara* - Merit, for what one aspires. The vision of *Brahman* is not for any and everyone. It requires arduous penance and *Tapasya*: A totally purified heart and genuine merit. How can ordinary eyes which cannot even look at the sun, stand the radiance of *Brahman* which is like the effulgence of billions of suns? Cultivation of a purified heart and total *Vairagya* - detachment are the pre-requisites for higher spiritual experience. All the devotees of Maharaj should learn from the experience of the weaver and understand that one's spiritual ascent progresses only step by step.

Once a *Varkari* - a devotee of Lord Vithal of Pandharpur came for the *Darshan* of Sri Swami Samarth. He was deeply impressed by Swamiji's divine appearance and awe-inspiring personality. He forgot his *Varkari* mission - that of visiting Pandharpur twice a year, and stayed with Maharaj at Mohol. He would sing devotional songs in ecstasy and others present would join in the *bhajan*. The atmosphere would become highly spiritual, soul elevating and blissful. One day while singing with intense devotion he got lost in a trance. After an hour he regained his normal consciousness, but his eyes were still beaming with ecstasy. All those present asked him to narrate his experience during his trance. He said he saw *Vithoba* (Lord Vithal) of Pandharpur, in the person of Swami Samarth. "Oh, what a splendid and glorious vision! Sri Swami is none other than "Vithoba". "Vithal" is here too"! He said in a rapturous tone. All those present had a glimpse of the divine splendour of Swamiji and had a supremely blissful experience.

Swami Samarth goes to Sholapur

After staying in Mohol for 5 years, Maharaj went to Sholapur and stayed in a corner of Datta Mandir (temple). It is said that when Maharaj first came to the Datta Mandir, it was time for the *Maha Prasad* and the seats were laid. Maharaj went straight in and occupied a front seat. The person in charge asked Swamiji to get up and sit at the back. Swami

Samarth left the temple immediately and went to the adjoining "Muth" where He sat playing like a child, near a pillar. A lady was wonder-struck, as she saw Lord Dattatreya in all His divine splendour, where Swamiji was sitting. She prostrated at His feet. (The pillar where Swami appeared as Lord Dattatreya is still venerated). She went and told the priest in the Datta Mandir about her vision. The people in charge of the Datta Mandir subsequently begged to be forgiven.

Mahatma or Mad Man?

Most people who saw Maharaj thought He was a mad man. One Chintopant Tol alone felt He must be a great *Mahatma*. Tol approached Maharaj with great hesitation when Swamiji shouted "What do you have to do with me, whether I am a *Mahatma* or mad man?" Tol was taken aback at his thoughts being read so clearly. He thought that Swamiji had some *Siddhi* (power). Again Maharaj shouted "What is it to you whether I have any, *Siddhi* or not? How does it concern you? Tol realised that the stranger was a *Mahapurush*. He prostrated at His feet and requested Him to visit his house. After this visit, Tol used to invite Swamiji occasionally for *Prasad*. Once when Swamiji had come and *Prasad* was about to be served, a friend of Tol's talked disparagingly "How can you serve food to such a person (Swami Samarth was almost naked and looked like a lunatic - He was an *Avadhoot* after all) along with other holy and respectable Brahmins? Keep his seat separate in a corner away from others." Tol was taken in by his friend's words and did accordingly. Swamiji walked away saying "When you have doubts in your mind, I cannot accept food from you." Tol repented deeply and prayed for His pardon and begged Swamiji to forgive him and come back. Maharaj relented, and came back and ate the *Prasad.*

Sri Swami Samarth did not approve of any distinction between people - all were the children of God and all were alike in the eyes of God, specially when serving food whether it be high caste or low caste, rich or poor, all should be revered as *Narayana* (the Lord). It was not charity, indeed it is deemed to be a privilege to serve and feed the Lord, who is residing equally in all. This is the moral Swamiji wanted to teach Tol.

Never too late

On another occasion Tol invited Swamiji for a meal. His son, Vishnu, was a clerk in the Collector's office. As he was getting late for work, his father asked him to have his meals. Meanwhile, Tol worshipped Swamiji and carried out all the rituals with love and devotion. It was 10 a.m., even so Vishnu did not want to have his meals before Swamiji, as it was against tradition. At last Swamiji had His meal and Vishnu could eat. He then rushed to his office, worried that he was very late. All staff members had to sign the muster and mark the time of arrival. The Head Clerk was very strict and Vishnu went to him with great trepidation and requested the muster, whilst muttering apologies for his late coming. Looking at Vishnu in surprise, the Head Clerk enquired why he

wanted the muster when he had already signed it
and why he was apologising for coming late! Finding
his own signature and time already marked
punctually in the register, Vishnu was wonder-struck.
He narrated the whole episode to his colleagues, with
tears rolling down his cheeks all the while. Maharaj's
protection is ever present and He never fails His
devotees.

Tol retired from service and was offered a post by the
king of Akkalkot. Swamiji was by then staying with Tol
in Sholapur. When this offer came, Tol requested
Swami Samarth to accompany him to Akkalkot.
Swamiji refused saying it was too hot, but promised to
visit during the rains, (as if He could not bear the
heat!) He who could wade through floods, could defy
the fury of storms, need not have given this reason.
The words of Swamiji were cryptic and the reason was
apparent later. In this case, He foresaw the death of
Shahaji the king of Akkalkot. The king died and was
succeeded by Maloji and Swami Samarth decided to
shift to Akkalkot. It was the rainy season.

CHAPTER 5

SRI SWAMI SAMARTH AT AKKALKOT

The splendour of Sri Swami Samarth and His glorious mission became more fully manifest, after His arrival in Akkalkot.

Akkalkot, formerly known as *Prajna Puri* (town of wisdom), was a great seat of learning in days of yore. The town gained special significance because of the long stay of Maharaj there, for 22 years from 1856 onwards till his *Mahasamadhi.* Its spiritual magnetism has not waned even now, as is indicated by the constant flow of thousands of pilgrims to Akkalkot. Those who go there for a Darshan of the Samadhi, still feel the subtle power of Swamiji. They feel a definite response to their prayers; some are cured of their suffering; others find their desires fulfilled. More than that, they feel guided onto the right spiritual path.

During British rule, Akkalkot was a small princely state with a total area of 498 square miles and an annual revenue of Rupees 2,35,000 in 1881.

Swamiji's advent in Akkalkot coincides with a very crucial period in Indian history; the country was politically enslaved, economically impoverished and religiously humiliated. Islamic oppression existed for 300 years before the Christians had arrived. The spiritual morale of the people was at the lowest, unable to withstand the aggressive Christian missionaries.

At this critical time, Swamiji took up His Divine Mission to redeem the people, restore their morale and to revive their spiritual vitality. Like a spiritual beacon, He extended His influence far and wide, enlivening the drooping spirit of the people, in fact He re-lit the spiritual flame of our ancient land.

When Swami Samarth agreed to go to Akkalkot, both Tol and his *guest* started out on horseback. After they had gone some distance, a messenger arrived saying that Tol was urgently wanted back in Sholapur. Tol asked the servant to wait on the Master and went back. On returning, his servant reported that Swamiji had disappeared, he knew not where or how. Tol searched everywhere anxiously, but Maharaj was not to be seen anywhere. Utterly dejected, Tol reached Akkalkot and began his search in temples and holy places nearby. He was able to locate his missing spiritual guest at last in the *Khandoba* temple and he fell at His feet with great joy. To his frequent requests to stay with him Swamiji gave negative replies, saying that His residence was to be at a different place.

Test of an Auliya

Tol was at first overjoyed because Maharaj was nearby and he thought He would frequently have food at his house, but that was not to be. Swamiji wandered on the outskirts of the town and attracted the attention of a military officer named Ahmed Ali Khan, who was acquainted with the ways of *Auliya's*. He wanted to test the Swami, offering an empty pipe with mock respect, he enquired whether Maharaj would care for a smoke. Maharaj began heartily smoking the pipe, exhaling smoke even though the pipe contained no tobacco! This made Ahmed realise his folly; he was face to face with an *Auliya* and he apologised with total humility. He went in search of a house which could supply good food for the *Sadhu.*

Ahmed located one Cholappa and arranged for food to be served. Cholappa invited the Swami with Ahmed to his house. As food was served, Swamiji asked Ahmed to bless it. It was a strange request he thought, but on being pressed, he blessed the food and then Swamiji began to eat. The Swami never made a distinction between Hindus and Muslims - to Him all were, children of God.

Staunch Devotee

Swami Samarth continued to stay at Cholappa's house, after having food. Cholappa became His close devoted disciple, serving the Swami faithfully with devotion. Swamiji put him to severe tests and created problems for him. He used to insult and trouble Cholappa, annoy his wife and tax their patience to the extreme. Yet Cholappa remained a staunch devotee, never wavering in faith, he won the Master's favour and grace completely. He won Maharaj's love; he became so dear to Him that the

Swami, a *Mahavairagi*[18] lamented like a child when Cholappa died.

All Kinds of Devotees

Sri Swami Samarth's name and fame as a spiritual Master spread far and wide. Streams of devotees used to come to Cholappa's house for *Darshan,* from morning to evening.

Chatur Vidha Bhajante Mam Janah Sukriitino Arjuna[19] - four kinds of people worship me, Arjuna; the afflicted; those who desire private gain; the wise who know; those who enquire. These were the four types who came daily, however many came out of pure *Bhakti* - devotion, for the "darshan" of Swami Samarth.

Maharaj used to bless the disciples, giving them dates, sugar candy, or sweets as *prasad.* During festivals whether Hindu or Muslim, special gifts were offered to devotees, Sadhus, Fakirs, Auliyas etc. Many Jews, Parsis and Christians, too visited Akkalkot and received His grace and favour. Many foreigners from USA, Germany & Great Britain also were blessed by HIM.

Joy and Bliss for all

Sri Swami Samarth had to be cared for by others - He never asked for food or clothes. He was an *Avadhoot*

---

[18] Vairagi is one who has mastered "vairagya" - detachment. Thus "Mahavairagi" is one who has absolute detachment.

[19] Geeta, Chapter 7.16

unconcerned with the world, always contented. Swamiji could understand many languages - the minds of others were an open book to Him - He was *Omniscient* and could read the innermost thoughts of those who came to Him. His replies were cryptic and often accompanied by gestures, His subtle language understood and explained only by His close disciples. Generally a glance, a gesture, a word was sufficient for the devotee to be filled with joy, bliss and a sense of fulfillment.

Often, Maharaj would toy with metallic rings, which He used to give apparently at random to some of the devotees; whosoever got one was sure to find the picture of his favourite deity on it.

No Distinction

Swamiji never made any distinctions between devotees; whether male or female, rich or poor, Hindu, Muslim, Jew, Parsi or Christian, from the West or East - all were treated alike by Him. He used to bestow His attention and benevolence more readily and lavishly on low castes, the needy and the afflicted. To appease another's hunger by serving food, is the most meritorious act according to Indian tradition. Swami Samarth was particularly fond of serving food to hundreds of people at a time. There was never dearth of food, it never seemed to run out. Many were the times when such miracles were seen.

SOME MIRACLES OF AKKALKOT MAHARAJ

Miraculous events and Avataars seem to accompany each other. These Miracles are spontaneous events flowing from an Avataar's knowledge and use of subtle laws that operate in this cosmos. Our ignorance and lack of understanding make us gasp in awe.

Imagine a tribal community in the deepest jungles, away from towns or even villages. If a hologram was to be displayed to them, they would probably look upon those operating the holograms as God's or Avataar's!

Are Miracles necessary?

Why are miracles necessary? When Christ was asked by a rich man to heal his dying son at Caperaum, Jesus is said to have said wryly "Except ye see signs and wonders, ye will not believe" (John 4: 46-54, Bible).

Incurable diseases and insoluble problems require "signs and wonders" i.e. miracles for their solution.

The ultimate purpose of miracles is to shake dull, cynical human beings out of their spiritual "sleep" and awaken their desire to progress towards union with God.

Feeding the Multitude

Rawji Patil and his wife Vithabai stayed in Rampur, a small village near Akkalkot. They were devotees of Swami Samarth, who used to grace their house by His occasional visits. On one such occasion, Rawji and his wife took a vow, that they would feed 40 Brahmins, on the next visit of Maharaj. Accordingly, during the next visit of Swamiji they cooked food, enough for 40 - 50 people. Rawji duly worshipped Swamiji and requested Maharaj to take His food first. The news of Maharaj's arrival spread rapidly, as a result, hundreds of devotees from neighbouring villages eagerly came for Swamiji's *Darshan.* Maharaj said "let all the devotees who have come, have their meal first and then we shall eat".

Rawji and his wife were worried about feeding such a large gathering. Swamiji understood their plight and ordered some baskets to be bought. After these baskets were bought, all the food available was filled in them. The idols of Annapurna and other gods from their shrine were kept on top of the food, in the baskets. Swami then asked the host and hostess to carry the baskets on their heads and do *Pradakshina* (circumambulation) around the *Tulsi* plant thrice. Then they were asked to start serving food, but warned that they should not look into the baskets. They started serving food to the hundred of devotees. All were sumptuously fed and Rawji requested Swamiji also to eat. However He said "Not yet! Our parents and grandparents have yet to eat". Just then another bunch of devotees arrived from Sholapur and they too were fed. Only after the last devotee had taken food, would Maharaj agree to eat.

Food prepared for only 40 - 50 people was served to hundreds of devotees and yet quite a lot was left over! The words of Maharaj were infallible[20].

Averting Death

There were many occasions when Swami Samarth like Sri Narasimha Saraswati, averted the death of His devotees and prolonged their lives. Jadhav, a potter, was a great devotee of Swamiji. Maharaj one day warned him about his impending death, saying "O potter! there is a summons coming in your name". The potter understood that his death was approaching, fell at the feet of Swami Samarth and cried "Maharaj save me! I am not afraid of leaving this world, but I do not want to forfeit and forego the privilege of serving you. Please do not deny me this blessed privilege".

Swami Samarth was touched by his devotion. As if addressing someone who was invisibly standing there, He pointed towards a nearby bull and said in a commanding tone "go to the bull". The bull instantly fell down dead. Swamiji thus saved His devotee from death and at the same time released the bull from its lower animal state and speeded up its evolution. Rescued from death, Jadhav turned into the

---

[20] The five sensory stimuli are regulated by "Pranic vibrations". Masters create food by using "Pranic force" to rearrange vibratory structure, according to Paramahamsa Yogananda.

staunchest devotee of the Swami and lived long, doing dedicated service to Him.

Once Sri Swami Samarth went along with some of His devotees to a village. Jadhav was also with them. When the Swami was sleeping, a farmer who had been bitten by a serpent, was brought into a nearby temple. The farmer's condition was critical, the poison spread all over and he was in a coma. Jadhav quickly took the leather sandals of Swamiji and put them on the farmer's head. At that juncture Swamiji got up, saw what Jadhav was doing, was angry and started scolding him, shouting "Why have you put my slippers on that corpse"? Jadhav was shuddering in fear at the fury of the Swami.

Swamiji then seemed to cool down a bit. He said "You, fool! What do you think you were doing?" Then in a normal tone He said "Wake him up by calling his name thrice. He has slept enough". Jadhav did as he was told and the farmer slowly opened his eyes! He got up and felt embarrassed wondering why he was lying there and why so many people were around him. He was then told what had happened subsequent to the snake bite.

Destiny had to run its inviolable course. The course of destiny is not to be interfered with - the pre-appointed time of death had come for the farmer. Thus, Maharaj had become furious with Jadhav. Sri Swami Samarth could overrule nature or destiny, but not unless circumstances specially warranted it, and there was a Divine purpose to be achieved. He rescued the farmer from death, to inculcate spiritual faith in the people who were observing the event, as well as to demonstrate the power of His *Padukas.*

There is nothing impossible for a *Mahapurush,* even death has to retreat at His command. A similar miracle was performed by Sri Narasimha Saraswati[21]. A widow wanted to commit *Sati.* On her way, she met Sri Narasimha Saraswati and prostrated at His feet. The Avataar blessed her with the traditional blessing *Astaputra Bhavah* - "may you enjoy your married life and have eight children". She cried "Swamiji, how is it possible? My husband is dead and I am about to join him as a *Sati".* The blessing of a *Mahapurush* can never be false. Sri Narasimha Saraswati accompanied her to the cremation ground and sprinkled holy water on the dead body of her husband. Lo! The dead man got up!

Similar miracles have been performed by saints like Sripad Sri Vallabhaa, Jnaneshwar Maharaj, Ramdas Samarth and Jesus Christ.

Feeding Fire with Water

There was a devotee named Appa. During harvest season he invited Sri Swami Samarth to his farm. He went there with a number of devotees. They all enjoyed roasted grains from the new harvest. Instead of pouring more fuel to feed the fire, Swamiji poured water! To the wonder of all, the fire continued blazing as if oil had been poured on it. Maharaj's disciple

---

[21] See "Guru Charitra", Chapter 32.

Shirdi Sai Baba, had also filled lamps with water and the lamps burned brightly the whole night!

Once when Swamiji was resting in Khas Baug, He suddenly got up and said "Come, I shall show you a great soul." His devotees followed Him, after a few steps they saw a big cobra coming out of an ant hill. The cobra lifted its hood and bowed as if paying obeisance to Sri Swami Samarth. Swamiji said "This is a very great soul." All the persons present bowed down to the cobra.

Ramanna Maharshi, the great saint of Tiruvannamalai, used to say that great souls often came in animal bodies for the express purpose of *Darshan* of *Avataars*. Sri Adi Shankara also had expressed the same viewpoint.

Maharaj's love for animals

Once a monkey started causing havoc by entering houses and destroying everything it saw. The police officer had the monkey caught and ordered that it be killed. Swamiji heard this and ordered that the monkey be brought to Him. When the monkey was brought to Him, Swamiji patted it, fondled it for a while and said "Don't trouble others henceforth - Go!" The monkey became completely tame and gave up its mischievous ways! Thereafter it used to come daily for *Darshan* of the Swami.

An elephant named *Jawahar* went rogue and started hurling stones at random with its trunk. It was beyond all control. Sri Swami Samarth went and stood in front of it with His hands on his waist. Wonder of wonders! The mad elephant became completely calm and quiet.

He had a mother's love for all beings; dogs, cats cows, elephants, serpents monkeys. All received His love. They in turn responded to His love. Love is indeed the greatest subduer and Sri Swami Samarth was the *Premavataar* - the Incarnation of love itself. At times, Maharaj used to speak to stones and trees, as if they were His kith and kin.

He spoke very little, never gave sermons or wrote anything. His actions sometimes seemed strange and childish, but His *Darshan* was sufficient - just a glance was enough to imbibe spiritual knowledge. This method of transmitting spiritual knowledge is known as *Drik Diksha*. Often His silence itself was a sermon and cleared all doubts of devotees. This method is known as *Sankalpa Diksha*.

The Muslims used to revere Him as a great *Auliya* and He gave them occasional proof of His saintly powers. He visited Muths, mandirs (temples), dargas, pirs and mosques. He Himself was beyond all conventions. He was an *Avadhoot*!

Restoring eyesight

Once when Sri Swami Samarth was sitting in Desmukhwada, a woman approached Him with her son and said "Maharaj, my boy, Ganesha, lost his eyesight soon after his thread ceremony. Earlier his eyesight was perfect. Be gracious and favour him with eyesight again." Swamiji replied "Five demons are coming to test me. This boy will have his eyesight back at that time." There were many devotees present. As soon as Swamiji uttered these words, five bulky hugely built, dark complexioned Brahmins came there and began to talk in Sanskrit and Kannada amongst themselves.

None of the devotees could understand what they were saying. For some time the Brahmins talked angrily with great contempt and looked towards Maharaj.

Sri Swami Samarth called the blind boy and said "Ganesh, come here, state the questions these Brahmins wish to put to me and give them the answers." Ganesh pleaded ignorance with folded hands and said "Maharaj, what do I know? What answers can I give?"

Swami Samarth took off a Rudraksha bead and gave it to the boy. He also touched his eyes with a flower. Immediately, a wonderful thing happened! The blind boy stood up and reeled off all the questions, the five had planned to ask! Further, he answered them too! The questions were very difficult, spiritual problems involving complex interpretations, which would have stumped many a *pundit* or scholar. Upon this stunning incident, the five Brahmins were shamefaced and nonplussed and they prostrated at the feet of Swami Samarth.

Maharaj said to their leader "All of you criticise me and came here to test my *Shakti* (power), because I eat food given by anybody and visit mosques and dargas. Well, what about your mother's character? She committed adultery with a Muslim and you are born of Imambaksh, a Muslim. Did you know that?"

This fact was known only to the leader himself and he fell at Swamiji's feet and prayed for pardon for his misdemeanour, in trying to test the *Shakti* of a *Dattavataar*! He also prayed for advice as to what he should do for *Prayaschitha* (atonement). Swamiji asked him to go on a pilgrimage and take purificatory bath in the Holy Ganga.

The blind boy, Ganesh, too recovered his eyesight in the bargain with the grace of the Swami.

Swami Samarth - The loving mother

One Bhimrao had a huge swelling on one side of his head, which made him look very ugly. He became a butt of ridicule and felt miserable. Once he approached Maharaj, prostrated at His feet and place flowers there. Swamiji said jocularly "Look at this 2 headed monster!" Bhimrao felt mortified - even Maharaj was making fun of him! - even the Mother was ridiculing her child! He returned home feeling thoroughly miserable. During a nap that afternoon, he had a dream wherein Maharaj appeared and gently and lovingly passed His hand on the swelling, like a very affectionate mother, and went away.

Bhimrao woke up and lo! The swelling was no longer there. He ran to where Sri Swami Samarth was and broke down with gratitude. Maharaj smiled and looked at him with a mother's love, understanding the inexpressible feeling welling up in the child's heart (- are we not all children before God?). Only the mother can understand her child's feelings!

In Maharashtra, Jnaneshwar is commonly addressed as Mouli (in Marathi) reflecting the mother-child relationship between the Saint and His devotees. Swami Samarth is also referred to as Mouli by many devotees. There are some paintings of Him in the guise of a mother! In Bhakti Yoga one of the methods by which a devotee can get closer to God is by assuming the role of a child. Sri Ramakrishna Paramahamsa always regarded Himself as the child of Goddess Kali, whom He always referred to as Mother.

Greed and its control

Devotees are sometimes assailed by irrational urges. There was an old Brahmin, Sheshacharya, who was a staunch devotee of Sri Swami Samarth and worshipped Him as Lord Venkateshwara, his family deity. One day he got a craving that he should get sweets, from those presented to Maharaj. A *Sadhaka* (one who does *Sadhana*) should try to have perfect control over his or her appetites. Swamiji knew his desire and purposely avoided looking at him that day. Sheshacharya knew the reason for this indifference and repented. He then went and ate cowdung as self punishment!

Afterwards, he approached Maharaj and confessed "I committed the sin of craving for sweets and of desiring them from offerings made to You. If I make such a mistake again I shall punish myself by eating cowdung, just as I have done now." Swamiji had a hearty laugh and thereafter he was able to get Darshan every day. By subduing his mind and desires more and more, he made good progress spiritually too. Maharaj's way of teaching devotees was often indirect. The wise ones understood and flowered by His grace refined into spiritually advanced disciples.

Tasty chilly!

Once a person seeing Swamiji eagerly accepting sweets and fruits from His devotees, had doubts whether the Swami was saintly, because a saint is supposed to demonstrate *Aparigraha* - non covetousness or non desirousness. As soon as the thought arose, Swamiji threw away all the rich and tasty food and asked for some chillies to be brought. He chewed and ate them with as much gusto and relish as if He was eating sweets! His seeming likes and dislikes were only to please and satisfy His devotees. This reminds us of Lord Krishna who ate parched rice offered by His poor devotee Sudama, as if it was the tastiest meal He had ever eaten!! Saints have complete mastery over their senses; they are *Jitendriya* i.e. They have total control over senses.

You will have a son

Sometimes foreigners were among Swamiji's visitors. Once a European engineer visited Swamiji. He had no children and he and his wife were pining for a son. Hearing about the spiritual greatness of Maharaj, in

Sholapur, he had come to the Swami to seek His blessings for a son. But after seeing the queer ways of Swamiji, he cursed himself for having come with high hopes. He thought these Indians are stupid to put their faith in such a near lunatic and to glorify Him as a saint. While such thoughts were coursing through his mind, Swami Samarth looked at him and said "You want a son, do you? You will have a son in a year's time".

The engineer was surprised at the omniscience of this "mad" man. It was a strange and unexpected fulfillment of his desire and he bowed down in overwhelming gratitude. If we take but one step toward Him; he takes nine steps towards us! From then on, he turned into a staunch devotee of Swamiji and was a frequent visitor to Akkalkot. Needless to say, in due course he became the proud father of a son!

The "I" Specialist

One Jewish doctor working as an eye specialist in J. J. Hospital, the largest hospital in Bombay, came for Swamiji's *Darshan*. He was haughty and proud. Sri Swami Samarth glanced at him and said "You have treated thousands of eye patients, but how many of them have lost their eyesight   due to you for ever?" The doctor was taken aback as this was the first time he was visiting Swamiji and nobody knew him in Akkalkot. All his conceit and vanity at his being an eminent eye specialist tumbled down in a trice. The big balloon of his ego deflated - the "I" malady of his ego was cured and his "I" vision repaired. He became a staunch devotee of Swamiji and settled down at the Master's feet after retirement.

Who can defy scientific process?

Photography was new and was in early development at that time. The Kodak company had just set up their office in Bombay. They made plans to photograph great people and publicise them, to popularise the art. They were very keen to get a photograph of Sri Swami Samarth, as His name and fame as a *Mahapurush,* miracle performing saint had spread far and wide. Kodak felt that if they could photograph Swamiji, they would get a great amount of publicity which would promote their business. Therefore they deputised their best photographer, an American who was a senior officer in Kodak.

After arriving at Akkalkot, he approached the disciples and expressed his desire to photograph Swamiji. He was told that without the explicit permission of Maharaj, His photo could not be . taken. The photographer was highly confident of his skills and thought that he would take the photo without anyone noticing it, especially when Swami Samarth was unaware.

He thought, the camera is no respecter of . great people, who can defy science? Waiting for an opportunity, he surreptitiously exposed his plates on Maharaj, "without" Him being aware of it. He developed the prints and brought them proudly to

Swami Samarth and asked Him to have a look. Maharaj took them and asked His disciples to have a look. One said it was a photo of Sri Rama, another of Vishnu, a third Bhavani, a fourth said it was Khandoba and so on.... Everyone saw in it their own family deity.

The photographer ridiculed them, that they could not even identify the picture of their Master properly. He asked Swami Samarth, Himself to look at the photo. Swamiji looked at it and burst into a loud laugh and said "Is this my picture? Do I look as funny as this?" And Lo! everyone now saw a picture of a monkey on the print. The photographer felt highly embarrassed. He realised his folly in not obtaining permission from Sri Swami Samarth before taking the photo. He had relied on his skills and the "supremacy" of science and learnt his lesson.

He sought Maharaj's pardon and prostrated at His feet and requested Him to permit him to take His photograph again. He said "Ours is a new company, I have been specially sent here to take your photo with a view to propagating photography and to popularise it, as well as for our company's progress. Your picture is sacred and is worthy of being kept in everyone's home. Please be gracious and kind enough to give permission".

Sri Swami Samarth indicated His consent with a smile. The photo was allowed to be taken and it came out so well - fully capturing the manifestation of the Divine personage that was Maharaj! Everyone was delighted to see this picture.

Maharaj's fame had spread far and wide, as a result of which many photographers used to come to Akkalkot to try and photograph Swamiji. If they succeeded this was a passport to fame and money for them!.

Too late for a photo

With this motive, one Phadke came and was given advice which was unless Maharaj permitted it, no photograph would develop, so he prostrated before Swamiji and humbly asked for permission to photograph Him. Maharaj smilingly assented and asked Phadke to come at 5 o'clock (in the evening) and take the photo. Phadke was present ahead of time, eager to photograph Swamiji. However, Swamiji was giving Darshan to devotees and the time passed by. Phadke was waiting expectantly for the signal to "shoot", but had no such luck! It was 6 o'clock and Swamiji asked Phadke to prepare and hold the hukka, while He smoked it. Finally, at 7 o'clock, Swamiji gave permission to Phadke, but it was dark and Phadke tearfully said it was not possible to take His photo (flash had not yet been invented at that time).

Maharaj laughed and told Phadke to develop the photographic plate. Phadke couldn't believe his ears - no photograph had been taken, what was the point in developing the plate? However, Maharaj's words are ever true and Phadke went to his room and developed the plate. Lo! there was a wonderful image of Maharaj smoking the *hukka* as if He had posed for a photograph! Phadke was speechless!

This inability to photograph a spiritual personality or even an idol has been experienced by many people. One Chowgule who travels frequently on the Bombay Ratnagiri road, has had this experience on more than 17 occasions at the holy Parashuram temple at Lote Parshuram, near Chiplun. He has tried with 5 different cameras under all conditions, at different times, over the last 6 years, with the same result - the camera does not work or if the camera does work, no image is formed, there is only a blur! Pictures taken immediately afterwards, outside the temple, come out very well!

Similar episodes have been related by his Paramahamsa Yogananda about his Paramguru (the Guru of his Guru) Lahiri Mahasaya.

Doubt and repentance

Once Babaji Sootar, who was Superintendent of post offices, came for the *Darshan* of Sri Swami Samarth. After his *Darshan* he sought permission to leave, as is customary when one visits any saint. Swamiji asked him to sit down. Babaji did not know what to say; he had to attend office the next morning and it was therefore necessary to leave immediately. After some time, he again requested permission to leave. Swami Samarth told him "Sit down, the river is in flood". Nobody knew about this in Akkalkot and Babaji wanted to get away somehow. When Swamiji was talking to other devotees, he slipped away and went to the railway station, which was 7 miles away by bullock cart (there were no cars in those days). When he reached there, he found that the Krishna river was in flood and the railway bridge across was damaged. All trains had been cancelled. Babaji had to wait at the station the whole night in the cold, as it was not possible to go back to Akkalkot. He disregarded the advice of Sri Swami Samarth and had to pay for it now. He repented greatly and prayed incessantly from where he was, to Swamiji for forgiveness. Swami Samarth was Omniscient and could foresee impending danger.

Aspiring devotees should have complete faith, sincerity, surrender and devotion to Sri Swami Samarth - He will protect them and ensure their welfare.

CHAPTER 6

RAJA DHIRAJA YOGIRAJ
AKKALKOT SWAMI MAHARAJ

When Swami Samarth came to Akkalkot, there was already a king, *Raja* Maloji Rao but Swamiji was regarded as the real ruler - hence He was extolled as *Raja Dhiraj* Emperor and *Maharaj* meaning supreme King. *Yogiraj* means King of Yogis.

The passage of time has seen the ruling family lose its former status, while the mendicant Maharaj continues to rule Akkalkot, even after He is no longer in bodily manifestation. The spiritual empire established by *Raja Dhiraj Yogiraj* still continues to expand. Thousands of pilgrims still pour in to worship and to get spiritual guidance, to Akkalkot.

Emperor of the Soul

When Maharaj began showing His *Leelas*, the king Maloji Rao heard about the great and holy *Sanyasi* from a courtier. Maloji Rao said "How do you know he is great? I shall accept his greatness only if he appears before me, just now"! *No sooner* had he said these words, Sri Swami Samarth manifested Himself in court, right in front of the king! Maloji Rao knelt at His feet and offered his respect. Maharaj left as suddenly as He had appeared and Maloji Rao decided to go for His *Darshan* on Thursday.

He went for Maharaj's *Darshan* with all the paraphernalia of state, accompanied by all his retinue. Maloji Rao was seated on a howdah, atop the royal elephant and his courtiers were all marching alongside. The procession came up to Cholappa's house, where Swamiji was staying. Maloji Rao approached Swamiji and bowed at His feet. Swami Samarth gave him a tight slap and reprimanded him "Don't exhibit your 'greatness' before Me. I make and unmake kings like you. Why try to show rank and status here"?

Maloji Rao stood up in fear and was trembling uncontrollably. He begged "Please forgive my stupidity". Swamiji was later to show great love and affection to Maloji Rao, but he wished the king to understand that while regal splendour is fine in court, it was unsuited in the presence of a spiritual Master, who was *Emperor of the Soul.* Displaying status and rank, prevents a devotee from shedding his ego and surrendering to God.

Maloji Rao became a pious and ardent devotee of Maharaj and thereafter, when he went for Maharaj's *Darshan* he would go without escort, dressed in simple attire and in all humility. He was no ruler in Swamiji's presence. Maharaj displayed complete indifference to rank - He treated all alike. Swamiji would visit the royal palace whenever it pleased Him, and He used to stay there as long as He wished. All members of the royal family were His ardent devotees.

Gift of an heir

The King had no children and this was a cause of unhappiness for him. He prayed to Maharaj and he had two daughters in quick succession. He prayed to the Swami for a son, to be heir and successor to him. When his wife was pregnant, Maloji Rao was anxious to know whether it would be a son. Swamiji replied "Fire the cannon", indicating that a prince would be born. The birth of the prince was celebrated in grand and lavish style. By the Swami's blessings, Akkalkot state got an heir to the throne.

Maloji Rao gifted horses, cows, palanquin etc., for the use of Swamiji. Whenever the Swami stayed in the royal place, devotees would throng there for His *Darshan.* Swamiji would stand on the balcony and give *Darshan.* He would call some people from the devotees below and bless them and give *prasad.* This was not partiality to some; it only meant that those whom He called would be needing His solace and encouragement immediately. They may have been in great distress or encountering some problems in their spiritual sadhana. Words of solace and blessings were needed by them at that moment and He offered them readily.

The visitors were numerous and of all castes, creed and colour, rich and poor, Rajas (Kings) and paupers; spiritual aspirants, people in distress or stricken by calamity. Sri Swami Samarth used to give them *Darshan* at various places and different times; Sometimes in the palace, sometimes in the Muth, many a time under a banyan tree or even on the roadside. He would be sitting on a silken cushion or in the midst of thorny bushes, depending on His will. Wherever He went, His *Das* (devotee dedicated entirely to His service) Bhujanga, Cholappa and Sunderabai accompanied Him and constantly attended on Him.

Humility and Piousness attracts Blessings

The ruler of Gwalior state, Jayoji Rao Shinde, was a pious, religious devotee. In spite of his wealth and power, he was very simple and egoless. He used to visit saints and places of pilgrimage. Once he came for the *Darshan* of Sri Swami Samarth. Swamiji was in the state palace in those days, and Jayoji Rao found it difficult to get *Darshan* as Maharaj did not allow anyone to meet Him in the palace. Knowing the sincerity, earnestness and nobility of the king of Gwalior, Swamiji out of His infinite mercy, came out and seated Himself under a tree. Hearing this news, Jayoji Rao rushed there and bowed at His feet, offering Him flowers and coconut, as is customary. Swamiji gave him a loving glance and greeted him with a smile. Jayoji Rao was thrilled with joy and sublime happiness. Swamiji answered all his queries and cleared his spiritual doubts. Jayoji Rao had never had such an experience in his life, though he had met many saints. Sri Swami Samarth made the deepest impact on him and the great spiritual power of Swamiji was a revelation to him. Jayoji Rao was blessed with an heir to the throne of Gwalior in due course.

Once the king of Indore state, Tukoji Rao Holkar and his son came to Akkalkot for *Darshan* of Maharaj. The king and his son knelt at the feet of Swamiji and offered prayers, "Sadguru Mouli! By the merit earned by my mother Ahalyabai and my father and their blessings, I have the unique fortune of your *Darshan* today. The last time, I was out of Indore, I had the great fortune of your *Darshan* at Mount Abu. Both these *Darshans* are the greatest incidents of my life". No one knew about Maharaj visiting Mount Abu. It was evident that Swamiji could give *Darshan* anywhere to His devotees - distance is no barrier to Maha yogis. By mere *Sankalpa* (will) they can cross oceans and mountains! Sri Swami Samarth smiled and stated "There are mango trees in your palace garden". Holkar replied with surprise "Yes Maharaj there are 2 mango trees". Then Swami took off the cap on his head and tossed it to the king. Tukoji Rao picked it up as Prasad, garlanded Sri Swami Samarth, distributed sweets offered "dakshina" in a regal way to Brahmins. He returned to Indore happy that he had obtained the grace and blessings of Maharaj.

Pomp & glory get short shrift

As opposed to the humble and pious way in which the kings of Gwalior and Indore approached Akkalkot Swami, the Maratha ruler of Baroda went about boasting that he would 'bring' Sri Swami Samarth, to Baroda! This plan was doomed to fail, with disastrous consequences!

Malharrao Gaikwad, king of Baroda state, had heard of the spiritual prowess of Akkalkot Swami and also about the visits of the other two Maratha rulers (Gwalior and Indore). He had an earnest desire that Swamiji should visit his state, as it would then prosper[22] and his stature would rise. He announced in his *Durbar* to all present that he would not mind spending any amount to get Swamiji to Baroda. He assigned this task to one of his best commanders, one Tatya. Tatya set out for Akkalkot with plenty of money and fabulous gifts to be offered to Swami Samarth. On reaching Akkalkot, he tried to bribe those devotees of Swamiji whom he perceived as close to Him. He showed off, spending money lavishly, showered gifts and talked of the grandeur of the royal court he belonged to.

He was very confident of his success, as he believed that money was supreme and that there was nothing that money could not buy. When he got no nearer his goal, he offered Cholappa a bribe of rupees ten thousand (which was a huge amount in those days) provided he could prevail upon Swamiji to visit Baroda. Cholappa was poor and a simple person and told Swamiji about the offer! Swamiji just smiled and did not comment. After some time the stake was increased; In addition Cholappa was offered a *Jagir* (agricultural land along with farm workers).

---

[22] Akkalkot State was tiny & had miniscule revenue compared to Baroda State. The presence of Sri Swami Samarth placed Akkalkot on the map, with 3000 people visiting it every day! In fact the British government had to open a new railway station here, in view of the huge profit potential.

Cholappa again told Maharaj about this and tried to persuade Him to visit Baroda. Swamiji said "He has no bhakti". On hearing this Tatya hired a Brahmin to read *Guru Charitra* and organised religious gatherings, mass feedings etc., but Swamiji was not fooled about the king's or his commander's *bhakti*. The Baroda king had no true devotion, it was only for pomp and status that he wanted Swamiji to visit Baroda.

Tatya then changed his tactics. He decided to *abduct* Swamiji! His plan was that Swamiji would be persuaded to sit in his palanquin and the procession would detour to the railway station, where the Baroda state train would be waiting to whisk Maharaj away to Baroda. It was easier said than done! Tatya bribed all the palanquin bearers lavishly and went over the plan again and again, to eliminate any hitches.

The Swamiji got in the palanquin and the procession started! The palanquin bearers detoured to the railway station. Once they reached there, Tatya went and opened the door of the palanquin to find it empty! Hundreds had seen Maharaj get in and now it was empty! Tatya, the foolish man, realised he was dealing with a powerful saint and departed post haste to Baroda, having wasted thousands of rupees and lavished gifts by the ton - all to no avail!

Saints not recognised

Most people fail to recognise saints, because they appear in a human body and appear to have the bodily frailties that common people have. It may be recalled that even the great Vivekananda had doubts about Sri Ramakrishna, when he lay dying of throat cancer. This is one of the reasons why they perform miracles - to jolt us awake from our spiritual stupor - and to *prove* to us that They are saints or *Avataars.*

However some people never learn! Malhar Rao was still keen to bring Swamiji to Baroda. He decided to take another chance and he chose one Yeshwant Rao to do the task. Rao reached Akkalkot and offered the Swami, his master's *Nazrana* (tribute) - costly ornaments, rich clothes and valuable gifts. Swami Samarth was enraged "Trying to buy me with wealth? Take back all that you have brought" he thundered. He added "Handcuff this man and confine him in prison". Rao lost all his courage and returned to Baroda. Subsequently, he got implicated in a plot to poison the king, was handcuffed and confined in prison!

Satyabhama had tried to entice Krishna with her fabulous wealth but failed, while Rukmini could win Him over with a mere Tulsi leaf! It is sincerity and devotion that binds the Lord, not worldly wealth and power. What a small prayer offered in all sincerity could have achieved, the king of Baroda tried to accomplish by subterfuge, using his wealth and power and failed! Lord Krishna says in the Geeta - "I happily accept flowers, fruits, leaves (of Tulsi) or water from a true Bhakta"[23] - nowhere is money mentioned.

---

[23] Chapter IX . 26

He knows what is best

Dadasaheb Vinchurkar was Regent of Akkalkot state and a great devotee of Sri Swami Samarth. The Swami sometimes visited his house, when Vinchurkar would give a bath to the Swami and after worshipping Him, used to feed Him and thereafter receive *Prasad.*

vinchurkar developed an unsightly skin disease with white spots appearing and spreading on his thighs. He was very worried. When he went to Swamiji, He asked Vinchurkar to remove the costly diamond ring on his finger and give it to Him. At first Vinchurkar hesitated, but after a moment removed it and put it at the Swami's feet. Later Swamiji gave this ring to Cholappa to sell and build a temple with the proceeds. As the temple came up, his skin disease progressively reduced, until it disappeared completely not leaving any trace.

Vinchurkar was a blessed person indeed. One day the Swami went to the office of Vinchurkar and told him he should pack up bag and baggage and leave Akkalkot. Vinchurkar anxiously asked where he should go. Swamiji answered "To a place where you will be respected by thousands".

Not long after this incident, difference of opinion arose between him and the king. Vinchurkar resigned his job and went away to his *Jagir* at Vinchur. There he led a life free from worries, peacefully, devoted to spiritual pursuits. Sri Swami

Samarth knew all - He knew what was best for everyone.

Come, Come, Come .....

After the 1857 War of Independence was lost, the British persecuted and victimised those who had directly or indirectly participated or helped in the war. Many innocent rulers suffered victimisation. The ruler of Jamkhindi state, Appa Patwardhan was dethroned and his state annexed to British territory. He was kept in Vengurla jail and his estates in the custody of the Collector of Belgaum.

One Harlikar, a faithful servant of the state went to the Swami, whose devotee he was. He prayed to Swami Samarth on behalf of Appa Pathwardhan. Swamiji looked in the direction of Jamkhindi and said "Come, come, come" while making gestures with His hands. After a few days Appa was fully exonerated and was released. His state was restored to him and he was reinstated as ruler. It was all by the grace and blessings of Swami Samarth.

His creation

Once Swamiji went to the palace, He was received with great respect by Maloji Rao and taken to the family shrine. Thereafter both sat on a swing. A rat was running here and there and trying to eat the Prasad. The priest who was making sandalwood paste, saw this and killed the rat. The priest was about to throw out the dead rat, when Swamiji snatched it from his hand and started playing with it.

He took it in His palm and said "Get up and play, my dear fellow". The rat came back to life immediately and started running here and there, as before. The priest was stunned by this miracle. Maharaj said "You have no right to kill. All life is created and looked after by the Almighty. All is His Creation". The priest repented and learnt the lesson of mercy to all.

Fixing a Royal Alliance

One Appa Moné was greatly worried as he could not secure a suitable match for his daughter, who was of marriageable age. As with all devotees, he narrated his problems to the Swami. Swami Samarth said "Why Worry? I have fixed a royal alliance for your daughter. The bridegroom's name is 'Khandya'". By 'Khandya' he meant the Prince of Baroda, Khanderao Gaekwad, before long this marriage took place.

A son is given

Bhausaheb Ghorpade was a senior courtier in Baroda. He had no son. Hearing of the power of Swamiji, he deputed one of his assistants, Venimadhav, to approach Him for His grace and blessings. Venimadhav prayed to Swamiji to bless Bhau with a son. Swami Samarth said "Let him listen to *Harivamsa Puran*. He will definitely have a son". When this message was given, Bhau and his wife began to read *Harivamsa Puran* daily and soon they had a son!

Crossing the Ocean of *Samsara*

Sri Swami Samarth had innate knowledge of scriptures and could readily come to a sincere devotee's rescue as well as tear apart a deceitful person.

Joshi was a pundit in Akkalkot. He used to read *Panchdasi*, a text in exposition of Vedanta, daily. Many would attend these recitals daily. One day during the recital, Joshi came across a beautiful verse whose meaning he could not grasp. Stopping at that *Shloka* (verse) he and all those assembled went to the house of Cholappa for *Darshan* of Swami Samarth. As soon as they were seated, Sri Swami Samarth started explaining most lucidly the meaning of the same Shloka, in which Joshi had got stuck! The people were wonder struck at the Omniscience of Sri Swami Samarth, as well as His masterly knowledge of the scriptures.

A pundit named Maté from Poona was renowned for his exposition of the Vedanta in simple language. He was a great devotee of Swami Samarth and on coming to Akkalkot, did recitations for one week continuously. These recitations were graced by Swamiji's presence and was a unique honour. Sri Swami Samarth appreciated the exposition and recital of Maté as it was done with great devotion.

Once a recital was on at Khasbaug, which was attended by thousands. Sri Swami Samarth was also present, seated on a throne. When the recital was in full tempo, and the devotional atmosphere supercharged, Maté said "Where are those blessed

Feet, which alone can help us to cross this vast ocean of *Samsara*"? Swami Samarth lowered one of His feet at this point. Maté instantly ran to Swamiji, caught hold of that foot, held it tightly to his bosom and cried "Yes, Yes These Lotus Feet can easily take us across the ocean of *Samsara*"! Sri lowered His other foot and this too was immediately grabbed by Maté. He pressed both feet tightly to his chest and was overwhelmed by devotion. Thousands watched spellbound this spontaneous expression of the great devotion and total surrender of Maté and tears rolled down many cheeks that day.

Kaal Buva

Vishnu Narayan was a very pious man residing at Pandharpur. He always used to say "*Kaal* (time) is the supreme master", to whomsoever met him. Therefore he was known as Kaal Buva.

Kaal Buva was an *Avadhoot*, preferring to be left alone and used to avoid the company of others. He used to behave strangely at times and was considered almost mad. The ways of *Avadhoots* are strange and unintelligible to us, earthy people.

Once Kaal Buva slapped two Brahmin boys. Their father lodged a compliant with a senior officer at the Collectorate. Kaal Buva was summoned and asked for an explanation. Kaal Buva only replied "Time is the supreme master. It is all consuming and all devouring". The official thought him to be mad and sent him to the Sasoon Hospital, Poona for treatment.

There *Bramhanistha* Wamanbuva noticed him by chance and instantly recognised that Kaal Buva was not an ordinary person, but a great *Mahatma*. He got Kaal Buva discharged from the hospital. He said to him "Maharaj you are a *Sat Purusha*". Kaal Buva replied "I belong to the Datta Sampradaya - you too belong to it." We cannot comprehend the ways of the God intoxicated.

Meanwhile the Brahmin who had lodged the complaint coincidentally happened to visit Swami Samarth for *Darshan*. On seeing him, Swamiji admonished him for lodging a complaint against such a holy person. The Brahmin prayed for forgiveness and withdrew the complaint. Sri Swami Samarth knew all. His omnipresence was demonstrated once again.

Footprints Engraved

Tol who has been mentioned earlier, used to worship Swamiji as an incarnation of Lord Dattatreya. Tol offered *Tulsi* leaves to Lord Vishnu every day and had taken a vow to offer 10 million leaves (one crore). Swami Samarth would often visit his house at the time of worship. Later, Tol worshipped Swamiji too with *Tulsi* leaves.

On one such occasion, Sri Swami Samarth was extremely pleased with the devotion of Tol and there was a glow of celestial light around Swamiji's head. Tol saw this aura and he prayed to Swamiji, with tears in his eyes, to impress His Footprints permanently on the wooden seat on which Swami Samarth was standing like Lord Vithal (Vithoba). Swami Samarth replied *Tatastu!* (let it be so) and left. Lo! Tol saw the Footprints clearly on the seat, as if they had been engraved on it. Tol was overjoyed and tears of gratitude rolled down his cheeks. This wooden seat is kept in Joshibuva's Muth at Akkalkot and can be seen even now.

Con Man

One day a *Sadhu* in saffron robes came to visit Sri Swami Samarth, with a veena in his hands and *Rudraksha* beads round his neck. Swamiji said he was a con man and an immoral fellow. Soon afterwards he was totally exposed and everything about him came to light.

What a Yogi !

Baba Sabnis, who has been mentioned before, became a firm devotee of Swamiji. Once his brother-in-law, a *Puranik* (one who is an expert in the *Puranas)* came to visit him. One day he was reciting a *Purana* at the Muth. Sri Swami Samarth was reclining on a silken cushion and listening to him. The *Puranik* made sarcastic references to so called *yogis* using silken cushions. Sri Akkalkot Maharaj was an *avadhoot* and always used a rough blanket, but Baba Sabnis had offered Him the cushions, which the Swami accepted only to please Sabnis. Swamiji did not respond to the taunt by Puranik.

Later, one day, Swami Samarth asked the *Puranik* to accompany Him to the hilltop nearby. It was winter and it was already late in the evening when they set out. As they climbed up, a spine chilling wind began to blow and the *Puranik could* not stand it. He was shivering and he felt as if his bones would freeze. But Sri Swami Samarth was completely at ease. He stretched Himself on the bare rock and reclining as if on a silken bed, He smiled and asked "Puranik, how soft is my bed now?" The Puranik realised his mistake in criticising a *Maha Yogi,* for whom heat or cold, silk bed or hard stone did not make any difference. He repented deeply and fell at Swamiji's feet seeking forgiveness for his rashness.

Divine Grace

Sri Swami Samarth appeared in various forms and gave *Darshan* to his devotees as Dattatreya, Vithal, Krishna, etc., depending upon who their *Istadevata* (principal deity) was. He appeared at different places at one and the same time and fulfilled the wishes of His devotees. Whoever had full faith in the Swami drew the Divine grace in full, and if they were sceptical, denied themselves His grace. If we approach fire we get warmth; If we keep afar, we shall be cold. Just as the sun's ray lighten up a house when the doors are opened, so also, if we keep the doors of our heart open in full faith, Divine grace will fill and flood our whole being.

One Vinayak Rao Vasudeo was working as an Oriental language translator to the government. He came to Akkalkot for *Darshan* with his wife. He was a close devotee and wanted to settle down at Akkalkot when he retired. Maharaj advised him to settle down near the seashore at Bombay. After some time his wife became seriously ill. He prayed to Swamiji for her recovery and she recovered by His grace. Sri Swami Samarth sent him His *Atma Linga* Padukas, as a token of His grace through one Raoji. (These *Alma Linga* Padukas were produced by Maharaj from his mouth. They have very clear auspicious markings and a *Darshan* of them is enough to alleviate the suffering and misery of devotees). Vasudeo built a temple at Mahalakshmi, on the seashore and installed the Padukas in it.

Vedantic States & Intellect

Bramhachari Vishnubuva, was a great scholar well versed in Vedic scriptures. He was a great orator and was respected and honoured by Kings and Emperors. The ruler of Akkalkot once invited him to deliver lectures on *Vedanta*. All this honour and respect created an inflated ego and vanity in him during his stay. He visited the Swami and challenged Him to explain the meaning of *Bramha Tadakar Vritti*. Sri Swami Samarth merely smiled and did not reply. Vishnubuva thought that the question was beyond the Swami's capacity to answer and that He was ignorant of the meaning! His conceit rose all the more and he started making slighting and derogatory remarks about the Swami, that He did not know the basic tenets of Vedanta and was considered a *Mahatma* by ignorant, illiterate and credulous people. Even then the Swami did not respond.

One night Vishnubuva dreamt that thousands of scorpions were crawling on his body and he was desperately trying to get them off, when one of them stung him! He screamed so loudly, that a Parsi friend sleeping next to him woke up in fright. He then woke up Vishnubuva who was still shouting, his face contorted with fright. Afterwards, when fully awake though not yet out of the fear the nightmare had produced, he told the Parsi about his dream.

After some days, Vishnubuva visited the Swami and arrogantly asked again about *Brahma Tadakar Vritti*. Sri Swami Samarth said "You stupid fool! You could not discriminate between a dream and reality; you screamed so loudly in your dream that you frightened that poor, Parsi. Do you think you have become a great Yogi just because of your reading Vedas and giving eloquent discourses thousands of times? Do you think that the supreme state of *Brahma Tadakar Vritti* is such a simple thing, that it can be experienced by any fool? Or that it can be talked about? Your dialectics would be of least help in making spiritual progress. First, knock out your conceit and become humble".

Later on when Vishnubuva approached the Swami with true repentance and humility, Maharaj explained the spiritual significance and import of that supreme state - the state of supreme absorption in Brahmic consciousness and blessed him with a glimpse of that state. Vishnubuva became a saint of renown in later life. He wrote several spiritual and religious books. Swami Samarth saved Vishnubuva from conceit and intellectual approach to spiritual progress, put him on the right path and made a saint out of a *theoretical Vedantin.*

Wavering Faith

A similar incident occurred when one Shastri, a pundit from Sringeri Muth accompanied a devotee of Akkalkot Maharaj called Bavadekar. At the first meeting he took Swamiji for a lunatiç. He thought "How can such a 'man' guide anyone on the spiritual path? I am far better than him". He told this to Bavadekar, who, in spite of being a devotee, became sceptical and his faith, in the Swami wavered. Both of them were sleeping in a room that very night, the door bolted from the inside. The doors opened with a crash and there appeared on the threshold, Swami Samarth who said to Bavadekar "When will you also become a Shastri, well versed in scriptures? Poor Shastri of Sringeri- 6 masters have got hold of him - *Kama, Krodha, Lobha, Moha, Mada, Matsarya* (sexual desire, anger, greed, delusion, arrogance and envy). He is their servant; They make him dance to their tune without respite - he has no freedom; a great self-styled scholar that he is". Having said these words, Swamiji disappeared and the doors closed by themselves. Bavadekar approached Swamiji with folded hands the next morning and prostrated at His feet. He prayed to be pardoned and Swami Samarth blessed him and sent him away.

Not only the intellect, but the heart also has to blossom - only then will the soul blossom too. *Hridaya Vikas* leads to *Atma Vikas.*

Feeding 1000 Brahmins

A wealthy businessman from Bombay had no children. He and his wife went to Ganagapur and prayed to Lord Dattatreya, undertaking to feed a thousand Brahmins if they had a son. Within a year a son was born, but business losses reduced the couple to poverty and the businessman died. The pledge to feed 1000 Brahmins remained unfulfilled and his widow was conscious of this. She went to Ganagapur with her infant son and begged pardon of Datta Sriguru. That night she had a vision of Gurudev Datta who said "Feed Sri Swami Samarth at Akkalkot and your vow will be fulfilled".

She was very happy and she proceeded to Akkalkot. She came across Him and He like a child, demanded that she feed him! The woman was overjoyed and fed Sri Swami, albeit a poor and meagre meal. Swamiji, however seemed to have enjoyed the meal very much and said "Do not worry any longer, you have redeemed your pledge". With the blessings of Swami Samarth the happy woman returned home.

Arrogance cured

The hydraulic engineer (called *Bumb Saheb* in Marathi) was one of the senior officials of Akkalkot state. Once while on his rounds in the Khas Bag

Gardens, he saw Kondu Anna washing his feet at the garden well. This was a minor infraction of rules, but Bumb Saheb lost all restraint and started kicking and beating Kondu Anna mercilessly. Anna, a devotee of the Swami went and narrated to Him how ruthlessly he had been beaten, for a minor misdemeanour.

After some days Swamiji went to the bungalow of Bumb Saheb, who was quite surprised and quickly arranged for a seat and requested Maharaj to be seated. Maharaj said "You will be unable to eat or drink anything apart from *Kanji* (rice water)" and went away. (Only the poorest people have *Kanji*)

Bumb Saheb was taken aback and he could not understand what Swamiji meant. A few days later, he was bitten by a poisonous serpent and suffered unbearable pain. He survived, but his foot was in a bad shape and doctors urged him to have his foot amputated. Through a friend, Moro Pant, who was a devotee of Akkalkot Maharaj, he begged the Swami to save his life. Swami Samarth took pity on him and advised him to stop all food and take only *Kanji* (rice water). This the Bumb Saheb did and within 8 days he recovered so that he could stand on his feet. Sri Swami Samarth cured his foot completely and along with it, he cured his haughtiness and arrogance too.

Time has not come

Vasudeo Phadke was one of the foremost Maharashtrian revolutionaries, fighting for independence from Britain. After the 1857 war of independence, there was great repression by the

British rulers and the condition of the people was pathetic. The Christian missionaries having the full backing and patronage of the rulers offered economic security and could lure many Hindus to undertake conversion to Christianity. All these conversions provoked many right thinking, peaceful Hindus.

Vasudeo hailed from an aristocratic family near Panvel. Shivaji's life was a great inspiration to him and he planned to raise armies from among Koli and Ramoshi people to fight and vanquish the British.

He was a great devotee of Lord Dattatreya and he had composed devotional songs under the name *Datta Lahiri*. As Sri Swami Samarth was the incarnation of Gurudev Datta, he wanted to seek His blessings, before taking any action. He knew that unless there was divine grace, nothing could succeed. As Ramdas Swami put it:

> Saamarthya aahe chalavaliche
> Jojo kareel tyache,
> Pari tethe bhagwantache,
> Adhistan pahije

(Every movement gathers strength from the efforts which men make; nevertheless Divine blessings are necessary.) Vasudeo therefore came to Swamiji and placed his sword at His feet, prayed to Him to bless his efforts. Swamiji looked at him, took the sword and asked for it to be taken away. He said "The time has not yet come".

Vasudeo continued with his revolutionary activities, however, and he was caught, tried and confined to prison in Aden, where he died at the age of only 38, in 1883. As Sant Tukaram said " *Tuka mhane, thethe na lage tatdi, prapta ghadi kaal alyaveena.*" Tukaram says: "Impatience will serve no purpose, for the right moment must dawn."

Similarly, Anna Patwardhan was a renowned physician and was a great patriot too. He felt restless and wanted to free India from the foreign yoke. Having a decided spiritual bent, he believed more in Divine grace and strength for success, than in human effort alone. He wanted to immerse himself in *Yagna* and intense *Tapasya* for achieving independence.

Before starting on his *Tapasya*, he went to Swami Samarth for His blessings. Swamiji told him "God Almighty has set this world in motion and this cosmos is going on according to a scheme planned by HIM. Every event has to wait its turn and without His grace even a blade of grass cannot move."

Swami Samarth further told him that the time was not ripe and the country had still to wait for freedom. He was told to go and serve Narasimha Saraswati[24] at Alandi and first strive to attain the freedom of his own soul, through the grace of his Guru. Freedom of the soul is the true *Swarajya* (self-rule). Swamiji assured him "India will not continue in bondage for long. She will surely attain freedom in a few decades".

---

[24] Not to be confused with Datta Avatar Sri Narasimha Saraswati: Refer to Chapter VII under Sri Vithal Swami.

Ineffective Hair

A barber used to come regularly to shave the Swami and he would also cut his nails. He knew the great power of the Swami and began collecting the hair and nail parings and distributing them to the afflicted devotees as talismans. They were very effective and there was great demand for them. Tempted by greed, the barber started selling them for money. Once he started doing this, the hair and nails stopped giving relief and lost all their powers. As long as they were given free in all faith they proved highly efficacious, but when greed and selfishness stepped in, Swamiji made them ineffective.

Sceptical Mind - True Healer

One Athalye went to Akkalkot along with Madhav Vaidya, a well known physician, for the darshan of Swami Samarth. When they prostrated at His feet, Sri Samarth offered one thread and some rice grains as prasad to Athalye and to Vaidya HE gave a handful of earth. The prasad to Athalye indicated that he would never experience any dearth of food or clothing; the earth was given as medicine to Vaidya.

As they were returning, at the outskirts of the Akkalkot, they came across a man suffering severe stomach pain. Vaidya thought that this was a wonderful opportunity to test the earth-medicine. He gave a pinch of earth to that man and he had instant relief! It worked a miracle! It ought to, having come from the Divine hands of Swami Samarth, Lord

Dhanvantari* Himself. But the human mind being sceptical, Vaidya wanted to test it and make sure. That night the Vaidya was given "darshan" by Sri Swami Samarth in a dream. HE said "That man had no need of your ministrations, as he was under my care. He would have been cured anyway".

Both these experiences convinced Vaidya that human beings are only instruments in the healing process - the real healer is GOD. He gave up his "practise" and spent the remainder of his life in prayer and devotion.

Making Of An Ustaad

Balkrishna was a renowned musician. He ran away from home when he was just a boy, to learn music. He went in search of a musical guru. First, he went to Sri Annabuva who was a musician of some repute (and a disciple of Swami Samarth) Annabuva did not allow him to stay, but told him to go on seeking a guru. Balkrishna wandered from place to place, but could not find his guru.

He went to Indore and approached one Ustad Joshibuva, a great singer, who turned him out.

He then went to Akkalkot for Darshan of Sri Swami Samarth, who looked at him and asked him to go North, with His blessings. He would definitely find a guru there.

---

* The physician of the Gods

The boy went to Benares and sat by the river Ganga. By coincidence the master musician of Indore came there. He saw him and called out to him, saying "Are you not the same boy who had come to see me at Indore?" The boy replied in the affirmative. The Ustad took a liking for him now. He now appreciated the boy's earnestness and strong resolve for learning. He asked him to come to Indore as his son, stating that he would teach him music.

Accordingly Balkrishna went with him to Indore, learnt music and became a master himself. It was all by the grace of Akkalkot Maharaj.

CHAPTER 7

SWAMI SAMARTH - THE SADGURU
SWAMIJI'S SPIRITUAL HEIRS

It would be impossible to enumerate the spiritual disciples of Sri Sadguru Swami Samarth, because apart from the known spiritual heirs of Swamiji, *Avtaari Purush* (incarnations) often have *Gupta Sishya* (secret disciples) for reasons which we cannot ever understand. They often initiate disciples at a distance of hundreds of miles by *Sankalpa Diksha*. Naturally, we cannot know about these disciples. Sri Ramanna Maharishi, initiated disciples across continents and once rebuked a disciple and his wife for having come from Colombia (in Latin America) to India in search of Him, after he had given them *Darshan* in their garden. Indeed, Dr. Paul Brunton embarked on his *Search of Secret India*, after Sri Ramanna Maharshi's *Darshan*, while he was fishing in the Thames river on outskirts of London, 4,200 (plus) miles from Tiruvannamalai, where Sri Ramanna Maharishi used to stay!

These 'Gupta Sishya' may not all be in the public eye, nor have any disciples or do any visible spiritual work. As Paramahamsa Yogananda* writes "Invariable rules may not be formulated about saints, some perform miracles, others do not, some are inactive while others are concerned with large affairs; some teach, travel, accept disciples, while others pass their lives as silently and unobtrusively as a

---

* Ibid

shadow". He also mentions Babaji the great Yogi, who moves round with his secret band of disciples.

Thus, very often devotees of certain saints do not know that they (the saints) are the *Gupta Sishya* of some Sadguru. In addition, sometimes a saint may have *Upaguru's* that is additional Gurus, to whom they may be sent by their guru for some specific instruction or they may be given *Darshan* spontaneously by an *Upaguru* e.g. Ramakrishna Paramahamsa. Dilip Kumar Roy was a staunch disciple of Sri Aurobindo. Yet following an inner urge, he went to live in Ramannashram and attained the transcendent state of *Samadhi* under the guidance of Sri Ramanna Maharishi, who thus became his "Upaguru".

As will be seen later, Gondvalekar Maharaj and Vithal Swami also had *Upagurus*. Why even 'Vishnu Avataar' Sri Rama whose guru was Vasistha, had scores of Upagurus during His 14 years of exile from Ayodhya.

How then would we know about these *Gupta Sishya?* Very often the Sadguru Himself tells one of His spiritual heirs and commands it be kept secret, (for unknown or for revealed reasons), until their *Mahaniryan,* when it may or may not be revealed. Great saints are not interested in recognition and praise of their achievements as we are!

1. As we have seen Sri Swami Samarth travelled all over India, after emerging from the ant-hill. During the course of His journey to Gangasagar, He gave *Darshan* to Sri Ramakrishna

Paramahamsa at Dakshineswar. After Swamiji blessed him, Sri Ramakrishna is said to have uttered "Alakh Niranjan! I feel most blessed by your Darshan!"

2. Sri Sai Baba of Shirdi

There is a period of 17 - 22 years which are a blank to Sai Baba's devotees. He used to serve Sri Swami Samarth at Mangalvedha, while still a boy. Maharaj is said to have blessed him by placing His divine hand on the boy's head. The boy turned into a *Jnani* and *Mahayogi* by this *Sparsha Diksha* (initiation by touch) of Swamiji. Later he travelled far and wide and finally settled down in Shirdi, when he became known as Sai Baba.

Bharadwaja* writes that:

a) When Swami Samarth was about to take "Mahaniryan", Keshav Naik, one of His devotees said, with tears in his eyes "Maharaj, if you go away, what support have we ?"

Akkalkot Maharaj gave his "Padukas" to Naik to be worshipped and said "My manifestation will be at Shirdi. Go there and be devoted to Him. If you do so, you will not suffer my absence and you will be happy."

After the "Maha Samadhi" of Akkalkot Maharaj, Naik with his son and two Brahmins went to Shirdi.

* "Sai Baba, The Master" by E. Bharadwaja, Shree Guru Paduka Publications, Ingole, 1993.

On the way they were told that Sai Baba was a Muslim and Brahmins should not bow to him. When they all arrived at "Dwarka-mayi", Sai Baba said to Naik "You and your son may come and visit me. The two others are zealots".

Then they were asked to bring some margosa leaves and all four were asked to eat them. Naik and his son found them sweet, but the brahmins found them unusually bitter. Sai Baba thus confirmed the statement of Akkalkot Maharaj in the mind of Naik and his son.

b) Harish Pithale had a son who suffered from epileptic fits. He took his son to Sai Baba at Shirdi and he was cured. After spending some days in Baba's blessed presence, the Pithale family sought his permission to return home. Baba called Pithale near and said "Bapu, I had given you Rs. 2 earlier. Now, I give you Rs. 3. Keep these also in your shrine and worship them. You will be benefitted. Pithale could not understand how Baba could have given Rs 2 earlier, as this was his first visit to Shirdi. Pithale's mother solved the problem. She said 'Your father visited the great Maharaj of Akkalkot when you were a small child. Swami Samarth blessed your father and gave him Rs. 2 and told him to keep them in his shrine. Your father did so carefully till his death. Thereafter, worship was neglected and the 2 rupees could not be found. Now it is clear that Akkalkot Maharaj has manifested Himself in the form of Sai Baba and gave you the clue to recognise Him."

Pithale's joy knew no bounds - he realised saints not only bless their devotees but care for their children too.

The Padukas of Akkalkot Swami are installed under the neem tree, behind the Samadhi Mandir, near the Dwarkamayi mosque. The devotees of Sai Baba worship the Padukas there first, before offering worship to Sai Baba at the Samadhi Mandir.

The Padukas were installed in 1912 with due ceremonies and religious rites conducted by Upasni Maharaj and Dada Kelkar.

Similarly, Gajanan Maharaj of Akola and Sri Anna Buva of Miraj, were Guru Bandhus (brother disciples under same guru) of Sri Sai Baba and Gupta Sishyas of Sri Swami Samarth Akkalkot Maharaj.

Countless were the spiritual heirs of Swamiji and it is not possible to give an account of all of them (for gupta shishyas are unknown to us for reasons adduced above). Just as the Sun illuminates the Moon and all planets and makes them shine, so Sri Swami Samarth illumined many souls and left a legacy of many spiritual luminaries.

4. Vasudevanand Saraswati

Vasudev was a great devotee of Lord Datta. He was well versed in *Shastras* and repeatedly went through the *Guru Charitra*. As a result of his ascetic life he attained great spiritual heights. He composed *Datta Puran* and *Narmada Lahiri*. Once he had a vision in which he was directed to go to Akkalkot. He visited Akkalkot and when he got the *Darshan* of Sri Swami Samarth, he saw in the celestial form of Swamiji, the *Paramahamsa* of Narsimhawadi, Dattavatar, Sri Guru Narasimha Saraswati! He later became famous as Tembe Swami.

5. Sri Krishna Saraswati

Sri Krishna Saraswati was a Jeevan Mukta Mahapurush (great soul who is no longer subject to any karma) and an Avadhoot. He was born in the year 1836. His father was Appa Bhat and His mother Annapurna Bai. They had no children and longed for a child. They prayed to Lord Dattatreya for a child, and Gurudev Datta pleased with their long and arduous devotion, appeared in their dream one night and told them that HE Himself would take birth as their son. Some months later a son Krishna was born to them.

Krishna's coming

Even at a young age, the boy displayed all traits and characteristics of an Avadhoot. One day when He had gone for Darshan to his Kooldevata, He had the Darshan of Khandoba (Lord Shiva) who ordered him to go to Akkalkot for Darshan of Sri Swami Samarth.

For days before His coming to Akkalkot, Sri Swami Samarth was saying "Krishna is coming, my Krishna is coming". None of the disciples or devotees could understand the significance of this. When the boy Krishna came, Swamiji got up and taking hold of the boy's hand, led him into the dense jungle. In the deep jungle they sat together, Swamiji on a stone slab the boy at His feet. The boy started reciting *Stotras* in praise of Swamiji, who then blessed him saying "Your are a part of ME and have taken this *Avatar* for the spiritual upliftment of mankind".

Krishna's Going

Swamiji then laid His hand on the boy's head. This *Sparsha Diksha* (initiation by touch) sent the boy into *Nirvikalpa Samadhi* for 8 days! On the 8th day, Swamiji stroked his back lovingly and brought the boy back from the transcendental state to terrestrial consciousness. Maharaj then named him *Krishna Saraswati* and commanded him to stay at Kolhapur and spread the divine light from there. HE also gave him *His Atma Linga Padukas* as a sign of His grace and blessings. After they returned to Akkalkot, Maharaj started saying "Krishna will go, Krishna will go". Sri Krishna Saraswati left for Kolhapur after a few days.

One day, Swamiji started looking in the direction of Ganagapur saying "Why has our Brahmin not come?" He said this several times and nobody understood the meaning. After some time a Brahmin afflicted with leprosy came to Swamiji. He had gone to Ganagapur first and there received a mystical directive to visit Akkalkot and seek Maharaj's blessings and grace. Having arrived, he prayed to Maharaj to remove his affliction.

Swamiji asked him to go to Kolhapur and serve Sri Krishna Saraswati. The Brahmin went and served Sri Krishna Saraswati with great devotion. The latter pleased with his dedicated service for many years, blessed him and completely cured him of his leprosy.

Sri Krishna Saraswati imbibed to the full the spiritual power of Swami Samarth, was deemed to be almost one with Maharaj. It is believed that vows made at Akkalkot could be fulfilled at the Kolhapur Muth, especially after the *Mahaniryan* of Swamiji. Sri Krishna Saraswati (being a highly evolved soul) could relieve the sufferings of the afflicted and fulfill their desires. Saints came to Him for guidance and elucidation of their doubts. It is recorded that while traversing India, Swami Vivekanand came for His *Darshan* and was blessed by Him with *Vachasiddhi* (he would succeed through speaking). Tembe Swami, Rangoli Maharaj, Narayan Maharaj of Kedgaon and Upasni Maharaj of Sakori, also visited Him for His guidance.

Displaying Leelas

Sri Krishna Saraswati displayed His *Leelas* throughout His earthly sojourn. He was never seen to eat, drink or sleep throughout His life, after coming to Kolhapur. It should be remembered that He had thousands of devotees, coming to him at all hours of the day and night.

He would, on the river path, unexpectedly touch a married woman and say "You will have a son soon" or touch a maiden and say to her mother "She will get married soon". Needless to say these words would prove prophetic.

Once while walking during a long hot summer, His devotees complained that their feet were scalded and requested that they be allowed to rest. Sri Krishna Saraswati looked at the sun and ordered "Give us a little shade". Immediately a huge cloud appeared and blocked the sun, simultaneously a cool breeze sprang up and cooled the environment. This lasted until they completed their walk after which the hot sun blazed again!

Sri Krishna Saraswati could make Himself as light as a feather or so heavy, that even 5 weight lifters would not be able to lift him!

He had a small tail and *Rama-Bhaktas* or *Hanuman-Bhaktas* who experienced doubts or were troubled, would be shown His small tail. They would be rid of their doubts ever after.

Once, a Brahmin took a vow at Akkalkot that if he had a son he would personally feed Sri Swami Samarth with *Peda* and distribute *Pedas* to all and sundry. Unfortunately, though his wish was fulfilled (he had a son), Swamiji gave up His earthly body, before he could fulfill his vow.

Feeling distressed, he stood before the *Samadhi* of Akkalkot Maharaj and wondered how to fulfill his vow. That night Maharaj appeared in his dream and said "I am now in the form of Hanuman, in Kumbhar Galli[25], Kolhapur as Krishna Saraswati. Come there and fulfill your vow".

The Brahmin was overjoyed and he left immediately for Kolhapur. On presenting himself before Krishna Saraswati, however he had doubts. Akkalkot Maharaj had said "In the form of Hanuman" but here was a human being. Sri Krishna Saraswati recognised his dilemma and showed him His tail. The Brahmin was stunned and he realised that Swami Samarth and Krishna Saraswati were one and the same. He fulfilled his vow and became a disciple of Sri Krishna Saraswati.

Sri Krishna Saraswati performed hundreds of miracles for 22 years after the Mahaniryan of Sri Swami Samarth. He took Mahasamadhi in 1900.

---

[25] Hence He was also known as Kumbhar Swami.

Sri Namdev Maharaj

Sri Namdev Maharaj was one of the most illustrious of the disciples of Sri Krishna Saraswati. The experiences of Vivekananda, Yogananda & Namdev Maharaj as *Sadhakas* (seekers of God) and disciples show us how a devotee can often go off at a tangent, even when the disciple is as highly evolved as Vivekananda, Yogananda or Namdev Maharaj and the Guru as great as Ramakrishna, Yukteshwar, Krishna Saraswati. They play these *leelas* for our benefit. Truly is it said that the spiritual path is like walking on a knife-edge!

Namdev Maharaj was born on the holy and auspicious day of *Gudi Padva* in 1841 and lived for 130 years[26]. His mother was a *Datta Bhakta* and had even in her advanced state of pregnancy gone to the *Datta Mandir* for her daily *Pooja* (worship). While circumambulating (*Pradakshina*) the holy *Audumber* tree she went into labour and gave birth to Namdev Maharaj. A Yogi who was praying there stated *"Sri Datta is born"*. His father was a very rich building contractor. He (Namdev) had four elder sisters and one younger sister. His mother died when he was only four years old and was taken away by his eldest sister, who was childless, to Madiyal which was his birthplace.

He will see Datta Maharaj

The *Datta Mandir* where he was born, was his sister's property. It was frequented by great saints and yogis.

---

[26] Some devotees state that he lived for 138 years.

Namdev loved to spend his days in the temple. He would attend the *Kirtans, Pravachans and Bhajans* which were on almost everyday. One day he had the *Darshan* of Rajaram Buva, a highly evolved soul who forecast that "This boy will have *Darshan of Datta Maharaj*" and gave him his *Datta Guru* idol, made of five metals (Panchaloha).

Once he was taken by his sister for the *Darshan* of Sri Bote swami, who was a disciple of Sri Swami Samarth. He too stated "He will see *Datta Maharaj*".

Sri Namdev Maharaj being the only son and heir of a rich father lacked nothing and was not interested in studies, which he stopped at the age of ten. His father died when he was fifteen years old. He had no interest in his father's business or in farming. He continued visiting the holy places and obtained *Darshan* of many holy men. There was a *Shiv-yogi* Naglingayya who was a *Naga* sadhu (naked). He used to live on top of a hill and was always surrounded by hundreds of cobras and poisonous snakes. If anyone ventured near, he would throw stones at them and drive them away. However, all this was a test. Namdev decided to have his *Darshan*, as he was one of the greatest saints in that region. Controlling his fear he started clearing a way between the snakes, while Naglingayya swami was throwing stones at him. He persisted in his attempts and saw that the Swami was not meaning to hit him or hurt him. Seeing the spiritual urge of Namdev, the Sadhu beckoned him to come near and said "You will definitely have *Darshan of Datta Maharaj* (Lord

Dattatraya) in Kolhapur, you have nothing to gain from me".

Just after this incident, his eldest sister's husband died and she decided to adopt him, as they were childless. Namdev Maharaj inherited 75 acres of land, the government contracts, building construction business, jewellery enough to fill a bath tub, in addition to what he had inherited from his father. His renunciation later assumes significance, in view of his great wealth. As Sri Yukteshwar Giri, the Guru of Yogananda had caustically remarked "A beggar cannot renounce anything, wealth has renounced him!"

When seventeen years of age, Namdev Maharaj was a great gymnast and wrestling champion. He could perform five hundred squats and equal number of pushups! When he was twenty two years, he was married to Gangabai, who was very beautiful and they resided in Kolhapur.

Namya's come

In Kolhapur, their house was on the path which Sri Krishna Saraswati used to take every day, while going to the river. Namdev Maharaj would go to his farm on the outskirts in a horse carriage every morning. One day he did not do so and was sitting on the veranda of his house, when Sri Krishna Saraswati came up to him and said "you have obviously forgotten what Naglingayya had told you. I am Datta Maharaj. You are part of me", and went away.

Namdev Maharaj now remembered the forecast! He made enquiries next day and found where Sri Krishna Saraswati stayed and went for His *Darshan*. On reaching His house he stood in a corner, waiting till he could be alone with Krishna Saraswati. However, saying "Namya's come, Namya's come", Krishna Saraswati asked Namdev to come near Him. He was stunned to hear his name from the saint as he had not mentioned it to Him in his previous, momentary meeting and he was now meeting Him for only the second time.

He prostrated at His feet - at last he had found his guru! Sri Krishna Saraswati said "You are bound to me now; where else can you go?" Then holding *Namya's* arm, He told the other devotees "He is the Namdev of Pandharpur". After this meeting, Namdev Maharaj's life revolved around Sri Krishna Saraswati.

For three years, Namdev Maharaj would spend the whole day with Sri Krishna Saraswati and return home only after the last *Aarti* at night. He was disappointed however, as he was not given any *Upasna*[27] to do, nor was any verbal guidance given to him. Only the fact that his guru's divinity was supremely visible, kept his impatience bottled up.

Experience of Samadhi

One day, Sri Krishna Saraswati suddenly came to Namdev Maharaj's house. All the women and children had gone out and he was alone. Sri Krishna

---

[27] Spiritual practice.

Saraswati led him to the cow shed. There was a pile of wood stacked there, for use as fuel. The guru removed wooden sticks from the pile and created enough space for Namdev Maharaj to sit in *Padmasana* (lotus-pose) and made him sit down. He touched Namdev's head and put him into *Savikalpa Samadhi* and replaced all the wood, so that nobody could guess there was anybody in the stack.

The members of the family came back and were surprised to find all the doors open and nobody at home. Servants were sent out to locate Namdev Maharaj. Next day his mother went to the Guru and asked about her son's whereabouts and was told to search properly, he would be found. All the women were in sorrow and were mystified at the disappearance of Namdev and presumed him dead. On the fourth day, Sri Krishna Saraswati came home and went to the cow shed. He started removing the wood with the household watching. When Namdev was uncovered, they all burst out in tears and lamentations, as he was frozen and unmoving. The Guru brought Namdev out of his state of *Samadhi* and asked him how long he had been sitting there. Namdev replied "You made me sit here, for maybe 20 - 25 minutes". The household was astonished, because this was the fourth day! Sri Maharaj asked him "Shall I give this faculty to you permanently?" Namdev, immediately replied "I do not want this type of Samadhi. On its ending all the old *Vrittis* come back. Give me the state of *Sahaja Samadhi* which you possess". Sri Maharaj smiled and said "Be it as you wish".

After this incident his mother and sister were convinced of the divine greatness of Sri Krishna Saraswati and did not object or oppose Namdev in his *Sadhana* in any way.

No Spiritual Practice

Once again Sri Maharaj did not give any *Upasna* or task for Namdev to do. He would ask Sri Maharaj from time to time for guidance or *Upasana* only to be told "We shall see". After a few days, He became impatient, for he thought he was not progressing spiritually at all. He was friendly with one *Naga* Sadhu and asked him how to progress spiritually. The Sadhu told him a yogic *Kriya* to be performed with the horn of sambhar deer. Namdev did this *Kriya* and after two days could not walk or sit or sleep. On the third day, he was at death's door. Sri Maharaj came home; Namdev was so weak that he could not even prostrate at his guru's feet. Sri Guru removed the horns and helped Namdev recover, saying "Namya, do you think you can progress spiritually by injuring your ribs? Progress is made by the blossoming of the heart". After his recovery, life continued in the same fashion.

There was one sadhu who had minor powers and could perform some *Siddhis*. Namdev heard about his *greatness* and went there with two of his *Gurubandhus*. While there the oil level in the lamp was low and the flame started spluttering. Namdev pointed it out to the Sadhu. He was asked to put water in the lamp and the flame rose high and bright

138

again! The Sadhu asked "Can your Guru do this?" All his disciples started jeering at Namdev.

Unclean

They then went for *Darshan* of Sri Krishna Saraswati in the evening. Sri Maharaj did not allow them to enter, saying "Nobody should touch them or talk to them, they are impure, wash yourself". They went home and had a bath and came back, yet Sri Maharaj would not allow them to enter, saying they were impure. They were puzzled, since all of them had had a bath; none were mourning* over any deaths in their family nor were any of them associated with any sacrilegious act to the best of their knowledge. This intrigued Namdev, who introspected deeply and soon realised why Sri Guru Maharaj would not let them in. Namdev apologised, "We made a big mistake in going to the sadhu, without your permission. Please forgive us." At this Sri Guru Maharaj allowed them in and said "Namya, the sadhu will be handcuffed and paraded in public tomorrow. He wants to see what I can do - so be it." The next day, they saw the sadhu arrested on some fraud charges, handcuffed and paraded around the whole town! Sri Guru Maharaj was referring to the impurity of their mind, caused by doubt. As such they had to cleanse their mind. This impatience and lack of absolute faith in the guru had also clouded the mighty Swami Vivekananda and Parmahamsa Yogananda in their earlier days - it is a lesson for all struggling *sadhakas*.

---

* The mourning period is considered to be inauspicious as per Hindu rituals.

Control of Sex Urge

For some time, Namdev was struggling vainly to control his sexual appetite. He wanted to get rid of the sexual urge and since he couldn't, became agitated mentally. With a view to finding some technique to eliminate the sexual urge, he met one sadhu who carried out *Aghori* practices. He advised that the organs should have a hole drilled in them and some locking mechanism inserted, whereby they would not be a hindrance to spirituality. Furthermore, he showed his own disfigurement, which convinced Namdev about this *technique*.

Namdev decided to carry out this technique the next day itself and did so in great secret. He developed infection and after two days was again at death's door. On the third day Sri guru came early in the morning. He was in a terrifying rage and said "Stop this mad behaviour once and for all". He released Namdev from the *Aghori* technique in a trice. Later, Sriguru advised him "Sexual enjoyment is very deep rooted and cannot be eliminated instantly. The *Indriyas* (senses) have to be directed into different channels. Patience is required. *Viveka* (discrimination) has to be used. Instead of trying to control sex urge or anger, the mind should be focused on God and Moksha. Instead of trying to control externalities, control the mind instead."

At Death's Door

The years sped by and Namdev's faith increased and he surrendered body, mind and soul to his Sri guru.

Namdev developed a urinary infection and the kidneys also got infected. He tried herbal medicines, but to no avail. Sri Maharaj advised him to stop all medicines. His condition steadily worsened. Meanwhile, Sri guru used to come to his door, call his wife and when she appeared, wipe the *Kumkum* off her forehead[28] and leave without a word. No Indian women would have tolerated this, but she too had developed faith in Sri Krishna Saraswati and was puzzled, but kept quiet. After ten days, Namdev was sub conscious so when Sri Maharaj came and called her, she covered her forehead with her sari, went to the door and burst in tears. Krishna Saraswati left without a word and He did not come thereafter. After three days it seemed that Namdev was on his last legs and his wife ran out panic stricken, to search for Sri Maharaj who could not be found anywhere. She ran helter-skelter and finally found Him at the river *ghat*. She collapsed at His feet saying "Take my life first, but save him". Sri Krishna Saraswati set right the *Kumkum* which had spread on her forehead, lovingly, and said "Take two buckets of water from your neighbour and wash your doorstep with *Haldi-Kumkum* and then do a *namaskar* (salutation) and your Namya will be well".

She ran back and did what she was told speedily. A miracle took place! Her husband who was literally on his last legs and could not even speak, started calling out vigorously to her "I am hungry, give me something to eat." He had recovered

---

[28] This act amounts to indicating impending widowhood.

141

instantaneously! "Medicines have limitations, the divine creative force has none". Thus Sri Yukteshwar Giri used to say, and we see the force of his statement above.

Renunciation

After this experience, Namdev's spiritual progress was rapid. Two years later, Sri Krishna Saraswati suddenly asked him to renounce all his wealth, saying "If you do so, only then you are mine, otherwise do not show your face again." His wife was also present when this happened. Namdev asked his wife "Do you want all this wealth and Samsara (worldly life) or do you want me?" Without hesitation she said "I want you". Both of them immediately started the task of distributing their great wealth to their relatives and friends.

Having completed this distribution, Namdev ran for his Guru's Darshan. When he was twenty feet away, his guru said "You are now really clean, from now on you are mine for all eternity. Then, stroking him lovingly, his guru said "Today your victory is total". After this both Namdev and his wife lived like Sanyasis. They would eat only if offered something or starve for days, but they had their guru's grace and progressed spiritually, and attained Vairagya (detachment).

One day Sri guru came and calling both husband and wife, said "Here is a rupee, go to my maher (mother's place) serve God, do not beg" The couple left immediately for Sri guru's birthplace, thinking that, that was what He meant. When they reached there, they got a telepathic message that maher meant

Narsoba wadi, after all Sri Krishna Saraswati was a *Datta Avatar* . They also visited Audambar, Pandharpur, Tulzapur and Akkalkot. They would always be offered food mysteriously and they did not have to beg. At Akkalkot they got the command "Worship the Padukas at the sangam". On reflection they realised that that meant they should go to Ganagapur. Even though public transport was available, they had to walk many miles as they had no money, often on empty stomachs. But they never once begged or asked for anything. They had to undergo a lot of travail and trouble, including the suspicion that Namdev had abducted his lady companion, (who was none other than his wife), an extremely beautiful lady, while he looked like a wrestler! Finally, they reached Ganagapur.

There was a person who used to collect basketfuls of *tulsi* leaves and sell them to devotees. He approached Namdev of his own accord and asked him whether he would do this task, as he wished to go to his native place for sometime.

Sri Namdev Maharaj was thrilled at this *bonus*. He was able to do the *seva* (task) ordered by his Sadguru, that too without begging. The devotees used to give food, clothes or a little money to Namdev unasked, maybe as recompense for the *tulsi* leaves he gave to them. Ten months sped by in this manner.

One night, Namdev had a clear vision of his Sadguru asking him to return to Kolhapur. At the same time one devotee was ordered to worship Namdev

Maharaj and give *Dakshina* (money) to him, by Sri Krishna Sarswati. When Namdev Maharaj shied away, Sri guru told him "Consider this worship is reaching me through you." By coincidence, Namdev Maharaj's family happened to come to Ganagapur and they travelled back together. Their return journey was very happy and comfortable.

Make the Foundation Firm

Meanwhile, the end of Sri Krishna Saraswati's Avatar was near. He had already made the preparations. When Namdev Maharaj came, he said, "Namya, the task of building up the *Datta Sampradaya* is yours. Make the tree grow strong and with firm foundations." Saying thus, Sri guru gave up His body and merged with the Absolute.

Namdev ran to tell his wife about the sad event and many devotees saw a divine globular light following him to his house, enter behind him and then vanish into the *Padukas* of Sri guru. These *Padukas* are now enshrined at the Akkalkot Swami Muth at Apta Road, near Bombay.

After the *Mahaniryan* of Sri Krishna Saraswati, Namdev Maharaj set up a Muth in his house, where devotees could come and worship his Guru's *Padukas*. Cobras were often seen traversing the *Padukas*, as if caressing them and worshipping them. Similar sights have been seen even after these *Padukas* were transferred to Apta. Namdev Maharaj would often sleep in the Muth and these cobras would often crawl over his body. He often referred to them as his 'bodyguards' and had no fear of them.

Namdev Maharaj would often be seen talking to an invisible person. At these times a sacred atmosphere would manifest and a perfume at once wonderful and unearthly could be smelt by the lucky few. Later, he would state "Sriguru had come." On other occasions, he would be lost to the world, singing *bhajans* or singing *"Guru Maharaj Guru, Jai Jai Parambramha Sadguru"*

Namdev Maharaj spread the principles of *Datta sampradaya* to the south. He visited Madras and today there are many devotees of Sri Krishna Saraswati and Akkalkot Swami there*. Apart from Madras, there are devotees in Belgaum, Dharwar, Narsobawadi, Miraj, Pune, Kedgaon and Sakori.

VITHAL SWAMI ALIAS NARASIMHA SARASWATI OF ALANDI

(We shall refer to Shri Narasimha Saraswati of Alandi by his former name Vithal Swami, in order to avoid confusion with *Datta Avatar Sri Narasimha Saraswati*)

Vithal Swami was a resident of Pandarpur and was a Yogi well versed in all scriptures. He was considered an eminent scholar and had advanced spiritually. He was stuck with some subtle spiritual problems and with a view to seeking guidance from Sri Swami Samarth, he came to Akkalkot for His *Darshan.*

* Akkalkot Swami Padukas have recently been installed in Madras.

Akkalkot Swami knew that Vithal Swami was coming and directed that a seat (of deerskin) be kept near Himself. By this gesture Sri Samarth indicated that a person of some spiritual advancement was coming to see Him.

Transcendental Bliss

On his arrival, Swamiji recited a Sanskrit verse on the *Ajnya Chakra,* (one of the mystic chakras of the *Kundalini*), and cast a glance at Vithal Swami, who at once plunged into a deep trance and experienced spiritual ecstasy. He remained in that transcendental bliss for two hours. Sri Swami Samarth again cast a glance and Vithal Swami slowly surfaced to his earthly senses. What he could not achieve by years of arduous practice, was given to him by a mere glance, by Swami Samarth! The Swami lifted and rocketed him off spiritually, by *Drik Diksha* - transmission of spiritual power through a glance. The anecdote below demonstrates what great power *(Siddhis)* he came to possess and to what spiritual height he rose through the grace of Sri Swami Samarth.

Degenerate Place

Vithal Swami was asked to proceed to Alandi, by Swamiji. When he arrived, he was disappointed at the degenerate atmosphere prevailing at that time, in such a sacred and hallowed place. Sacred traditional practices had been discarded and indulgence in depraved activities had become the vogue. Instead of reciting the *Jnaneshwari* or the sacred *Vedas,* the Brahmins were singing vulgar and sensuous songs.

Vithal Swami was deeply distressed and decided to do something to restore the sanctity of Alandi by the use of *Siddhis* (yogic power). He invited all the Brahmins for lunch and mysteriously created several heavenly dishes and gave them a sumptuous feast. The Brahmins were greatly attracted and impressed by his powers.

Vithal Swami promised them a heavenly feast daily if they recited the verses from the *Jnaneshwari* every day. This enticed the greedy and gluttonous Brahmins to learn and recite the *Jnaneshwari.* This work is so sacred, that the chanting purified their hearts and minds and brought a great transformation in them. They reverted to the sacred traditions with all their heart and took to study and recitation of holy texts. This remarkable work of restoring and reviving the spiritual splendour of Alandi, hallowed by the *Samadhi of Jnaneshwar Maharaj,* was made possible by the grace of Swami Samarth.

You have not left the "randi"?

Later, Vithal Swami again came for the *Darshan* of Swami Maharaj. Sri Swami Samarth was at that time in the Sri Rama temple, with His disciples and devotees. On his arrival, Vithal Swami prostrated at Swamiji's feet, who immediately said "What! You have still not left the *randi?"* None present could understand how these words could be addressed to a Yogi of the stature of Vithal Swami: he however immediately understood their significance and said "Maharaj! Now that you have warned me, I shall leave her for ever... but I cannot do so without your grace."

Sri Swami Samarth had a hearty laugh and ordered a tiger skin spread for Vithal Swami to sit. Thereafter they had a long talk covering his complex spiritual problems and Maharaj cleared the doubts of Vithal Swami. Finally, Vithal Swami departed after taking the blessings of Sri Swamiji.

Siddhis not worth having

The word *randi* means prostitute of the lowest type, but Swamiji's use of it implied *siddhis* or yogic powers. HE equated *siddhis* with the lowest kind of whore, and wanted to caution Vithal Swami not to get trapped by them. *Siddhis* distract the yogi from his onward progress. The goal of spiritual sadhana is not acquiring and displaying *siddhis* but the realisation of the *Self, the absolute.* Vithal Swami understood the warning and desisted thereafter from using his yogic powers. He pursued his spiritual practices with unswerving devotion to Maharaj and attained Realisation.

Vithal Swami had a wooden chariot, made, for carrying the *padukas* of Sri Jnaneshwar Maharaj. The chariot was heavy and required a number of people to draw it. One day, the chariot would not move at all and the procession could not start. Vithal Swami was at that time in deep *Samadhi.* He slowly became aware of the situation and he came to the chariot, got on it, took the reins in his hands and lo! - the chariot started moving immediately!

Vithal Swami was an ideal Yogi and spent 12 years in Alandi. He used to deliver discourses and engaged himself in a number of social and philanthropic activities. He started feeding the poor and built *Dharamshalas*. He got stone pavements constructed on the Alandi river banks. He would chant the name of Sri Swami Samarth incessantly.

His Muth and *samadhi* are at Alandi. There are a large number of disciples and devotees of his, including Maharishi Patwardhan and Madhavnath Maharaj.

It was Sri Samarth's grace that made Sri Vithal Swami (Narsimha Saraswati of Alandi) into a great yogi. It is like a candle being lit from a lamp, which is the main source, being used to light other candles.

BIDKAR MAHARAJ

Ramanand Bidkar was born in 1838 in a *Desastha* Brahmin family. He lost his father while quite young. From childhood itself he was religiously inclined and would visit places of holy pilgrimage like Pandharpur, Saptashringi etc. In adult life, he settled in Poona. He was skilled in jewellery making and also dealt in perfumes and sandalwood. He became rich and started money lending. Along the way, he somehow succeeded in learning alchemy and was able to turn base metals into gold.

Debauch

Along with wealth, he acquired other vices and enjoyed the company of debauches. Once, when on a business tour to Gwalior, he was infatuated by a beautiful courtesan and he became a slave of hers and was willing to make her a partner. Luckily for him, the woman died. His lust for women grew and he chose another woman and carried on his sensuous life, in spite of having a good wife.

By coincidence he came across a holy man at this stage. When he saw him, regret at his immoral ways gnawed at his heart and he told the sadhu he would like to become a yogi. The sadhu told him that yoga required total dispassion and non-attachment. It meant a life of total renunciation and is not for people who could not live a day without a woman.

Repentance

Bidkar took this to heart and radically changed his lifestyle. He started visiting the Hanuman temple and reciting the *Anjaneya Kavacha*. Hanuman is an embodiment of purity, celibacy and self-restraint. Bidkar gave up his old ways and was greatly purified by prayer.

True repentance draws divine forgiveness and grace. One night Bidkar had a dream, that he should pay a visit to Akkalkot and seek the grace of Sri Swami Samarth. When he arrived at Akkalkot, Swami Samarth was staying in the palace and therefore he could not have *Darshan*. He decided he would not leave the spot, nor would he have food or water until he had the *Darshan* of Maharaj. Seating himself outside the palace, he started chanting Sri Swami's name ceaselessly. Two days and nights passed thus. Of course Swami Samarth knew all and was pleased. When He came out of the palace, Bidkar prostrated and clasped His feet firmly. Sri Maharaj asked him why he was holding His feet so tightly. Bidkar replied that he was holding them tight, so that his spiritual foundation would be firm and unshakeable. Swamiji lovingly pointed to a deer skin and Bidkar could not understand whether Sri Swami Samarth was asking him to sit on it. This would be an exceptional honour and Bidkar rightly hesitated and said "Swamiji, I do not understand." Strangely, Maharaj's mood changed and he started shouting at and abusing Bidkar. Seeing the fury of Sri Swami, the devotees tried to draw him away from Swami Samarth's presence. They advised Bidkar to leave the place. Bidkar however felt he deserved all this and much more for his past debauchery. He boldly said "Maharaj, whatever you may do, I shall not lose hold of your feet. They are my sole succour and refuge now".

Swamiji's mood seemed to change again. He had tested Bidkar's faith. He said tenderly "You can leave now. Your task is done. The purpose of your visit has been achieved." Bidkar was overwhelmed with joy and tears of gratitude welled up from his eyes. He was ecstatic, a thrilling sensation passed through his body, his whole being, as if all the nerves and cells in his body were about to burst. It was the arousal of the *Kundalini* through the mere glance of the Master.

Bidkar returned to Poona, a transformed person. He was now filled with a sense of strength and confidence in the Guru's protection. His Guru's abuses had burnt off all his past sins. The Swami had ushered in a new glorious phase in his life. Bidkar took intensively to *Japa* of *'Sri Swami Samarth, jai jai Swami Samarth.'* His chanting became continuous, almost as natural and spontaneous as his breathing.

The Mango is ripened

After a year of this intensive *Nama Japa Sadhana,* he again paid a visit to Akkalkot, impelled by an irresistible desire to have his Sadguru's Darshan. Swamiji glanced at him and said "Ah! The mango is getting ripe" to indicate to Bidkar that he was progressing well in his *Sadhana.* Bidkar returned to Poona greatly encouraged in his efforts.

After another year, he again felt an irresistible yearning that he should visit the Swami, serve Him and bask in the sunshine of His grace for some days. Swamiji allowed him to stay and serve Him. One night, Bidkar was massaging the Swami's feet, feeling exhilarated at this unique honour. Swamiji fell 'asleep' and since He did not ask Bidkar to stop, Bidkar continued massaging while chanting His name, feeling thrilled and marvelling at this rare privilege. Suddenly a cobra appeared with a raised hood, hissing nastily, and about to strike. Bidkar kept on massaging Swami's feet, feeling what a blessed death it would be, holding the feet of the Swami, while chanting His holy name! Thus, he did not stop massaging his Sadguru's feet, perfectly content whether the cobra bit him or not.

Sri Maharaj got up and said "What an obstinate fellow you are." He lightly touched Bidkar's cheeks, while yelling at the cobra to get out. Bidkar lost all consciousness and was moved to a nearby room. After some time, he slowly came back to his senses. It was spiritual awakening that Maharaj's touch had given him; he was transported into an experience of ineffable bliss; he had dived into the inner divine realms of his Self. When he fully surfaced, he shed tears of gratitude at Swamiji's feet, for having bestowed on him the highest experience of transcendental bliss. Later, he returned to Poona, highly elated in spirit, having passed another test of faith.

Dakshina

Thereafter Bidkar occasionally came to Akkalkot. During one of his visits Maharaj said "Am I indebted to your forefathers, when are you going to feed me?" Bidkar immediately understood that Swamiji wanted him to do mass feeding. He decided to feed at least 1000 people and returned to Poona to arrange the money. He also took very expensive perfumes as an offering to Maharaj. On the way to Akkalkot, the horse he was riding became unruly and all the expensive perfume bottles were smashed to pieces. It was apparent from this incident that Maharaj did not want anything for Himself.

On reaching Akkalkot, he arranged the mass feeding. Swami Samarth also graced the function and partook in the meal. Bidkar felt blessed. Swamiji then asked "How much *Dakshina* will you give me?" Bidkar replied "Whatever you desire Maharaj." Swamiji said "Give me a promise that you will no longer indulge in alchemy." Bidkar promised that he would no longer practise alchemy or even think of it. *Kamini* (sexual excess) and *Kanchana* (lust for gold) are enemies of spiritual life; they are like water which douses the spiritual fire. Swamiji wanted him to have a thorough cleansing of his mind and heart *(Chitta Shudhi)* so that he could make real lasting progress in his spiritual pursuit. Hence His testing of Bidkar's faith and his various directions to him. It was like the caring mother who wants to wean the child away from evil and danger. Bidkar understood the cryptic words of Maharaj and corrected himself.

Narmada Pradakshina

Bidkar paid his fourth visit to Akkalkot after some time. Swami Samarth told him he need not come to Akkalkot again and His grace would always be on him. He asked him to do *Narmada Pradakshina* i.e. circumnavigate the Narmada river. This is a very arduous task as it involved travelling from the river mouth, along the banks to its origin, in the jungles of Chitrakoot, and back down on the other bank, to its exit into the Arabian sea. The course runs through dense forests, steep cliffs and perilous rocks and there is always the danger from reptiles, wild beasts and dacoits. Thus, completing the *Pradakshina* involves austere discipline, great forbearance, total mastery over the senses and mind and great courage.

With total faith in Swami Samarth, Bidkar set out on the holy pilgrimage. When Guru's grace is there acting as armour and umbrella, what harm can ever come to one? Even the lord of death desists from approaching such a person. Bidkar had many narrow escapes from tigers and snakes and cobras, but every time he faced danger, he found the invisible hand of Sri Swami Samarth protecting and rescuing him.

When Bidkar was at Maheshwar (on the banks of the Narmada river), he heard of the *Maha Samadhi* of Sri Swami. His grief was unbounded. He wished to discontinue his pilgrimage and return to Akkalkot. But, the same night, Swamiji appeared to him and said "I am ever alive; don't grieve WHEREVER YOU ARE, I AM ALWAYS WITH YOU. WHENEVER YOU CALL, I SHALL RESPOND. Fulfill your vow of *Pradakshina*, don't break it. Not only Mine, but Goddess Narmada's blessings are also on you." (This assurance of Maharaj is eternal and has been experienced by many devotees even to this day). Bidkar felt greatly consoled and relieved. He was again infused with courage and continued his pilgrimage. A Guru's benediction helps one to achieve the impossible. Somewhere, towards the end of his *Pradakshina*, he was honoured with the vision of Goddess Narmada who blessed him.

Meanwhile, Bidkar's wife was anxious about his safety and set out to search for him. By Maharaj's grace, she met him at Omkareshwar. Concluding the *Pradakshina* successfully, Bidkar went to other holy places like *Kashi, Prayag,* Audumbar, Narsoba Wadi, Dehu, Alandi, etc..

After completing his pilgrimages, Bidkar built a Muth at Poona and settled down to a totally ascetic life. He came to be known as Bidkar Maharaj. He cast off his body on 4th April, 1913. Amongst his disciples, one Baba Sasrabudhe was very highly spiritually evolved.

The alchemist Bidkar had himself undergone a spiritual alchemy! The sensuous and lecherous Bidkar was transformed into a saint, by the *Spiritual Alchemist* Swami Samarth!

BRAHMANISTA WAMANBUVA

Wamanbuva was a resident of Wambori village in Nagar District. He was a devotee of Lord Datta from his childhood. He had met many holy men and worked at various jobs and was not happy spiritually or materially.

One day, while he was in Poona with his mother, a Brahmin came and in course of the conversation said "A life without the grace of a *Sadguru* is totally wasted". Wamanbuva was impelled to ask "Where can I find a *Sadguru?*". He was told to go to Akkalkot and try and get *Darshan* of Sri Swami Samarth, the Avataar of Datta guru manifest in human form.

Darshan and Initiation

On hearing this, Wamanbuva immediately left for Akkalkot but Swamiji had gone to Honde, a village across the river. Wamanbuva rushed to the river bank. There was no way Wamanbuva could have reached Honde, as the river was in flood. He felt frustrated especially, because on the other side he could clearly see the celestial figure of Swami Samarth. He prostrated to Him, from his side of the river bank. Swami Samarth walked across the river and Himself came to him! Wamanbuva again prostrated, this time his heart was overflowing with gratitude for Swamiji's solicitude and compassion for him. Swami Samarth said "You are my child, be with Me, serve Me, I bless you. You will attain *Bramhanista*. Renounce the world completely". Wamanbuva at once threw away all his clothes and belongings and wore only a *Kaupin* (cod-piece). Sri Swami Samarth gave him a *Kamandalu*, (water pot carried by renunciants) as a token of His initiation and blessings.

Wamanbuva took to ascetic life and became a staunch disciple of Swami Samarth. He would visit Akkalkot twice or thrice a year. Wamanbuva went to Nasik, Trambakeshwar and then to Wani for a *Darshan* of his family deity *Saptashringi*. After offering worship to the goddess, he requested the priest to be given *paan* (betel-leaf) from the mouth of the goddess, as *Prasad*. This was a strange request and was not the custom there. The priest refused, as it had never been done before, but Wamanbuva was so keen and set upon getting it, that he started praying earnestly to the goddess, "Mother, if your grace be on me, you must favour me with the *paan* in your mouth, as *Prasad*". The goddess seemed to have heard it! The *Prasad* fell into his hands! All the people present were wonder struck at this act of grace. Wamanbuva felt really blest. Taking the holy Godavari water, he went to Pandharpur, where he washed the feet of Lord Vithal with it. As he did so, he saw the celestial figure of Sri Swami Samarth, in the place of the idol of Vithal.

After his pilgrimage, he came to Akkalkot for Swamiji's *Darshan.* Sri Maharaj said "You went to *Saptashringi* and became so crazy for getting the *paan*, I had to come there to satisfy your demands and give it to you. The pot on your shoulders (i.e. His head) is still unbaked (meaning that spiritually he had not evolved much at all). Instead of wandering from place to place on pilgrimage, why don't you stick to one place and peep into yourself? You will find all the deities of all the places there. Don't wander, dwell within yourself". Following up on this advice, Wamanbuva stayed at Akkalkot for some years, doing *dhyana* (meditation) and contemplation. Later with Swamiji's permission he left.

Suffering: A spiritually cleansing process

After three years, his health deteriorated, he had all sorts of complications and he could not bear the suffering. He sent a letter to Swamiji, praying that He should cure him by His Grace. There was no reply and his condition worsened. He felt that he could find relief only in death and wanted to commit suicide, by drowning in Surasagar Lake. At the very moment that he was to jump in, Sri Swami Samarth suddenly manifested Himself, caught hold of him and slapped him. Swamiji admonished him saying "You want to escape from paying your debts. You had incurred heavy *Karmic* debts in your former life. All the present suffering of yours is in settlement of this old account. What *Karma* you sowed in your previous life, you have to reap in this one. Even *Maha Purusha's* cannot escape *Prarabhda* (accumulated Karma) even if they purify themselves completely, in the present life. By committing suicide do you think you can escape from your suffering? After suicide it will be far worse; the unsettled accounts will haunt you life after life, increasing many fold with compound interest. Have forbearance, let not your faith be shaken by these physical ills and ailments. Such faint heartedness does not befit a man of your spiritual stature. Your body is meant for achieving a far nobler purpose than to be thrown into a watery grave, to rot there. Seek your Self and attain it." Further, Swami Samarth said "Do you think I did not know about your suffering? You should know that it is a cleansing and purifying process. The gold has to be put in the fire and hammered, before it frees itself of its dross and attains purity and shines resplendently. The hardships thrown on man by destiny are by way of similar process, meant to cleanse the mind, heart and self of man, so that the divinity innate in him, will get manifested in full and he will be worthy of being God's child."

Sanyasa and Realisation

Wamanbuva fell on Swamiji's feet, hugging them and bathing them with tears welling up from his eyes. Swami Samarth disappeared as suddenly as He had come. Wamanbuva went home filled with renewed strength, courage and wisdom. Soon he recovered from all his ailments too. He visited Akkalkot after his recovery to pay homage to Swamiji. He was like pure gold now, mellowed, mature and grown in wisdom, with a heart flooded with love and devotion for Swami Samarth, who had not only redeemed his body, but his soul too. Wamanbuva was a gifted poet; he composed *Guru Leelamrit* delineating the spiritual glory of Sri Swami Samarth. This book has 56 chapters, each poem profound in meaning and spiritually uplifting. Wamanbuva took *Sanyasa* and spent the rest of his life in contemplation and attained realisation.

Ignorant Sanyasi

There was a *sanyasi* from North India, who had learned alchemy and had attained a few *siddhis*. He was vain and boastful. He came to Nasik and met Gholap Swami who was a very saintly person. Gholap Swami told him that *siddhis* were no measure of spiritual attainment and nothing more than a hindrance on the spiritual path. For this correct guidance, the *sanyasi* tried to manhandle Gholap Swami!

Wamanbuva happened to visit Nasik at that time. He learnt about the *sanyasi* and his abuse of spiritual power. When the latter met Wamanbuva, there ensued a discussion on spiritual matters. As the *sanyasi* was ignorant, he always tried to divert the discussion to alchemy, *siddhis* and boast about himself.

He asked scornfully "Who is your Guru?" Wamanbuva replied, "Sri Swami Samarth Akkalkot Maharaj is our Guru." The *sanyasi* taunting him asked "Does your Guru know alchemy like me?" Everybody started laughing. Wamanbuva said "There is no use telling you anything. We pity you. If you wish to save yourself go to Akkalkot and seek Swami's blessings and grace." The *sanyasi* left in anger.

After this incident, whenever he carried out his alchemy practices; instead of gold, charcoal would come out. He thought it was something done by Wamanbuva and wanted to kill him. He threw a heavy stone at Wamanbuva. Lo! The stone stopped in mid air and reversing hit his own head injuring him seriously. When he regained consciousness, he apologised to Wamanbuva, Gholap Swami and his disciples, for his misbehaviour and impudence. He then realised that the advice they had given was sincere and for his own well-being. He also realised what a great Guru they had. He went with repentance in his heart to Akkalkot. When he approached Swami Samarth, He said "What a slave to greed and anger are you! Because you get charcoal instead of gold, you tried to kill the holy Wamanbuva. Why wear the garb of a *sanyasi*, when you cannot control your greed or anger. You want gold, gold, gold, nothing else!" Saying thus, Swamiji ordered him to look at the Neem tree. When the *sanyasi* looked he was thunderstruck - liquid gold was flowing down from the tree!

He fell at the feet of the Swami, prayed for forgiveness, blessings and grace. Swamiji then advised him with a mother's love, to go to Mahurgarh and take to penance there. This is a lesson for all aspirants not to be tempted by *siddhis* or to wander into by-lanes away from the royal pathway, to the goal of realisation of the divine. One should choose the right Guru. Guru's grace is the real gold that one should aspire for, not metallic gold.

Wamanbuva came to be known as *Bramhanista*, Wamanbuva Bramhachari. He took samadhi in 1901. Another great soul, Wamanbuva was the handiwork of Sri Swami Samarth.

BALAPPA MAHARAJ

Ballappa hailed from Bijapur District of Karnataka. He was a Brahmin landlord, money lender and jeweller, and was the richest person in his locality. At the age of 30 he turned to spiritual life and left for Ganagapur in search of a Sadguru. On his way he met one Chidambar Dixit at Murgad. Dixit was a realised soul and deemed to be an incarnation of Shiva. It is said that Swami Samarth was present at one of the *Yajna* conducted by Dixit. Dixit, later served Swamiji during *Prasad Bhojan*. After staying with Dixit for 3 days, Balappa went to Ganagapur and started *Tapasya* at the *Padukas* of Sri Narasimha Saraswati. He maintained himself by begging alms from door to door.

Darshan

After spending a fortnight there, he was directed in a dream to go to Akkalkot, but did not go there. Two months later, he again got the command that it was time for him to proceed to Akkalkot. He also had the vision of Sri Swami Samarth in *Digambar* state. He proceeded to Akkalkot on foot and as he set out, there were many auspicious omens.

When Balappa arrived at Akkalkot and had his first glimpse of Sri Swami Samarth, he recalled the vision he had in Ganagapur; the form of Swamiji in *Digambar* posture. It was an ecstatic experience. He ran and prostrated at the feet of Sri Swami Samarth, clasping His feet tightly. Swamiji also seemed happy, seeing Balappa. Balappa had now found his Sadguru and surrendered body mind and soul in loving dedication to Him.

Swamiji then stayed in the palace for 8 days. As Balappa could not go in, he started doing *Tapasya* outside. One day he had the opportunity of having the *Darshan* of Maharaj and offered some dates to the Swami, who distributed them to all present, excepting Balappa! Balappa felt disappointed, until he learnt that Swamiji never gave *Prasad* to one whom he wanted to retain, close to Him. He was very happy at knowing this and started serving the Swami earnestly. He never spared himself and no work was too lowly or beneath his dignity. He knew he had the rare and most unique privilege of being near and serving the Supreme Lord Himself.

Once while plucking flowers for worship, Balappa got hurt by a thorn and his finger was swollen. It became very painful and he prayed to Swamiji for relief. The Swami asked him to apply cow urine to the finger and Balappa felt immediate relief. One day Balappa had severe fever and the suspicion was that he had been poisoned. With the Swami's grace he recovered and was completely well.

Serving Swami

All valuable articles offered to Sri Swami Samarth, were passed on to Balappa for safe custody. He also acted as the store keeper and it was his responsibility to supply whatever was asked for by the Swami, immediately. There could be no delay or default in his work, as he would be upbraided severely by the Swami.

Sunderabai, who was the main attendant, became jealous of Balappa and disliked him, but Balappa cared for none but the Swami and his duty. In spite of his devotion to Maharaj, Balappa used to perform daily *puja* to his family deity. Sri Swami would taunt him "Balappa is knitting rough blankets", to indicate that when one has found a sadguru, no other sadhana is required except dedicated service to Him. Sadguru is the physical manifestation of all deities - His grace is the sunshine for us to bask in; what necessity is there for blankets, when sunshine and warmth are there?

Swamiji once asked Balappa to fetch water from the house of a *shudra* (untouchable). Balappa had already finished his bath and was hesitant to do this, but Sri Swami Samarth insisted and he had to obey. All are equal in the eyes of God - Swamiji wanted Balappa to realise this.

Balappa found it difficult to concentrate during meditation. He told Swamiji about this. Maharaj patted him on his back - Lo! Just this pat was enough to put him in a transcendental state. For quite some time he remained in this blissful state. Later Swami Samarth blessed him with a rosary of *tulsi* beads and asked him to use it during japa. Thereafter, Balappa's *dhyana* (meditation) practice progressed very fast. Balappa never left Akkalkot in spite of Swamiji's visits and stay at nearby villages. He stuck to his duties at Akkalkot with the same love, sincerity, care and dedication, as if the Swami was there. Balappa always got first preference in worshipping Swami Samarth. The Swami presented a gold ring to Balappa, with His name inscribed on it. Maharaj said "You have to keep the spiritual torch burning. I am blessing" you." Balappa fell at the Swami's feet, shedding tears of gratitude. He asked Balappa to start a separate Muth under the *audumbar* tree and gave him a saffron coloured flag. He also gifted His *padukas* and *Kaupin* (cod-piece) to Balappa. This Muth is known as Balappa Muth.

Ballappa Muth

Before setting up the Muth, Balappa travelled all over India and spread the message of Sri Swami Samarth Akkalkot Maharaj and held aloft the banner of *Datta Sampradaya*. He revived religious and spiritual faith among the people, at all the places he visited. After his travels, he returned to Akkalkot and set up the Balappa Muth. The *padukas, danda* (stick) *kamandalu* (water-pot) rosary, given by Swami Samarth to him, are enshrined there.

On Swami Samarth's *Mahaniryan*, Balappa Maharaj broke down and felt as if life had ebbed out of him too. He decided to fast unto death and sat down at Swamiji's samadhi in sorrow and despair.

On the third day of his fast, Swami Samarth gave him His *darshan* and talked to him and comforted him. The grief that had filled his heart cleared. He realised now that Swamiji was *Nirakar* - beyond all form. Balappa Maharaj now fixed his mind on the *padukas* of Swami Samarth - they were the representation of Swamiji for him. He used to offer elaborate worship to them daily. Even when he was ill, Balappa Maharaj never missed the worship and offering of *abhisekh* to the *Padukas*. As Balappa Maharaj was advancing in age and his health was declining, he sent for Gangadhar, who was at Bilaspur and chose him as his successor. After making all the arrangements, Balappa Maharaj attained *Samadhi* in 1910.

During his lifetime, Balappa Maharaj travelled all over what are now the states of Orissa, Bihar, Uttar Pradesh,

Madhya Pradesh, Rajasthan, Bengal, Karnataka and Maharashtra. For 32 years after the departure of Sri Swami Samarth, he carried out his Master's mission with the selfless dedication.

Disciple and Successors

After Balappa Maharaj, Gangadhar Maharaj kept up the high traditions of the Muth.

Gangadhar was born in 1868 and lost his father when only a child. He used to worship the Shiva *Linga* all the time. He started working as a peon under an English officer. He picked up speaking English well and his hand writing was very good. The officer appointed him as a clerk in his office, as he was very impressed by the behaviour and hard work of the boy. Later, he joined Ralli Brothers.

In 1901, Balappa Maharaj visited Nagpur. He was very impressed by Gangadhar's spiritual yearning and devotion and felt that he was a fit person to succeed him. In 1910, just before taking *Mahasamadhi* he asked Gangadhar to come to Akkalkot immediately. After his arrival, Balappa Maharaj invested him with the insignia of the Muth and declared him successor.

After Balappa Maharaj's *Samadhi* Gangadhar Maharaj used to take only milk and fruits. He was *Ajanabahu* like Sri Swami Samarth. He was a renunciate and used to distribute alms and clothes liberally to the poor. He composed many *Abhangas* and used to recite them daily.

In 1937, his health started deteriorating and he attained *samadhi*. Before his samadhi, he entrusted the responsibility of the Muth to Gajanan Maharaj.

Gajanan was born in 1918. His father was a great yogi and lived a detached life. When he was young, his grandfather took him for the *Darshan* of Upasni Maharaj at Sakori, in 1922. For a few years, he was brought up under the guardianship of Sri Upasni Maharaj, who used to say, "Gajanan is no ordinary boy, he is a rare spiritual gem". When he was 7 years old, Upasni Maharaj himself performed his thread ceremony. Gajanan started learning all the scriptures and rituals and he progressed fast.

When he was 8 years old, his grandfather took him to Gangadhar Maharaj and entrusted him in his care. Under the guidance of Gangadhar Maharaj, Gajanan became proficient in yogic, religious and spiritual practices.

According to tradition, Gajanan was married and entered *Grihasta Ashrama*, which matures and mellows a man's mind. *Grihasta Ashrama* is the main pillar of Dharma, on which depends the welfare of the whole community.

In 1937, Gangadhar Maharaj invested Gajanan with the headship of the Muth.

Gajanan Maharaj revived the *Vedic* rituals, especially the sacred *Yajnya samaradhana* - worship to *Agni* (fire). He also restarted worship of Bhargava Rama (Parashuram), one of the 10 incarnations of Vishnu, and sage Bhrigu - extolled as the perfect *Rishi* or sage by Lord Krishna, in the *Geeta*. He has composed Sanskrit verses *Bhargav Kavacha Stotra.*

He is a *Maha Tapaswi* like his idol Bhrigu Rishi and has kept the torch of the Datta Sampradaya alight. He has spread the Vedic message in USA, Germany etc.

TAT MAHARAJ

His original name before he took to *Sanyas Ashram* was Rama Chandra Baradkar. He was a Saraswat Brahmin and was a resident of Bombay. He used to deal in medicinal herbs and roots. From childhood, he had devotion and attraction to Lord Shiva and would regularly visit the Shiva temple, at Babulnath. One day he had the vision of Lord Shiva in a dream, saying that He was residing in human form at Akkalkot and that Baradkar should go and have His *Darshan* there.

He left for Akkalkot and had Swami Samarth's *Darshan* and narrated to Him his dream and the directive he had received. As he said this, to quote his own words "In place of Sri Swami Samarth, there was a dazzling and effulgent form of Lord Shiva Himself. It was too blinding a vision and I began to tremble and perspire. It was too brilliant and august a vision for my human eyes to withstand. Sympathising with my plight, perhaps, Swamiji changed from the terrible form of Rudra[29] to the benign form of Vishnu and then Bramha - thus He blessed me with the vision of

---

[29] Lord Shiva

all 3 aspects of *Dattatraya*, who He really was. I was not ready for such a *Darshan*, as it was too much for me to withstand and I prayed to Swamiji "I want to see only your present human form, as Sri Swami Samarth. Please re-assume that form which is a delight to my eyes; which I can bear to look and adore." The transcendental vision passed and there appeared again the form of Sri Swami Samarth, gently smiling and saying "I am always with you, I am always in you. You have my grace and blessings." Saying this He touched my body and I lost complete consciousness of my body, mind and senses and was plunged into a state of inexpressible bliss. It was my first experience of the *Samadhi* state. It took quite some time for me to get back to my normal awareness."

Baradkar progressed very fast spiritually, after the above touch of grace by Swamiji. He attained *siddhis* by which he could perform miracles, relieve the distress and afflictions of people and cure their diseases. He came to be known as *Tat Maharaj.* (Tat means grandfather).

When devotees came to him for relief from disease, Tat Maharaj would pour *Tirtha* (holy water) onto their palms, chant the name of Sri Swami Samarth and taking back the water, swallow it himself. Thus, he seemed to be taking upon himself the ailments and problems of the devotees, which were unbearable for them, but nothing more than a trifle for him, being a great yogi.

Tat Maharaj by the grace of his Guru, kindled the spiritual light in others. One Balkrishna Suratkar came to meet Tat Maharaj. He had been much influenced by Swami Dayanand's lectures and had lost faith in idol worship, traditional religion and a personal God. Hearing about Sri Swami Samarth from Tat Maharaj, changed his mind. Later, Tat Maharaj, by his yogic power, touched him and sent him into a trance which lasted for 8 days continuously! This rocketed off Balkrishna's spiritual ascent and he became a great yogi like his master, Tat Maharaj, who in turn had imbibed his power from his master, Sri Swami Samarth.

From one Primal light, small lamps get lit up. This light is perennial in the sacred and spiritual land - India.

Balkrishna Maharaj established Sri Swami Samarth Muth at Dadar, in Bombay. He always used to say "My dear sons, the *Avatar* of Sri Swami Samarth is of recent origin and His presence is felt fully even now. If you call to Him with a devout heart He will respond and be with you."

GONDAVALEKAR MAHARAJ

As a boy he was spiritually inclined and ran away from home at the age of 12, in quest of a Guru. His father searched for him, found him at Kolhapur and brought him back home. His father got him married, thinking that this would divert his mind away from spirituality.

The boy could not resist his spiritual yearning and again left home, leaving a message for his mother that they should not search for him and forget him, as he would not return home under any circumstances.

Young Gondavalekar set out, wandering from place to place, to find a Guru who would accept and initiate him. He went to Miraj and met Annabuva, who was a disciple of Shri Swami Samarth. Annabuva blessed him, but about becoming his Guru, said he should seek an advanced saint. Marks of spiritual greatness were already apparent in Gondavalekar and Annabuva recognising these, knew that he needed a fully evolved Master.

He then went to Nasik and approached Dev Maharaj to accept him as his disciple. He too told him "You deserve a far greater Master, you will find him, my blessings on you."

Gondavalekar then proceeded to Akkalkot, for Darshan of the Swami, who knew all; He announced that a worthy spiritual aspirant was coming to seek His grace and Blessings. The morning the boy was to come; Swamiji told all his disciples and devotees "He is coming; what a worthy lad! All of you must treat him well." Soon after He said this, Gondavalekar arrived. On seeing Sri Swami Samarth, he felt a deep thrill permeating his body and he fell at Swamiji's feet.

His eyes filled with tears of ecstasy and devout emotion surged up from his heart - was it not HE whom he was seeking so restlessly?

Gondavalekar was a born yogi, only his spirituality was dormant so far and needed to be aroused. By a mere glance from Swamiji, who was the Master of spiritual Masters - *Yogiraj* (King of yogis) and *Yogeeshwar* (Lord of yogis) incarnate, he received the necessary fillip for spiritual take off. Swamiji put His hand on the boy's head and blessed him again, telling Gondavalekar that his progress would be unhampered thereafter, while so far as the Guru was concerned, he would find him at the appropriate time.

Gondavalekar actively pursued his spiritual life and due to Maharaj's grace found a Guru, became a realised soul and came to be known as Brahma Chaitanya Gondavalekar Maharaj.

ANANDNATH MAHARAJ

Anandnath was a dealer in medicinal herbs. Once in Bombay, in the shop of one Bhende, he chanced to hear the name and a description of the glory of Sri Swami Samarth. He instantly felt a deep yearning that he should have the Swamiji's *Darshan* and started for Akkalkot. On the way, he washed his feet in a lake and a twig fell on his head from the banyan tree. He looked up. Lo! Seated in the branches above was the beautiful and charming form of Sri Swami Samarth, Himself, holding his hand in *Varad Mudra* (benediction). What a golden-hued body! What lustrous eyes! What bewitching beauty! Anandnath totally forgot himself in the bliss of that celestial vision - the experience changed the course of his life completely. He took *Sanyasa* (renunciation) and stayed at Akkalkot for 6 years. He would be usually half naked with indifference to his body.

Anandnath was a gifted poet too, he composed many devotional songs, singing the glory of Sri Swami Samarth. He used to often sing in Swamiji's presence too.

Sri Swami Samarth was very pleased with the devotion and asceticism of Anandnath and He asked him to start Muths at different places in the Konkan. Swamiji materialised small *Padukas* of an unknown metal from His mouth and gifted them to Anandnath, as a token of His grace. The *Padukas,* tiny though they were, they had clear auspicious marks and impressions on them. As directed by Swamiji, Anandnath went to Konkan and set up Muths at 3 places - Yewala, Hodawade and Dhavade in Ratnagiri District. The *Padukas* given by Swami Samarth are installed in the Muth at Dhavade.

Anandnath Maharaj composed many devotional *Stotras, Abhangas and Aarti* songs in praise of Swami Samarth, which became popular and are sung even today. He took *samadhi* at Vengurla in 1904. At the Vengurla Muth, his own *Padukas* are installed. Anandnath Maharaj was another great and worthy disciple indeed.

ANAND BHARATI

His original name was Laxman. He was a fisherman and had great devotion for Sri Swami Samarth and used to visit Akkalkot for *darshan.*

Once Laxman was caught in a severe storm when he was fishing. His was about to sink and he was unable to control the vessel. In his desperate state, he invoked the name of Sri Swami Samarth and prayed to be rescued. At that time, Swami Samarth was playing a game of chess at Akkalkot. Suddenly whilst playing, he shouted "Laxman is drowning". He swiftly plunged His hands downwards and then lifted them up. Lo! His hands were dripping wet and water was streaming down them! All those present could not fathom what was happening.

Next day, Laxman came to Akkalkot, fell at Swamiji's feet and said "Swamiji, how did you save my life yesterday? You rescued me from certain death. You have given me a new lease of life. I now pray that you must give me spiritual illumination too. I do not want to go back to my family life. This body and life are now entirely yours. Please accept me at your Lotus Feet".

Laxman stayed at Akkalkot thereafter, serving the Master, body, mind and soul. With Swamiji's grace, he progressed spiritually and came to be known as Anand Bharati. His *samadhi* is near the *Dattatraya* temple at Thane, near Bombay.

PEER SAHEB

A Muslim policeman was residing at Maindargi, a village near Akkalkot. He was in charge of the prison there.

One day, one of the prisoners escaped and the policeman was extremely scared at the disgrace this entailed, apart from the fact that he would definitely lose his job. He desperately searched for the prisoner in every conceivable place, without success. The prisoner had hidden himself in a deep ditch away from the road.

The Muslim policeman was at his wits end and when all his efforts failed, he thought of Sri Swami Samarth. He offered ardent prayers and made a vow that if the prisoner could be found and got back, he would serve the Swami for the rest of his life.

Next morning, the escaped prisoner surrendered to a person riding by the ditch on horseback, who brought him back to the jail. The prisoner was in a shattered state of mind. He stated that he had hidden himself until nightfall and then tried to run away. But there was a Sanyasi there, who prevented him from escaping. He frustrated all the prisoner's efforts throughout the night and this had led to his surrender.

The Muslim policeman realised how Sri Swami Samarth had responded to his prayer and come to his help. He resigned his job, with a blemishless service record (thanks to Swamiji) and came to

Akkalkot for the Swami's *Darshan* and stayed on to serve the Swami.

Since he had no money, Swamiji asked Cholappa to give two bread loaves to him every day. He was asked to go back to his village after 8 days, by the Swami. He gave His leather sandals to him as *Padukas* for worship and as a token of His blessing and grace.

Excommunicated

The Muslim policeman went home and used to worship the Swami's *Padukas* morning and evening, without fail. His family and relatives did not like this at all - a Muslim worshipping the sandals of a Hindu Sadhu! It was most unbecoming! Besides he had no money - why should they maintain him! Being thus annoyed with him, they drove him out of his own house. He took shelter in a dilapidated house on the outskirts of the village. However, he did not give up worship of the *Padukas*.

Although excommunicated by his community, by the grace of Swamiji he used to be offered food daily by somebody or the other. Soon the news of the power of the *Padukas* to relieve disease and fulfill desires spread. Many people came there praying for relief and ask the Muslim for *Vibhuti* (holy ash). Not having any, the Muslim with his deep faith in the Swami, simply used to give a handful of the earth below the leather *Padukas* as *Vibhuti*, which gave unfailing relief and satisfied the desires of all. In the course of time this Muslim came to be revered as *Peer Saheb*, an

Auliya (mystic) and a great *Siddha Purusha*. Even Brahmins came and prostrated at his feet.

As he became famous and revered by all, there was no dearth of money and costly gifts given to him. His family members now pleaded with him to come back home and requested to be forgiven. He built a big temple and installed the leather Padukas there. This temple in Maindargi attracts lots of people and unfailingly gives relief to the diseased even now.

With Sri Swami Samarth's grace a simple Muslim policeman turned into *Peer Saheb*. This is the spiritual alchemy of Akkalkot Maharaj. As Tukaram says "Aapna sarikhe kariti tatkal, nahi wela kala taya lagi." Saints need hardly any time to raise others to their own spiritual level.

SWAMI SOOTA

Swami Soota (son of the Swami) was known as Haribhau, before taking *sanyasa* (renunciation). His life was a saga of devotion to Swami Samarth. He hailed from a respectable Maratha family and was a landlord in Ratnagiri. He was sent to Bombay for studies when he was 8 years old. After schooling for some years, he took a job in the Bombay Municipal Corporation. After 5 years of service, the course of his life, suddenly veered towards the spiritual.

It happened thus: Haribhau with a friend, Khatri, speculated heavily in the Stock Market and suffered losses with heavy debts. To repay these, they went to one Laxman Pandit. Laxman happened to be a

staunch devotee of Sri Swami Samarth. Hearing of
the spiritual power of the Swami, they desired to
accompany Laxman Pandit to Akkalkot, for *Darshan*
of the Swami.

My Son

When Haribhau had the *Darshan* of Sri Swami
Samarth, he was stirred to the depth of his very being.
He had never had such a blissful experience ever
before.

Swamiji addressed them "Oh, speculators and
Stockbrokers". Their life was an open book to Him
who was Omniscient! To Haribhau He said "Leave
your job, give up all you have and come away to live
with me here, my son!" Haribhau was in a fix, on the
one hand there was great joy in his heart at Swami
Samarth calling him "my son"; on the other, could he
act as directed, leaving a permanent job, giving up
property and take to a life of renunciation?

Next day, Swamiji asked Laxman, pointing to 3
pictures on the wall, who they were. Laxman replied
that they were Hanuman, Shiva and Sri Rama. Swami
Samarth told them that Haribhau was an aspect of Sri
Hanuman, Khatri of Lord Shiva, and Laxman of Sri
Rama, implying that each of them should meditate
on their respective forms. Swami Samarth recited
Sanskrit verses on each of these Gods. They all felt
profusely blessed and returned to Bombay.

Haribhau was a totally changed man now. He felt
disgust for routine life and lost interest in all worldly

things. Getting silver *Padukas* made he went to Akkalkot before long. Swami Samarth accepted the *Padukas* and wore them for a fortnight. He called Haribhau on the 15th day and told him "Now the time has come for you to break away from your old life. Leave your job, build a Muth on the sea shore and set up the great banner (of Datta Sampradaya)." He patted and caressed Haribhau like a father and gave him the silver *Padukas* sanctified by the touch of His feet. Swamiji then told him to install the sacred *Padukas* in the new Muth, which he would build in Bombay. Sri Swami Samarth said those *Padukas* embodied and symbolised His divinity to the core.

On the last night of his stay Swamiji got up and came near the tree under which Haribhau was sleeping. He said "Get out - my Bal Govind is asleep." As He said this, a bright globular body came out of the tree and floated away. Haribhau woke up and seeing Swamiji fell at His feet. Swami Samarth talked to him for a long time and then gave him His clothes consisting of *kaupin* (cod piece) and *Chaaati* (gown) assured him that the *Padukas* He had gifted him, would be an eternal guide, provide protection and give spiritual power to him.

Sanyas

Haribhau returned to Bombay with the *Padukas*. He started wearing the ochre robes and lived the life of a renunciate. He donated all his substantial wealth to Brahmins and charities. He took to constant singing of *Namavalis and bhajans* and would get so engrossed that he used to lose consciousness of his surroundings and himself. He composed many devotional songs under Swamiji's inspiration. As Swami Samarth had called him "my son", he began to be called Swami Soota[30], the son of Swami Samarth.

Swami Soota built a Muth at Kamathipura, in Bombay, which people from all communities visited. He used to visit Akkalkot occasionally. While there, he would stay at the Murlidhar temple as instructed by Swamiji. Swami Soota used to be lost in meditation.

A lawyer once came and performed *Aarti* to Sri Swami Samarth, who said "You have come here without offering worship to my Hanuman first. Perform service there first, only then will I accept worship here." The lawyer did not understand what Swamiji meant and it was explained by devotees, that Swami Soota was the Hanuman referred to, and service was to be first performed at the Murlidhar temple. Thereafter, the lawyer would first light a lamp at the Murlidhar temple and only then visit Sri Swami Samarth. He was later blessed with a son, as he had desired.

Yoga Samadhi

Some years later, Swami Samarth told Swami Soota that he would be giving up His body and he would have to carry on Maharaj's mission on his own. Swami Soota was shocked to hear this. He could not

---

[30] Soota means "son" in Sanskrit.

bear to live in a world without Swamiji. He returned to Bombay, heart broken and all his courage had deserted him. His health broke down and he fell seriously ill.

Swamiji knew everything and he sent two disciples to bring Swami Soota to Akkalkot, but Swami Soota refused to go and took *Yoga Samadhi* (voluntary death). His mother was at Akkalkot and she broke down in grief. The ever compassionate Swami Samarth comforted her by saying "Please do not grieve. From now on consider me your child. I will fill his place hereafter." He slowly added "You do not know what a blessed soul your son was, what a *Sad gati* (glorious after death state) I have sent him to."

Successor

Swami Samarth had already picked Haribhau's younger brother, Dada, who was 8, as Swami Soota's successor. After some time, He directed that Dada be taken to Bombay, for investiture as head of the Muth and gave 3 insignias - *Danda (stick), Chaati and Rudraksha mala* (garland of Rudraksha beads). At this the mother started crying and protested that she did not want her other son to become a sanyasi. Swamiji ignored her outburst and the boy was taken to Bombay, where he refused to be invested as head of the Muth, because of his mother's reluctance.

He came back to his mother at Akkalkot. Swami Samarth was angry at His orders being flouted and he sternly ordered the investiture ceremony be carried out then and there. Swamiji Himself participated in the rituals and the name of Sachidananda Swami Kumar was conferred on the new head of Muth.

Now the mother was thrilled with joy upon seeing Akkalkot Maharaj Himself participate in the investiture rituals. What a unique honour! A sense of pride and gratification welled up in her heart. The son too was elated. He realised how blessed he was. But all this lasted only for a brief while and the mother burst into sobs again. Sri Swami Samarth then took the boy on his lap and fondled and caressed him with motherly tenderness. He said "My dear boy, who is mother, who is the son? It is all an ephemeral relationship. How many mothers and fathers have you had, in previous lifetimes? They are countless. There is only one eternal Mother and you belong to Her. Develop attachment only to God and not to any earthly physical relationships, which are like bubbles, which may burst at any moment. Strive for *Shreyas* (lasting and eternal good) and not for *Preyas* (momentary pleasure or fleeting gains)."

A thrill of joy surged through the boy, at the combined initiation by *Sparsha* (touch) and *vacha* (speech). He felt as if he was in the lap of the Eternal mother. Any regret vanished and a new zeal and vision filled his whole being.

Swami Kumar dedicated himself body, mind and soul, to keeping aloft the banner of *Datta Samprada*. He worshipped Swamiji's *Padukas* with great devotion. After his *samadhi*, Siddhbai, the daughter of Swami Soota shifted the Muth from Kamathipura to

Chembur in Bombay, in compliance with the directive she received from Sri Swami Samarth. The *Padukas* there are as responsive as Swami Samarth Himself was, (and is even now).

GOPAL BUVA

In his later life Gopal Kelkar was an ardent devotee of Sri Swami Samarth. His parents were very poor and he could not pursue his studies in Ratnagiri. He joined the railways and rose to the position of station master and served in many places. He developed stomach trouble which was very painful and it became difficult for him to carry out his duties. He tried out all kinds of medicines, but did not get any relief. In despair he took a vow - "if God loves me, HE must cure me within 8 days. If I am cured, I shall leave my job and dedicate my life to His worship." Lo! His stomach troubles disappeared within a week. Immediately thereafter he rushed to Akkalkot for Swamiji's *Darshan*. He served the Swami for 2 years and was named Pritinand Swami Kumar and directed to go to Bombay to serve Swami Soota which he did for 4 months.

Chiplun Muth

Swami Soota sent Gopal Buva to Chiplun, asking him to set up a regular Muth there for the white marble *Datta Padukas*, which had been taken there earlier by another disciple. Gopal Buva set up the Muth and remained there devoting all his time to the worship of the *Padukas*.

Swami Samarth Appears

When Swamiji took *Maha Samadhi* in 1878, Gopal Buva received the news by telegram and was totally shaken. He could not bear the grief and he gave up eating, preferring death to a life without the Swami. On the third day of his fast, Sri Swami Samarth appeared before him in 'physical' form (i.e. body) to convince him that He was deathless, He was ever alive and would respond readily whenever called and protect His devotees.

Swami Samarth then admonished him for fasting and advised him that grief does not befit a yogi. He had no right to try to give up his God given body. It should be dedicated in service to God until it withered and fell off naturally by itself.

Gopal Buva now found consolation in the fact that Swami Samarth was always present. He gave up his fast and resumed worship of the *Padukas* and duties at the Muth with greater dedication and devotion. He used to beg alms on Thursdays - a sacred day in *Datta Sampradaya*. He attained *Samadhi* in 1919.

The Swami Samarth Muth at Chiplun, continues to be visited by a large number of devotees even today. The *Padukas and Danda* of Sri Swami Samarth Himself are in this Muth, which is now looked after by Krishna Buva.

SITARAM MAHARAJ

Sitaram Subhedar belonged to Satara and lost his mother at an early age. His father married again. The step-mother was ill disposed to him and he ran away at the age of 12. He came to Akkalkot and he was received very kindly by Sri Swami Samarth. Sitaram felt that he had found his long lost mother again in the Swami, who caressed his head. This touch was enough *(Sparsha Diksha)* to rouse his dormant *Kundalini Shakti.* With Swami Samarth's blessings and as directed by Him, Sitaram left for Mangal Vedha and settled down. He spent 40 years there and came to be known as Sitaram Maharaj.

Sitaram Maharaj used to live on alms. At midday he would go out for alms to any house. He would take in his hand whatever was given and eat it then and there. This provided him enough sustenance for the day. He would then go to the cremation ground and remain there absorbed in *samadhi.* He always advised those who went for his *Darshan,* "Never forget Sri Rama, chant His name ceaselessly, remember Him always, realise Him. He alone exists, He is in all beings. All that you see is Rama, this world is Rama. A life without realisation is futile."

Displays traits of an Avadhoot

Though a realised person and a great saint, he would often behave like a child[31] Seeing this, people who did not know about him, thought him to be mad.

---

[31] Avadhoots always behave thus.

One day as he was going through the fruit market, he saw mangoes laid out in a basket. The vendor, a woman, had gone away. Sitaram picked a mango and started eating it. Upon her return, she became furious when she saw him eating the fruits nonchalantly, without having made any payment for them. She started beating him with a stick.

All this while, Sitaram was addressing himself "Sitya, do you think you can have only mangoes and not the blows?" While this scene was taking place, a policeman who was a disciple of Sitaram Maharaj, happened to pass that way. Seeing his Guru being beaten upset him and he was about to arrest her, when Sitaram stopped him and said "Bring me a new blouse piece and sari, I want to give them to my mother." The policeman obeyed and Sitaram Maharaj gave them to the woman saying "Mother, you must accept these and wear them. These are your son's offering." The fruit vendor was so moved, she became a staunch devotee of Sitaram Maharaj thereafter. What a fortunate woman! Through this "leela" she found her guru. This incident reflects our life and desires - we often want only pleasures and not what goes with them - pain.

Sitaram Maharaj knew his end was near and he used to say "Mad Sitya will soon depart." His simple hearted nature and faith won for him the grace of Sri Swami Samarth, who transformed him into a realised soul.

SRIMAD SHANKARACHARYA OF SANKESHWAR PEETH

A few months after the arrival of Sri Swami Samarth, the King of Akkalkot invited the Shankaracharya of Sankeshwar peeth, to visit him as his guest. At that time few people had realised the greatness of Swamiji. There was heavy rush and nobody paid attention to Sri Swamiji Samarth or Cholappa. One Brahmin however got a seat and got Him (Swamiji) seated properly.

The Shankaracharya happened to look at Swami Samarth and instantly recognised His Divinity from his Divine splendour. He was awe-struck and felt that the great saint "Adi Shankara" must have looked like Him.

Some people started murmuring that Swami Samarth partakes of food given by anybody, from any caste or community, so he should be made to sit separately for dinner and not with the main group.

When the food was served, people found it foul smelling, infested with worms and nobody could eat it. The Shankaracharya realised that this was the consequence of showing disrespect to Swami Samarth.

The Shankaracharya approached the Swami and offered his respects and paid obeisance. He invited Swami Samarth to sit with him. The food turned wholesome and everyone ate well, after extolling the glory of Sri Swami Samarth and took the food as His *prasad* (sacred food).

Sri Swami Samarth wanted to teach them that all are equal in the eyes of God. The system of caste and community came into existence for a different purpose originally. The purpose was the overall welfare of all, by the division of duties according to the work orientations of people, resulting in increased efficiency due specialisation of work. It was certainly not intended to disrupt the harmony and kinship of the human race. All are children of God.

Ten years after the *Maha Samadhi* of Sri Swami Samarth, Shankaracharya again visited Akkalkot and offered worship at the Samadhi Muth. He also composed Sanskrit verses *Stotras* in adoration of Sri Swami Samarth, for verily is Swami Samarth not the prime Guru - the Guru of all Gurus and the Sad Guru Himself?"

SWAMI SWAROOPANANDA, PAWAS

The late Swami Swaroopananda was a realised soul. He held Sri Swami Samarth in the highest esteem and venerated Him as the greatest saint among saints and Divinity itself. He always had the picture of Sri Swami Samarth facing his seat so that he could always see Him.

VISHNUDAS MAHURKAR

Vishnudas was a great devotee of Goddess Renuka Mata. He was a gifted poet and composed a number of *Stotras* (Sanskrit verses) extolling the prowess of Renuka Mata. Earlier he had gone to Akkalkot for the *Darshan* of Sri Swami Samarth.

He had prostrated at the feet of the Swami and prayed for His blessings. Sri Swami Samarth on looking at him, at once said "What purpose will be served by your staying here? Go to Mahur and stay at Atri Ashram, where after a year you will get the *Darshan* of Lord Dattatraya".

Vishnudas went to Mahurgadh and stayed at Atri Ashram. The prophetic words of Sri Swami Samarth came true and he got the Darshan of the Lord Dattatraya after one year! (Also see Appendix I).

CHAPTER 8

THE BLESSED ONES

The sea does not invite the rivers to come to it; the river is drawn irresistibly to the sea. The flower does not invite the bee, but the bee is helplessly drawn to it.

Similarly, although Sri Swami Samarth never called anyone to see Him, all were irresistibly drawn to His lotus feet, they sought Him as a child seeks its mother. Like the sun, Sri Swami Samarth enlightened His disciples by removing the darkness of ignorance from their minds and hearts and purified them.

The following devotees are among the most blessed because not only did they seem to attract more of the Grace and affection of Sri Swami Samarth, but had the privilege of serving Him which is a rare and a unique honour for lay disciples, i.e. for non-renunciates. Besides, almost all of them had been given "padukas", personally by Akkalkot Maharaj!

1. CHOLAPPA

Cholappa was fortunate and blessed as he was the first to serve Sri Swami Samarth immediately after His arrival at Akkalkot.

As described earlier, Swamiji had food after 3 days in Akkalkot, at Cholappa's house. During His stay, Swamiji caused a lot of trouble for Chollapa's wife, Yesubai. He used to feed the cows with grain stored in the house, He would distribute alms freely to all beggars. Once Yesubai had stored some *dal* (lentils) for use on festive occasions. Sri Swami fed all of it to the cows. Cholappa's wife did not have the same devotion and respect for the Swami as Cholappa had. Swamiji was often a nuisance and she wondered whether she would ever be rid of this strange and queer guest. After 2 months, Swamiji left Cholappa's house suddenly. Cholappa felt very unhappy and pleaded with Swamiji to come back. After a great deal of pleading, Swamiji relented and returned[32].

The Raja of Akkalkot used to send food, grains and sanctioned a further amount of rupees five (which was a huge amount in those days) towards Swamiji's expenses.

Nuisance

Swamiji continued His curious ways of 'harassing' Cholappa and his wife. He would occupy the bed meant for Cholappa's children, distribute food as alms to beggars passing by, pour water in the hearth etc. Once when Cholappa was out of town, He drove out all family members and would not allow them to come in. After Cholappa returned in the evening, he cajoled and appeased Sri Samarth as if He were a child and only then were the family allowed in.

---

[32] Sometimes devotees are made to go through severe tests of love, faith and surrender by Saints and Avataars.

Once Yesubai was in labour, Swamiji entered the labour room and did not allow anyone to enter. Yesubai had a safe delivery by the grace of Swami Samarth. His ways of protection also seemed queer! One day Yesubai's hand was bitten by a scorpion and the pain was unbearable. Sri Swami Samarth threw one of His sandals to her and asked her to keep her hand on it. She did so and the pain disappeared at once! When she removed her hand the pain returned with greater severity than before. When she placed her hand on the sandal again, the pain again vanished. After a while Swamiji said "You can remove your hand now" and the pain totally vanished. After this incident Yesubai's faith in Swami Samarth increased and she understood that she had been tested by Swamiji until then.

Though extremely devoted, being poor, Cholappa had a weakness for money. When Tatya (mentioned earlier) offered him Rs. 10,000 for persuading Swamiji to visit Baroda, he was completely swayed. Swamiji once chided him for his lust for money.

Cholappa had no diminution of faith even after being put to severe tests; he had recognised the power of the Swami, hence he experienced several revelations and Swami Samarth performed His *Leelas* in Cholappa's house.

Acting on some mystic command, Cholappa built a *Samadhi* for Swami Samarth in his house. When Swamiji saw it He said "Cholappa, I will see you off first, before I depart". Cholappa died 6 months before the (Maha Samadhi) of Sri Swami Samarth.

Swami Samarth lost His jovial and jolly mood after Cholappa's demise. He once remarked "Cholappa's relationship with me has been that of son and father, for generations. Whom shall I show my Leelas in the absence of Cholappa? I may depart soon".

What a blessed soul Cholappa must have been to elicit such declaration of Prema (Love) from the Supreme Lord Himself!

After Akkalkot Maharaj's Maha Samadhi, His body was placed in the Samadhi place built by Cholappa in his house and this sacred place is known as Cholappa Muth. Sri Swami Samarth's sandals are also preserved in this Muth.

Cholappa was a great Das Bhakta* of Swamiji.

2. SUNDERABAI

Sunderabai was a widow and she was one of the main attendants of Sri Swami Samarth.

She used to suffer from severe foot sores which caused unbearable pain. She came to Akkalkot to seek the blessings of Swamiji for a cure. Her Darshan of Swami Samarth gave her great relief and she decided to stay at Akkalkot serving the Swami.

---

* One of the paths in Bhakti Yoga is the path of service to God, called "Das." Thus, Gurudas means one who dedicates himself heart and soul in service to his Guru.

Cholappa was unable to cope with the number or devotees, visiting the Swami, increasing by leaps and bounds. He needed someone to assist him and he found Sunderabai to be earnest, a willing worker and devoted to the Swami. Swamiji warned Cholappa that Sunderabai would manoeuvre and manage to displace Cholappa in course of time. He should be on his guard and should not let Sunderabai attend to everything.

Swamiji's Custodian

Sunderabai gradually took charge of all the chores, concerning the Swami and became His constant personal attendant. Even when the Swami stayed in the palace, she alone looked after His needs. Whoever came for Maharaj's *Darshan* had to get her consent first. People gradually believed mistakenly that she was the "custodian" of the Swamiji. Without her favour, Swamiji's favour could not be secured! This mistaken belief spread to such an extent that devotees who brought offerings and gifts for Swamiji, thought it was enough to hand them over to Sunderabai. She began to believe that she had gained powerful influence over Swami Samarth. She was honoured by all visitors, as if she was Swami Samarth, All this increased her conceit and pride. She was avaricious too. Later, she displayed carelessness and negligence in her service to the Swami. She used to serve Him stale food sometimes, but He never seemed to notice such things.

Cholappa Loses

At the palace (where Swamiji stayed), Sunderbai removed Cholappa from the service of the Swami, by manipulating the queen. Sunderabai was made the sole attendant. Cholappa had been warned by the Swami but he was not combative in nature and let her win. Cholappa used to come for *Darshan* every day. One day Swamiji said "Cholappa why do you keep quiet ? Why do you allow her to grab all the benefits? If you keep quiet,you will forfeit the harvest that is your due."

Swami Samarth knew everything. He was aware of her crafty nature and greed for money. He ceased to give any importance to her and let her do only routine service to Him. It was His all-forgiving and compassionate nature. He might have retained her, to act like a scarecrow to ward off the crowd!

Later on Balappa was entrusted with the task of service to the Swami, since Sunderabai needed someone to assist her. Balappa found the greatest joy in serving the Lord personally so she allowed him to continue. Her greed grew more and more and she began extracting money from all visitors. She used all possible tricks to obtain gifts from devotees and none could go in without paying her, for the *Darshan* of the Swami. On one occasion Swamiji got very angry with her and flung his sandal at her. She had misappropriated Rs. 25 (which was a huge sum in those days) from the offerings by devotees.

Divine Grace Forfeited

On account of her continuing excesses, Sunderabai finally forfeited the grace of the Swami. Complaints were made to the police against her. There was an investigation and the charges were proved to be correct. She was dismissed from service and her property was confiscated.

Wealth, greed and conceit blurs the vision and fouls the mind. Sunderabai misused the rare and unique privilege of serving the great master and thereby forfeited Divine grace. She thought she could hide her petty minded schemes and manipulations from Him the 'All-Knowing'. She was under the *Kalpa Vriksha* (wish-fulfilling tree) itself and she could have got even *Moksha* (Total freedom from birth and death) for mere asking; but she desired common earthly things. She chose the snares of glittering paltry coins discarding the precious treasure of' Divine grace.

Her case is a warning to those who obtain the blessed privilege, of getting close to great Masters and misusing it. It amounts to playing with fire, or walking on the razor's edge. Unless the body is disciplined, all desires vanquished and the mind totally purified, we yield to delusions. God's ways are strange. HE dons the veil of *Maya* and deludes our foolish minds letting us miss His Divinity and take Him to be an ordinary being like ourselves.

Much later, Sunderbai genuinely repented her evil ways. Swami Samarth's ever-flowing divine love and compassion totally reformed her.

3. THAKURDAS

Thakurdas was a devotee of Sri Gurudev Datta and a well-known performer of *Kirtan*. From childhood itself he visited holy places like Ganagapur, Narsobawadi, etc., and took to spiritual *Sadhana*.

He was a profound scholar and philosopher, but because of his skin disease (leucoderma), he suffered from an inferiority complex and avoided the company of people.

He went to Ganagapur and worshipped the *Datta Padukas*. He had taken musk with him to apply on them, but he forgot to do so. That night he performed *Kirtan* with deep feeling and devotion. His intention was to go to sacred Benaras, but that night in a dream, he was ordered to go to Akkalkot and to have the *Darshan* of Swami Samarth. Accordingly he went there and enquired where he could see Sri Swami Samarth. In His infinite grace, Swami Samarth had gone to bless the new house of a concubine. Thakurdas went there and prostrated at the feet of Swami Maharaj, who said "Where is my musk? Give me my musk at once". Thakurdas' memory was jogged - he remembered now that he had forgotten to apply it on the *Datta Padukas* at Ganagapur. Thakurdas was wonder-struck. He realised that there was no distinction between Sri Swami Samarth and *Datta Guru Padukas* at Ganagapur. He immediately fetched the musk and offered it to Maharaj content that this was as good as offering it at Ganagapur.

Swamiji's Grace & Prasad

Later on when Thakurdas went for the *Darshan* of Swamiji, He flung a burnt piece of wood to him, which Thakurdas took as an indication of Swami's grace. He powdered it and mixed this powder with holy ash and applied it all over his body. The white spots gradually disappeared from his body and he was completely cured of his skin disease in time[33].

His wife wanted a son as they only had a daughter and offered prayers to Sri Swami Samarth who gave her his Gold-laced cap as *Prasad* - a token of Swami Samarth's grace and blessings. In due course she gave birth to a son, who was named Gurunath, who later on became a great devotee of Swamiji.

Sri Swami gave his *Padukas* to Thakurdas and instructed him to install them near Raghunath Mandir. Accordingly, Thakurdas installed the *Padukas* of Sri Swami Samarth on the right side of the hall, in the temple which he built. He kept a photograph of Swamiji there. Daily worship to the *Padukas* is performed there even today. A large number of devotees visit this temple at Thakurdwar, Bombay and offer prayers there. Swami Samarth's presence and

---

[33] The actions of Avadhoots are difficult to fathom and requires faith and devotion from the devotee, if they are to benefit. An average person might have left the burnt piece of wood behind.

blessings are felt and experienced by the devotees even now.

4. RAJE RAYAN

Shankar Rao Raje Rayan was a very rich landlord in the Nizam State, with an annual income of Rs. 6,00,000 in those days. But he was unhappy since he was suffering from Tuberculosis and poor health. He took treatment from the best doctors, but to no avail, his condition worsened day by day. He was advised by some friends to go to Ganagapur and he went there.

Visions

He lavishly distributed money and food to all. He worshipped the *Datta Padukas* daily. After 3 months he had a vision, whereby he was asked to go to Akkalkot and seek the grace of Sri Swami Samarth. Till then, although he had heard of Sri Swami Samarth, he did not have much faith in Him. Even after the vision he was sceptical and did not feel inclined to go to Akkalkot. He had a second vision after a few days and was told that unless he went for the *Darshan* of Swami Samarth, he would never be cured.

After the second vision he left for Akkalkot. When he reached there he met Sunderabai. He narrated his problems to her and she demanded Rs. 2,000 from him. He was prepared to give any amount provided he was cured. Sunderabai was very happy at this opportunity to make a lot of money.

Deliverance

She talked to Swami Samarth about Raje Rayan and requested that he be cured. Even as she was talking Swamiji rose and went out to the tomb of Sheikh Mursaheb. Raje Rayan followed with the rest of the devotees. Swami Samarth stretched out on one of the tombs and the fakirs there told Raje Rayan, that this indicated that he was delivered from death.

Raje Rayan was overwhelmed with joy. He distributed food, money and clothes to all the fakirs and the poor. Thereafter within 6 months, Raje Rayan got completely well without having to pay anything to Sunderabai, who had been dismissed from the service of the Swami by then.

He became a normal and healthy man again, all due to the grace of Sri Swami Samarth. Swamiji ordered him to build a Muth outside Akkalkot. Accordingly the Muth was built and is known as Raje Rayan Muth and the holy Swami Samarth *Padukas* are housed there.

5. MORESHWAR JOSHI

Joshi was a learned Brahmin well versed in *Shastras* and *Puranas*. In his youth he had done *Japa* and *Dhyana* and engaged in spiritual practices. Swami Samarth had appeared in his dream once. Hearing about the spiritual greatness of Swami Samarth, he decided to go to Akkalkot for His *Darshan*. He took a vow that he would not eat or drink unless he got His

Darshan. Due to fasting the journey became arduous and tiring for him.

Swami Samarth had gone to the top of a hill at that time and He knew that Joshi was coming for His *Darshan.* He said "What a mad fellow is he? He is coming from Sopara for My *Darshan* without taking food or water. Oh Joshi! I Myself came to you but you are not satisfied and want to see me in person". None of the disciples understood this soliloquy.

The "Madcap" arrives

As Joshi climbed up the hill, Swamiji remarked "Look! The madcap has arrived". Joshi prostrated at His feet. The Swami said "Why have you come here taking all this trouble? Did I not come myself to you in your dream? Go back at once to your house. Your wife is so much worried about you, that she has vowed to fast until you return home.

When Joshi was about to depart, Swami Samarth blessed him and presented His *Padukas* engraved in stone, on a brass plate. He said "You are a blessed person; you will have a happy family life. In later life you will take *Sanyas* (Renunciation). Preserve these *Padukas* and instruct your children to enshrine them on your *Samadhi.* Continue *Hari Kirtan*; its tradition will flourish and last for generations in your family".

Joshi returned home and found his wife fasting and praying for his safe return. Now that he had returned with a *Mahapurusha's* grace, she was overwhelmed with joy.

Joshi spent the rest of his life in performing *Hari Kirtan* and later took *Sanyasa* and was named Mayurananda Saraswati. He attained *Samadhi* at the age of 75. Sri Swami Samarth *Padukas* embellish his Samadhi and make it a hallowed place.

6. ABAJI RAMDASI

Abaji was a devoted disciple of Swami Samarth. He was a great scholar and a reputed *Kirtankar*. His academic learning and knowledge had evoked conceit and egotism in him. Therefore, when he went for *Darshan* of Swamiji, He completely ignored him. Abaji resolved, not to leave Akkalkot unless he got the *Darshan* and blessings of the Swami.

The next day Swami Samarth went out and seated Himself on a small hill. Abaji also went there and sat down. Swamiji asked one of the devotees to bring 2 jugs of water and when they were brought, turned them upside down and emptied them!

Donkey's burden

This was to indicate that one has to drive out one's ego. The heart should not be puffed up and fouled with pride. It is the shrine of the Lord and should be kept pure with humility and devotion. It should be hollow like a flute, only then can the Lord produce sweet and soulful Divine music from it. Mere learning has no value without purity. Without *Chitta Suddhi* learning is a mere burden. The mind must remain concentrated on the realisation of God. The aim of all our activities should be self-knowledge. A learned scholar without this realisation is like a donkey carrying *Shastra* and *Veda* - it is only a burden for the donkey. Abaji understood these truths and prostrated at Maharaj's feet, in repentance, gratitude and devotion. He remained at Akkalkot for a fortnight worshipping the Swami. Swami Samarth Maharaj blessed him and gave him His *Padukas*.

7. GOVINDJI AND KHANOJI

Govindji was a rich businessman of Bombay. During 1868 he went on a pilgrimage to Ganagapur accompanied by a Brahmin called Khanoji. There, while worshipping the holy *Padukas* he had a vision of Sri Narasimha Saraswati directing him to go to Akkalkot and have the *Darshan* of Sri Swami Samarth, saying "I am now at Akkalkot. Have my *Darshan* there. Your desire will be fulfilled".

Both of them went to Akkalkot and had the *Darshan* of Sri Swami Samarth. They were so impressed that they decided not to leave.

Khanoji used to cook food and offer it to Swamiji as *Naivedya*[34] daily. One day Maharaj ordered that the food should be offered to a Fakir and his dog on the outskirts of the city. They did accordingly and when they returned with the vessels, Swamiji pointed to the remnants of rice, milk pudding and bread and told them to eat it as *Prasad*. Govindji was unwilling to eat it, however Khanoji ate a little, though, he too was averse to eating it.

---

[34] One of the ways of performing worship.

Swami Samarth told Govindji "Your faith is still not steady, it is swinging like a pendulum between faith and doubt. Even so, I bless you. Take these sandals with you to Bombay and worship them". To Khanoji He said "You can also go back to Bombay. You will get a gift of Rs. 10,000 there".

Getting the Gift

Both returned to Bombay. Govindji installed the Padukas in his house and worshipped them daily. Khanoji was obsessed with getting the gift, which after all was a very large sum of money. He became restless and even went about without sleep, in case he missed the gift!!

Meanwhile a lady decided to make a Gupta Daan (secret donation), in memory of a relation who had died a few days earlier, to the first person she would see at dawn the next day. It happened to be Khanoji! He had set out on his search very early and he was hailed by this lady and given a bag containing Rs. 10,000!

8. BAPU KULKARNI

Swami demonstrated His "Omniscience" in a dramatic way, as follows:

Kulkarni was a Brahman residing in a village 20 miles from Akkalkot. He was suffering from cancer. There was a perforation in his throat and he could not swallow. He went to Ganagapur and stayed there reciting the name of Gurudev Datta and reading

205

Guru Charitra. He was a gifted poet and compiled 400 *Abhangs*[35] in praise of Lord Datta. But he had a peculiar problem - he used to get stuck at the fourth line - the concluding line - of each *Abhanga*. Thus they remained incomplete and unfinished. However much he tried, he could not think of satisfactory words to complete them and felt unhappy about this.

Bhanga to Abhanga

He had a dream directing him to go to Akkalkot. He went there and prostrated at the feet of Sri Swami Samarth. An amazing event took place. Swami Samarth began to chant the fourth line of each of the incomplete 400 *Abhanga* composed by Kulkarni! Thus the *Abhangs* were completed. In addition, by the grace of Akkalkot Maharaj, Kulkarni was completely cured of cancer, he was suffering from, for many years.

Thereafter, until the end of his life, he composed *Abhangs* and spent his time in spiritual activity and came to be known as "Das Bapu".

9. NANDRAM SAWKAR

Nandram was a famous contractor, who had built the *Sabha Mandap* (Assembly Hall) at Pandharpur and of the Ram Mandir at Poona. Nandram was suffering severely from inflammation of the prostrate gland. He had tried all types of treatment and remedies, but to no avail. One day an astrologer

---

[35] Literally unbreakable.

checked his horoscope and declared that his ailment could be cured only by the grace of a great *Mahatma*. Nandram queried how and where could he find such a *Maha Purush*. The astrologer told him about Sri Swami Samarth and told him to go for His *Darshan* and seek His grace.

He also gave Nandram some *Vibhuti** to be taken after chanting the name of Sri Swami Samarth. Lo! Chanting His name and the *Vibhuti* gave him great relief. The inflammation subsided within 8 days and Nandram became completely well.

Now he was eager to visit Akkalkot for Swamiji's *Darshan*.

He went there and prostrated at the feet of Sri Swami Samarth. He fed the poor, distributed alms, gave money and clothes to the poor.

Shiva Incarnate

Nandram was a devotee of Lord Shiva and went to the Mallikarjuna temple on a Monday, for *Darshan*. Maharaj was sitting outside the temple and Nandram prostrated at His feet. Swami Samarth said "I am not Lord Mallikarjuna, He is in the Shivalinga inside. Go and worship there". Nandram went inside, but could not find the Shiva Linga there. He was bewildered and coming out told everyone about it. When people excitedly entered the temple, they found Swami Samarth in place of the Shiva Linga, even

---

* Sacred ash

though they could see Swamiji sitting outside! All of them realised then, that Swami Samarth was not different from Lord Mallikarjuna. He was Shiva Incarnate! Thus did He demonstrate His OMNIPRESENCE.

Nandram was blessed by the Swami with His *Padukas* and returned to Poona. Nandram spent the rest of his life worshipping the Swami Samarth *Padukas*. He used all his wealth for charitable and religious purposes.

10. RADHA

There was a courtesan by the name of Radha, in Akkalkot who was a famed beauty. She was proud of her beauty and thought that no man could resist her beautiful figure and looks. She thought that she could tempt Swamiji too with her physical beauty, even as Menaka had Rishi Visvamitra. What a difference from snaring common men! What a grand victory it would be for her.

She approached the Swami one day, revealingly attired and throwing coquettish looks at Him. Swami Samarth glanced at her and asked "Why have you come? What do you want?" (He knew everything; the questions were His leela).

She wondered whether the Swami had ever known a woman. At this point, Swamiji asked her the difference between a man and a woman. She replied "Most obviously, the breasts". She added "I offer them to you". Swami Samarth said "I have accepted then - now you can go". Her heavy and beautiful breasts shrank and became flat (even though her health was normal). She was aghast; all her pride and vanity about her shapely form and beauty vanished.

With her "vanishing" breasts, her patrons also vanished. Like most beautiful women, she was narcissistic - full of self-love, which prevents one from loving God. Now her mind opened up, like light entering a dark room; realising the abominable beliefs and vices she had been pursuing all her life.

She again went for "darshan." Sri Swami Samarth looked at her with compassion and divine love. This touched her deeply and she felt deep revulsion and repentance for having tried to test the Lord incarnate. She felt great remorse for the life of sensuality she had been leading. She fell at His feet and their touch was enough to redeem her! Her *Deha Buddhi* (body consciousness) vanished.

With surrender at Akkalkot Maharaj's feet, all Radha's sins were forgiven and washed away. The woman who rose was a new Radha with a totally purified mind, surging with deep devotion and spiritual yearning. With Swami Samarth's blessings she became a *Yogini* and spent the rest of her life at Kashi and Vrindavan in spiritual pursuits.

One may be the most heinous sinner, but the doors of the merciful and compassionate Lord are ever open. He is equally solicitous and concerned about all His children.

11. SAYYED

Sri Swami Samarth was once sitting in Desmukh wada surrounded by disciples and devotees. A stranger named Sayyed (a Muslim) came there enquiring the whereabouts of Swamiji. Swami Samarth called him and as he looked at Maharaj, he immediately went into *Samadhi*. After some time he regained consciousness and started extolling. "Oh, Hazrat Allah! Uptill now I have come across a number of saints, sadhus, fakirs and auliyas but never have I seen a great soul like you. I feel blessed. I pray that you should command me how best I can serve you."

Swamiji advised him to go to Hyderabad and continue his spiritual pursuits. He went there and spent his life in spiritual practice and was known as a very holy man. Sri Swami Samarth was beyond all religions and did not differentiate between people.

12. GOVIND SHASTRI

Govind was a Brahmin suffering from acute poverty. He was in utter despair and decided to commit suicide. Before killing himself he wanted to have the *Darshan* of Sri Swami Samarth and went to Akkalkot. Swamiji understood his misery and advised him "Go and dig under the creeper in the backyard of your house. Your ancestors have left some treasure there which will take care of your sustenance. Devote all your time hereafter to spiritual pursuits".

When the Brahmin dug under the creeper as directed, he found a pot full of jewellery and gold coins. He was freed from poverty and could devote his body and soul to spiritual pursuits thereafter, due to the blessings of Akkalkot Maharaj.

13. RAMA SHASTRI DONGRE

Ramashastri Dongre, residing at Baroda decided to accompany his friends for the *Darshan* of Kartik Swami, On their way they stopped at Akkalkot for the *Darshan* of Sri Swami Samarth. While taking *Darshan,* Swami Samarth told Dongre that he should stay on for sometime, while his friends had His permission to leave. Rama Shastri was in a fix, but his companions and Baba Sabnis told him that, one should not leave until Swamiji gave His explicit permission. The Swami's asking him to stay was a rare blessing and presaged something good, so Dongre stayed on.

Later, on a *Poornima* (full moon day), Dongre went for *Darshan* of the Swami during *Aarti* (waving of lamps and lights in worship). He was stunned - he saw Kartik Swami in place of Sri Swami Samarth!

Dongre now realised that Swami Samarth embodied all saints, all *Mahatmas*, all incarnations, all deities in Himself. Akkalkot itself was the confluence of all holy places, therefore, going to other places was a superfluous act.

Dongre stayed at Akkalkot for 2 years; devoting himself to the service and worship of Sri Swami Samarth. Thereafter, he returned to Baroda on the bidding of the Swami and spent his life reciting *Purana* and performing *Hari Kirtan* in temples. Rama

Shastri's life was turned around and he became a spiritually evolved person, by the grace of Akkalkot Maharaj.

14. NANA REKHI JOSHI

Nana Joshi of Ahmednagar was an ardent devotee of Sri Swami Samarth. Nana was highly evolved spiritually and had learnt the subtle language of the *Pingala* bird and thus could unerringly predict the future.

At his request, Swami Samarth personally visited Ahmednagar and established a Muth there. Swami Samarth gifted His *Atma Linga Padukas* as a token of His grace and blessings to Nana Joshi. He installed them in the Muth and used to conduct regular worship to them, as representing Swami Samarth.

15. GAJANAN BORKAR

Borkar was a devotee of Gurudev Datta and recited *Guru Charitra* 52 times! The news of Swami Samarth's intention to end His *Leelavatar* spread all over and devotees flocked from all over India to Akkalkot.

Arrangements made

Borkar too went to Akkalkot and offered his prayers at the feet of the Swami and said "Maharaj, please bless me". Sri Swami Samarth laughed and said "I have already made arrangements for you; you will be transferred to a place where you will meet your Guru, Maruti Kaka Maharaj".

Borkar worked in the post office and was transferred to Rajapur, near Ratnagiri. He joined duty and started searching for Kaka Maharaj. No one could give him the whereabouts of Kaka Maharaj and Borkar became more and more anxious day by day.

As he had full faith in Swami Samarth he did not lose hope. One night he prayed to Swamiji. "Maharaj, you have tried my patience enough. Please shower your grace on me quickly". The same night he saw Kaka Maharaj in his dream, wherein he got him seated and worshipped him. He woke up feeling happy.

Next day he attended to his duties at the post office, ruminating over his dream. Kaka Maharaj came to post his letters! Borkar recognised him instantly, from his dream of the night before and at once prostrated at his feet. At this Kaka Maharaj showed surprise and pleaded that he was a simple ignorant man. Borkar told him "Swami Samarth showed you in a dream and led me to you. I shall never forsake your feet, now that I have found you".

Kaka Maharaj then blessed Borkar and accepted him as his disciple.

This incident demonstrates the fact that one does not have to search for one's Guru. "When the fruit is ripe, the birds come on their own"; similarly, when the Sadhaka (seeker) is ready, the Guru appears at his doorstep quite literally!

16. TATYA PURANIK

Tatya Joshi was a *Puranik* (Reciter of 'Puranas') at Akkalkot and a learned scholar in various *Shastras*. His recitals were sometimes attended by Sri Swami Samarth. Swamiji used to call him *Pandit* and used to visit his house from time to time. His wife *Mai* and he were a blessed couple indeed.

On one *Ekadashi* morning, Sri Swami Samarth came without any advance intimation, called Mai loudly and said "Mai I am very hungry, give me something to eat immediately." Mai was overjoyed to see Swami Samarth in their house on the holy *Ekadashi* day. She thought of feeding Sri Swami Samarth by making fresh *khichdi* along with milk and bananas and said "Maharaj, please come in and be seated, I shall prepare something for you soon".

Serve me

Swami Maharaj entered the kitchen and said "Mai, there is bread there, give that to me". Mai felt embarrassed, as Swamiji was pointing to stale bread, which had been kept there to be given to a stray dog. She said "Maharaj, I shall quickly prepare the *Ekadashi* food and serve you." But Swamiji was adamant, He wanted the bread. He said "Mai, give me immediately what I ask for, otherwise I shall leave at once". Mai had no choice, so she gave the stale bread, with milk to the Swami. He ate it with great relish and left in a happy mood.

At one o'clock, Tatya Joshi returned home and worshipped the family deities after his bath. Mai narrated the visit of Swamiji whilst cooking fresh food. When Tatya heard that Swami Samarth had been served stale bread, that too on a holy day he was infuriated. He took his wife's right hand and plunged it in the hearth, scalding it badly to the elbow.

The cure

That evening Mai did not attend the recital and Sri Samarth enquired from Tatya Joshi why she had not come, but Tatya kept silent. Mai attended the recital the next day and wished to ask Swamiji why this misfortune had befallen her even though she was blameless.

Swami Samarth called her and looked at her arm. It was swollen and bleeding. Maharaj asked her to untie the bandage and Lo! her wounds healed - her hand and arm became normal as if nothing had happened! Both prostrated at His feet and were blessed. One may wonder why Mai suffered, even though she had surrendered totally to Divine will. Sometimes such "leelas" are enacted to finish some Prarabhda karma. The significant point is Mai's hand was healed and she was freed from past karma in a trice, instead of suffering for years on end. Swami Samarth gave them a right-sided conch which brings prosperity and wealth.

17. SRINIVAS KADGAONKAR*

Srinivas's (alias Tatyasaheb) grand mother Sunderabai was the disciple of Sri Swami Samarth. When he was 4 years old he got the unique privilege of playing on the lap of Sri Swami Samarth. The leather sandals that Swamiji wore were given as *Prasad* to the child. In later life Tatyasaheb prayed to and worshipped them. He carefully preserved them, believing that he was always safe under the protection of Swamiji.

Tatyasaheb was active politically and he left government service, even though he had a position of stature, fighting for the freedom of India. In 1930, the British Government declared Martial Law and Tatyasaheb was charged with sedition and his house and property in Sholapur were confiscated. Tatyasaheb escaped and went to Hyderabad where he stayed as a guest of Raja Kishen Prasad. When he was fleeing to Hyderabad he was helped by the engine driver, who hid him in a large bowl, under coal. Tatyasaheb was chanting the name of Sri Swami Samarth throughout and the driver felt His protective presence throughout the journey.

A Muslim police inspector was assigned the task of arresting him. He was bent upon apprehending him at any cost and after searching for him widely, came to Hyderabad[36].

---

* All events were related by Kadgaonkar to his son.

[36] At that time, Hyderabad was ruled by the Nizam and was an autonomous state.

Divine Intervention

Tatyasaheb was known to be a good singer and one day at a musical concert in the palace of the Raja, he was ecstatically lost in singing. The police inspector happened to be present and found his quarry.

After the concert he showed Tatyasaheb the arrest warrant and told him he was under arrest. He asked him to hold out his hands for handcuffing. Tatyasaheb was calmly repeating the name of Swamiji, while holding out his hands, but Lo! The inspector saw a dog in Tatyasaheb's place! When this happened again and again he realised that a supreme power was at play and said "Tatyasaheb, I cannot arrest you, God is protecting you". Saying thus, the police inspector left Hyderabad and returned to his H.Q. totally foiled by Divine intervention.

Why fear? I am with you

Once Tatyasaheb felt worried and frustrated at some family difficulties and in despair he decided to commit suicide. With that resolve, he came to the river bank, but just before jumping in, there was a thundering voice asking him to go back. He felt nervous and could not move at all, he was stuck at that spot. Meanwhile his landlord got a mystic command and came searching for him and finding him on the river bank, forcibly took him home.

That night Tatyasaheb had a vision of Sri Swami Samarth who told him "Why fear when I am ever with you; don't act foolishly". Tatyasaheb recovered his courage and was greatly relieved.

When Tatyasaheb received the Swami's leather sandals from Sunderabai, he did not realise their value and kept them locked up in a box. One day, Akkalkot Swami appeared in the guise of a *Sadhu*. He gave him *Vishnu Sahasranama* (1001 names of Lord Vishnu) and the *Bhagwad Gita*. Then He asked him about the *Padukas* and advised him to worship them daily, but without fail on Thursdays (the holiest day of the week). Tatyasaheb thereafter took up regular worship of the *Padukas* till his death.

Sublime Voice

Tatyasaheb was once at the holy place "Parli Vaijanath". A musical programme was arranged, wherein half a dozen singers were to perform. Tatyasaheb's turn came first and he sang melodiously and the audience was lost in ecstasy. The other singers felt nervous and diffident and one of them was so jealous that he poisoned him. Fortunately only Tatyasaheb's voice was affected and he became hoarse. He felt disheartened and thought that he had permanently lost his god-gifted voice.

He went to Paithan (near Aurangabad) and while taking his purificatory bath in the waters of the holy Godavari, one *Sadhu* came and asked him to sing a devotional song to Gurudev Datta. Tatyasaheb expressed his inability, saying that his voice was permanently damaged. The *Sadhu* mixed some *Vibhuti* (holy ash) with water and said "Drink this holy water and then sing". Tatyasaheb drank it and a wonderful. thing happened! He regained his voice and it was far sweeter and more sublime than before. He sang *Dattatraya Stotras* pouring out melody and devotion. Meanwhile, the *Sadhu* disappeared and Tatyasaheb realised that He was none other than Swami Maharaj Himself! He realised that he was always under the eternal protection of Sri Swami Samarth. The *Padukas* of Swamiji are being worshipped even today by the family members of Kadgaonkar and other devotees.

18. UMABAI RASTE

Umabai had a niece who had lost her eyesight soon after marriage. All possible treatments were tried but were of no use. Umabai took her niece to Akkalkot for the blessings and grace of the Swami. Umabai prostrated at His feet and prayed "Maharaj, please restore the eyesight of my niece". Swami Samarth roared with laughter and said "Apply cat's milk to her eyes - she will get back her eyesight". Within a week she got her sight back by the grace of Sri Swami Samarth.

Umabai also witnessed another miracle. A Brahmin had served the Swamiji with dedication for 12 years. He was dumb from childhood. One day, Swami Samarth called him and gave him a little chewed betel leaf from His mouth and said "Eat this". The dumb man was overjoyed at this *Prasad* and ate it.

Lo! He got the power of speech. As the *Geeta* says - Mukam Karoti Vachalam - His grace makes the mute eloquent!

CHAPTER 9

MAHANIRYAN

Saints are deathless; they are immortal! They are ever alive and manifest themselves in response to a devotee's desperate call. As we have seen in the previous chapter as also in the next chapter, Sri Swami Samarth is eternal and responds readily to a distress call by a devotee.

The giving up of His physical body is only His *Leela* (divine play) - we are limited and conditioned beings and we cannot fathom the reasons why saints choose to 'die'. Their death appears real and affects even their chosen spiritual successors. Even a Paramahamsa, like Swami Yogananda was heart-broken and shattered when his Guru Sri Yukteshwar 'died'. Until he resurrected himself, Swami Yogananda moved around in a daze, heart-broken. So also, it happened to Balappa Maharaj, Gopal Buva, Bidkar Maharaj etc.

Swami Samarth manifested Himself again to all of them, to rid them of their grief, to awaken them from their slumber. and to impress upon them to forsake *Maya* (delusion).

Therefore, the following events only complete the historical record of the Divine existence in physical form of *Dattavatar* Sri Swami Samarth. Readers should rest content with the fact that Maharaj is protecting them at all times, now and in the future.

During Sri Swami Samarth's time, 2,000 - 3,000 devotees used to come for His *Darshan* everyday! HE devoted all His time attending to the needs and welfare of His devotees. Even during the last phase, when he was reclining on the bed covered with a blanket, He always used to keep His feet uncovered and exposed all the time, so that devotees could have His *Pada darshan* and do *Pada namaskar*.

Approaching Departure

After Cholappa's death, Swamiji started giving indications of His approaching departure, He went deep into the forest and camped there. People would flock even there for His *Darshan*, in spite of the difficult terrain and arduous journey.

Swamiji returned to Akkalkot and camped near the Jangam Muth. One day He asked one of His devotees to bring 500 dung cakes and pile them over the Shiva Linga. Swamiji Himself set fire to the pile. HE also ordered large quantities of fruits, dates, rice, coconuts, betel nuts etc. to be poured into the fire. Everyone was aghast but who dared disobey. The fire blazed and the news of this *Yagna* spread all over the town. The next day, Swamiji asked that the ashes over the Shiva Linga be cleared. When this was done it was found that the stone floor had cracked due to the intense heat but the Shiva Linga was shining far brighter than ever before.

Swamiji went to Naganhalli. While returning He started singing a Bhajan - normally He never used to sing Bhajans. After His return, Swamiji had temperature and the fever did not subside. He stopped taking food. He did not allow anybody to come near Him, except when it was absolutely necessary. The reformed Sunderbai was the only person allowed near Him. In spite of His fever, He looked cheerful at all times.

Time to Depart

Devotees were getting anxious about Swamiji's condition and begged Him to take a few morsels of food. He relented but took hardly 2 spoonfuls. Sunderabai asked Him "Swami Maharaj, when are you going to recover?" Swamiji replied "There is no question of my recovery, the time has come for me to depart". Everybody received a jolt at these words and doctors were rushed to the place. Sri Swami Samarth never bothered to take their medicines; He who had saved many from the clutches of death, did not need this piddling stuff. *Mahatmas* are not bound by *Karma* like us; they manifest for a divine purpose to put mankind on the right path, to ensure that *Dharma* which maintains harmony in creation prevails.

The devotees were now weighed down by anxiety and with tears streaming down their face, they gathered near Him. Although He had not had any food for a week, He looked quite cheerful. He greeted each one with a solicitous look.

He talked a little with each one giving them advice. He had a bath and a shave. Finally He gave advice, given to all humanity by Lord Krishna in the GITA (IX-

22), *"Ananyaschintayanto Mam Ye Janaha Paryupaasate, Teshaam Nityabhiyuktanaam Yogakshemam Vahamyaham"* meaning - For those who solely worship me thinking of no other and who are ever devout, I provide all their requirements and ensure their security too.

Swamiji said that one should always remember this assurance of the Lord and surrender himself totally - body, mind and soul - unto Him. This is the key to gaining happiness both in this life and the other worlds. This is the key for *Moksha* - liberation and merger in God.

Swamiji sat on the bed; His face was serene, radiating divine splendour and a celestial glow. He raised His hand giving His benediction to all, as if asking them not to lose courage or give themselves up to grief. Everybody realised that the sun was going to set any moment now, plunging their world in darkness. Pathos was writ large on the face of all those present.

The Sun sets

A devotee asked whether they should perform a special religious ceremony called *Anusthan*. Swamiji replied that a cow and calf may be set free - that was enough. As soon as they were set free, they ran to the Swami and went round His bed, touched His holy feet with their heads and slowly moved away halting and turning back and looking, as if unwilling to leave the Swami.

Then the Swami said "Meena (Pisces) is my Moon sign and Saturn is in that sign now; it is an auspicious moment". A devotee asked whether Maharaj would like to give any *Daan* (charity). Swami Samarth replied "What do I have to give ? I have only a cod-piece *Kaupin*, even that is no longer my own."

As usual, the queen came for *Darshan* but seeing Maharaja's cheerful look, she thought He was recovering. She had *Darshan* and returned to the palace.

Swami Samarth was then seated in *Padmasana* (Lotus pose). He gave His final message - "No one should weep. I shall always be present at all times, I shall respond to every call of the devotees". With these words, He closed His eyes. The peace and radiance on His face increased and three bluish white sparks flashed out of His mouth. Human nature being what it is, the devotees were still hoping, that their beloved and compassionate Master would still revive Himself and come back to life, but the divine will was irrevocable. Their Sun had set plunging their world into darkness.

Devotees broke down in inconsolable grief. Many sobbed and wailed while quite a few fainted. He was the father, mother, friend, philosopher, guide - God for them. With Swamiji around they had felt safe. He was their very life-breath. Now they felt orphaned.

Samadhi Muth

The news spread and thousands of people started coming for their last *Darshan* of their Master. The sobbing and wailing abated a little and a few started singing *Bhajans*. Some of the elders recovered and started making preparations for the last rites.

A flower-bedecked float was prepared and the Swamiji's physical manifestation placed on it. The king arranged for decorated elephants, caparisoned horses and infantry band to lead the funeral procession of the King of Kings. A mammoth procession went round the city in regal splendour. It was the saddest day for Akkalkot. The procession reached Cholappa's house. (We have seen that Cholappa had surreptitiously built a *Samadhi* vault in his house). It had been agreed by the devotees that Swamiji's body should be interred there. After all rituals the body was placed in *Padmasana* (Lotus posture) in the vault. This was closed, while thousands raised their choked voices chanting "*Anant Koti Brahmanda Nayaka Raja Dhiraj Yogiraj, Sri Swami Samarth Maharaj Ki Jai*" - Glory to the King of Kings, Sri Swami Samarth Maharaj, Controller of the entire cosmos. In the year 1878, Sri Swami Samarth wound up His earthly stay.

The Resurrection of Swami Samarth

Even today Sri Swami Samarth grants visions to devotees. He also appears in dreams, in His familiar physical form to bless them. He answers their prayers, fulfills their desires, protects them in time of danger and averts calamity. He guides devotees on the spiritual path. He responds readily to those who have full faith and devotion and have surrendered themselves to Him, providing perpetual succour to them.

We have already seen that Swami Samarth resurrected himself before Bidkar Maharaj, Balappa Maharaj, Gopal Buva. In each case He wanted them to transcend their attachment to His physical form and comprehend His true nature - the All pervading Absolute: *Brahman*.

Akkalkot Swami also gave *Darshan* to ordinary devotees after giving up His body:

Bhau Jagirdar was a staunch devotee and Maharaj had visited his house once. On *Datta Jayanti* day Bhau had come for Swamiji's blessings. He prayed that Swamiji should visit Nilgaon once again and bless his home. Swamiji said "Your desire will certainly be fulfilled."

A few months later, the Swami took *Samadhi*. Being at a remote place, Bhau did not get this news. Five days after the *Maha Niryan*. Swami Samarth appeared on the outskirts of Nilgaon and the news spread over the town. Bhau went there with his friends and had the *Darshan* of Maharaj. He again prayed to Swami that He should visit his home. Swamiji said "I shall come tomorrow" and asked them to go back.

The next day Bhau waited for Swami Samarth and since He did not come, he sat down for his lunch. Just then Swamiji appeared in front of his house. Bhau immediately came out, invited Swamiji inside and prepared to serve Him lunch. But, Lo! Swami Samarth disappeared, as suddenly as He had appeared.

A messenger came from Akkalkot with the news that the Swami had taken *Maha Samadhi* 6 days earlier. Bhau broke down in grief. But his heart overflowed with gratitude at Swamiji's compassion for him. He kept His word to visit his home, even though He had laid off His body! The promise He gave was infallible! He never fails His devotees.

Sri Swami Samarth is Eternal, He is All-Pervading;   He is everywhere, here and now.

CHAPTER 10

Swami Samarth manifests Himself even now: Memories and anecdotes of devotees' experience with Swami Samarth

Some of these anecdotes may seem simplistic and not worthy of incorporation. Only those who have had similar experiences or have the quality of empathy can feel the feel and the anguish and the uplifting sense of relief when their prayers are answered by Sri Swami Samarth. These experiences are very real and traumatic to the 'experiencer' and the reader may conclude 1. That Sri Swami Samarth is accessible to all, even today and 2. But for His grace, we could be in trouble. Most of the anecdotes have been reproduced from the previous books.

Nana Paranjpe, Bombay

P. B. Paranjpe known fondly as "Nana" is a very saintly person. He is the moving force behind this book and an earlier biography of Sri Swami Samarth Akkalkot Maharaj. He is the founder of the "Sri Swami Samarth Vishwa Kalyan Kendra", a charitable organisation set up to implement the ideals of the *Datta Sampradaya* and the teachings of *Dattavatar* Swami Samarth.

Nana was instrumental in the setting up of the Akkalkot Swami Muth at Apta Road, 7 miles from Panvel*. This Muth is by the river Patalganga and has a highly charged spiritual atmosphere. The presence

* near Bombay

of Sri Swami Samarth is felt there and hundreds of people visit this Muth and find relief from their afflictions.

Nana, himself, has guided quite a few devotees on their spiritual path and is in constant communion with Sri Akkalkot Swami. He writes on his experiences and early life: Most of my life has been spent in Bombay. We were five children. Born in a poor family, conditions were strained further with the death of my father when I was 5 years old. My mother brought us up under these difficult circumstances. She was a staunch devotee of Sri Shankara-*Lord Shiva*. Her devotion and worship created a deep impression on me. I endeavoured to gain the blessings of Lord Shankara, so that His grace and blessings may shine on my mother and reduce her burdens. This faith and conviction induced me onto the *Bhakti marg* (Path of devotion). The Japa "*Om Namoh Shivay*" was going on constantly in my mind, regardless of where I was.

Once, I had a dream vision as follows: Before I went for prayers to the Shiva temple I had the vision of Akkalkot Swami. I told Him that I was a *Shiva Bhakta* (Devotee of Lord Shiva) and hence did not feel like praying to any other God. Later when I went into the Shiva temple, I saw Sri Swami Samarth in the *Shiva Linga*. He told me "All Gods are the same - They are different forms of the Absolute. I am not different, I am the same as Lord Shiva".

Later, by the grace of God, I obtained residential premises in the Chembur Muth of Akkalkot Swami. I was fortunate in being able to render service to Swami Samarth at the Muth for 25 years. My spiritual progress was constant and by the grace of Maharaj, I had visions and experienced the presence of Swami Samarth on many occasions. Sometimes He would talk to me.

Every day before going to office I would take the Darshan of the Swami Samarth Padukas in my house. I never prayed for anything from Him except His blessings. Thereafter either on Thursdays or Saturdays, I used to get the Darshan of Sri Swami Samarth

One night at about 2.30, I saw in my dream that my Prana Jyoti had emerged out of my body leaving my physical body lifeless. My Prana Jyoti being subtle rose high up into the heavens. From that height I could see the earth moving round and round like a tiny ball.

Then, all of a sudden, I was flooded in a blaze of brilliant light and in its midst a magnificent palace of gold shimmered in all its glory. I was transported within. In the the inner chamber of the palace, was the majestic towering figure of Sri Swami Samarth wearing only Kaupin (Cod-piece) walking to and fro. When He saw me, called me and asked me to be seated near. He sat on a deer skin and told me "I am Akkalkot Swami, haven't you recognised me? My aspect is inhering in your body too. You will realise this fact later on".

Shri Swami Samarth then blessed me with a *Mantra* and assured me that I would always be safe whatever difficulties may come my way. He made me chant the *Mantra* which He had given me.

After His *Darshan*, I came out of the palace and to my dismay saw a dead body, with all kith and kin sobbing over the body. I shuddered at this sight and prayed to Swami Maharaj, I got your blessed *Darshan*, now why this ill omen? With these words I closed my eyes. Immediately there flashed in my vision the golden splendoured personage of Sri Swami Samarth seated on a large lotus flower. He said "Touch the dead body". I did so and what wonder! Instantly the dead body came to life. The man got up and went his way, his kith and kin following him joyously. I was amazed and prayed to Sri Swami Samarth to explain what this meant. Swamiji simply said "You will know its significance later on". He added: "I have made other arrangements for you." Then I had a vision of a saint, wearing white dhoti, shirt with a jacket and jari-bordered turban on his head. He was holding a thin stick and his eyes shone with spiritual power. With a smile, Swami Samarth said, "You will meet him in two years".

In exactly two years, my close friend Jnandev Katkar met me and told me "The principal disciple of Sri Krishna Saraswati has come to my house. Do come for *Darshan*." The moment I stepped into the house, I recognised the saintly person as the one I had seen, in the vision two years earlier. I was overjoyed and this saint said "The grace of my Guru's Guru is on you.

What more can I do?" At that time he was 125 years old and his name was Namdev Maharaj*.

By the grace of Sri Swami Samarth, I came in contact with Sri Namdev Maharaj of Kolhapur who was a devoted disciple of *Dattavatar* Krishna Saraswati alias Kumbhar Swami. Kumbhar Swami had the full grace and blessings of Sri Swami Samarth Akkalkot Maharaj.

I was fortunate to have his association for 8 - 9 years. On Guru *Dwadashi* He said "As per the command of Sri Akkalkot Maharaj, today I shall present you with a saffron coloured *chaati*. This *chaati* has *Guru Shakti* and will protect you always. May your desire to help remove the sorrows of the afflicted and the poor find fulfillment". Saying this he blessed me with his grace.

In my life since then, I have always had a sense of confidence. I have no other desire whatsoever, except that I should always be worthy of the grace of my Guru the Sadguru Maharaj Sri Swami Samarth and that the *Datta Sampradaya*, love and devotion should spread everywhere and every one should be happy.

Nana Paranjpe is one of the rare examples of extreme humility, pure devotion, selfless love and abundant piety and goodness.

---

* See Chapter 7.

As Tukaram says:

> Jeka Ranjale Ganjale
> Tyasi Mhane Jo Apule
> Tochi Sadhu Olakhava
> Dev Tethechi Janava.

He that acknowledges the afflicted and the poor as his own, can be considered a real sadhu and God incarnate.

It is as if this verse was written with Nana in mind!

2. Dr. Nandini Samant, M. Sc., Ph.D., Poona

My husband had a heart attack and I went to the Akkalkot Swami Muth near Rameshwar Mandir in Poona, to offer anxious prayers for his well-being.

A few days later, Swami Maharaj appeared before me, in the Image of Balkrishna, with peacock feathered crown on His head and bedecked with rose flowers. I was filled with wonder and joy and my heart over-flowed with gratitude to Swami Samarth for His response to my prayer and His kindness. This was during the auspicious *Datta Jayanti* week. When my father heard about this he replied "You need not have any anxiety at all about your husband, as Sri Swami Samarth Maharaj has blessed you".

The vision gave me strength, confidence and hope - of course my husband recovered from his illness before long. I pay my humble tribute and express gratitude to Sri Swami Samarth Maharaj.

3. P. S. Lele B. A., LL.B., Advocate, Poona

I was fortunate to have received the blessings of Sri Swami Samarth as a young boy, in a dream in which Swami Samarth had taken me on His lap and blessed me.

Later in life I had calamity after calamity. I lost my father when I was only 21. I lost all my money because two of the banks in which I had deposits, went bankrupt. But I braved all these with courage, with faith in Swami Samarth Maharaj. In 1962 I was on my deathbed. I lost all hopes of survival and lost the desire to live. I was already 72, quite a ripe age for taking leave of this world. One night Sri Swami Samarth approached my bed and sat there. I was counting my last moments. Suddenly I saw a tall figure on the threshold. He was a servant of *Yama-Dharma Raja*. Sri Swami Samarth ordered him to leave and go away. My death was thus averted. Sri Swami Samarth said "You are not to go yet. You are to carry out my work for another 12 years". Saying these words Sri Swami Samarth suddenly disappeared. Due to His grace I recovered my health soon.

Again when I was 82, I fell seriously ill and all hopes were given up. But again I recovered. I do not know what Swami's intentions are, in giving me fresh leases of life from time to time. I am 86 and surviving with the grace of Swami Samarth. I utilise my time in meditation and offering holy water, *vibhuti* and prasad to the devotees of Swami Samarth who approach me. Glory be to Sri Swami Samarth!

4. B. N. Mokashi, B. A. (Hons.), Poona

In one of the general elections I was appointed a Presiding Officer at a village near Poona. I collected all the election materials required, including the ballot papers and started for the village on the day previous to elections. To my great dismay I found that the ballot papers were missing. When I reached the village, this was a big shock and I was at a loss to know what to do. The dreadful prospect of dismissal from my job shattered my nerves. At that critical and dismal juncture, in desperation I sat and began to pray fervently to Sri Swami Samarth to save me. An hour passed and to my great surprise a farmer came to me and handed over a bundle and said "Are these your papers?" After uttering these words he immediately disappeared.

I opened the bundle and to my great wonder and joy, it contained all the ballot papers intact with tears flowing continuously I searched everywhere for that farmer, but in vain. I was fully convinced that Swami Samarth saved me from this most frightful situation. Throughout the night I sat in meditation and *Nama Japa* of Sri Swami Samarth. The next morning before the election, Sri Swami Samarth appeared in my vision and I was blessed by Him. What grace I experienced! I can never forget this event in my life.

5. Gurupriya, Management Consultant, London (U.K.)

I bow to the gracious Sri Swami Samarth, whose grace and blessings have enabled me to go through tremendous difficulties. I am honoured to narrate my experience, of the guidance and protection that Swami always extends to all His children for He is the *Mouli* - the eternally forgiving Divine Mother, always protecting her children.

Through the grace of Sri Swami Samarth, I met the holy saint Nana Paranjpe who gave me the biography of Akkalkot Swami. After reading this holy book, I was eager to know more about Maharaj and started visiting Nana regularly. In parallel with these visits, my experience of Maharaj's grace began.

After the completion of the Akkalkot Swami Muth, at Apta (near Panvel) the first festival was celebrated with great éclat and splendour in 1985. Huge number of devotees from Bombay and nearby places numbering over 5,000 had come there to celebrate this festive day in the presence of their Maharaj.

I dislike crowds intensely, thus when I arrived and saw this huge assembly my heart sank and I told my friend that we should just have *Darshan* of Maharaj and go. Because of my spiritual ignorance, I did not realise that one should not leave without partaking of the sacred *Prasad Bhojan*.

With the intention of taking *Darshan* we began moving to the *Garba Garh** where Maharaj's life-like statue is installed. Due to the huge rush of people, access was restricted to only select, really holy disciples of the Swami and I was wondering what to do. By the grace of Akkalkot Maharaj one of the disciples of Namdev Maharaj, happened to see me from inside the *Garba Garh* and asked the priest at the entrance to let me in. Thus, I and my friend could be present for the holy *Aarti* and got the sacred *Darshan* of Akkalkot Maharaj.

After the *Aarti* my plan to "escape" was foiled, because the same gentleman accompanied me outside and insisted that we have some light refreshment. After this, he kept talking about some common acquaintances until it was time for *Prasad Bhojan* to be served. Then he took my hand in his and escorted me to the hall where the *Prasad Bhojan* was to be served and arranged for 2 extra places to sit, be made and personally saw to it that we were the first to receive the *Prasad*. As if this blessing were not enough, I was seated right outside the *Garba Garh* and had the sacred meal literally in Maharaj's presence!

I feel really stupid now, when I recall, how I almost missed one of the most sacred meals I have ever had in my life.

The next year was very traumatic and only Maharaj's grace and blessings saved me from dishonour and

---

* Sanctum Sanctorum

bankruptcy. After being a successful business, consultant, I decided to start my own business. My blind faith in some unworthy business associates was the sole reason for the substantial losses I suffered, wiping out my entire capital and savings. In addition, I had pledged bank guarantees to my suppliers all of whom, too, defrauded me and their own bank. Their bank asked me to honour the guarantees I had pledged, failing which they would prosecute me for recovery of dues.

By 3rd quarter of 1986, I was penniless and had to repay a huge sum to honour my bank guarantees. In addition, I was asked to vacate the house I was staying in, because the owner wanted it for very genuine reasons. (I had been staying there on care-taker basis, rent free). So now I had to find a place to stay as well!

All through these troublesome months I had been experiencing the grace of Swami Samarth Akkalkot Maharaj, through Nana whom I was meeting regularly. Believe it or not, by the grace of the Swami and blessings of Nana, I did not lose a single night's sleep! I wonder at that, even today!

One day, Nana told me that Maharaj had said that my troubles would be over soon and that I should not lose heart. Within days, the Chairman of a large company where I had been consultant earlier, contacted me and offered me a job as vice-president of one of the divisions. The job came with house and all other perquisites. The company also gave me a loan, which was used to repay the money owed to the banks! In a matter of days all my problems were banished!

All kinds of problems keep cropping up, but with the protection of Swami Maharaj, the solutions also become available. After my experiences, quite a few of my friends have surrendered to Maharaj and have seen their troubles and afflictions vanish.

Ramakrishna Paramahamsa used to say "Cry to God with a trusting heart. HE will come; how can HE stay away? Like a mother who rushes to pick up her child that has fallen, HE too will rush to pick you up". In Akkalkot Swami we have the eternal protective *Mouli* who always saves us and looks after our welfare! May Swami Samarth protect us and bless us on the path to God!

6. Mr. Raghav, C.A., Chartered Accountant and Financial Consultant, Madras

I was defrauded in my business by my own kith and kin. I had pledged my house as security towards bank loans. In the heartless way banks have, my bankers threatened me with eviction and sale of my house to realise their dues. I was the sole bread-winner of my family and ruin was facing my family.

By God's grace, I met Nana Paranjpe and came to know about Sri Swami Samarth. Maharaj told me through Nana to do His *Nama Japa* with *Dal* (pulses) on His portrait. The *Dal* was to be accumulated for a week and fed to a black cow on Saturday.

I did this faithfully and on Saturday, asked my mother where I could locate a black cow. During the previous 3 days, I had kept a lookout for a black cow every time I passed a temple on my tour around Madras. I had not seen a single black cow. I had also asked the priests in nearby temples, but to no avail.

As I and my mother were discussing what I should do, to our surprise a black cow came in through the gate, mounted the steps, came up to our door and 'mooed' loudly as if asking to be fed! We fed her feeling grateful to Swami Samarth that He in His grace brought this cow to our door! I have never been able to find out how the outer gate and our door were open that morning, as we always keep them shut.

After this event, the bank regularly bawled vociferous threats for over 3 years, creating very tense times for me and my family, but under the protective umbrella of Sri Swami Samarth, they did not take any action.

Over a period of time, I could pay off my debts slowly and could finally settle my debts to bankers in 1992 a full seven years after they threatened to evict me!

Sri Ramanna Maharshi said "He that has won the grace of the Guru shall undoubtedly be saved and never forsaken."

Sadguru Swami Samarth is the ultimate Guru and one who has surrendered to Him, can never fail to win over all the trials and tribulations of *Samsara* (mundane life).

7. S. N. Bhat, Poona

On Wednesday, 22 October 1930 at 6 a.m. I had a clear vision of Sri Swami Samarth. In my dream I saw Him seated under the *Audumbar* tree in my courtyard. His appearance was majestic and full of splendour. I approached with folded hands and enquired His name and whereabouts. He replied "I am Akkalkot Swami I come here and sit under the tree whenever I wish. Get this stone pavement repaired". With these words he disappeared.

In 1934 my daughter caught polio and my family doctor told me there was no hope at all for her recovery. That night I saw in my dream, some people had brought a coffin for my daughter. All of a sudden Swami Samarth came and ordered the persons to leave. From the next morning she began to recover from her illness, She was saved from the jaws of death by Sri Swami Samarth's grace.

I was a regular visitor of Sri Swami Samarth Muth, near Srinath Cinema, in Shukrawar Peth from 1930 to 1937. On 25 August 1937, Shri Swami Samarth appeared in my dream* and told me "From tomorrow you need not come to this Muth for my *Darshan* as I have come to stay in your house. Now don't waste your

---

* After this vision, Mr. Bhat started a Muth at his residence. See Appendix IV.

time going here and there. I am residing in your very home."

I was transferred to Bombay, but Swami Samarth told me not to shift my family to Bombay, as the office would shift back to Poona. This is what happened!

Shri Swami Samarth gave me and my family many such experiences.

8. R. S. Pusalkar, Advocate, Kolhapur

I had one experience of Sri Swami Samarth's grace but I did not realise its significance. Later, one *Warkari* friend of mine told me to offer with devotion a coconut at the Datta temple every new moon day. I started doing so.

After some time, I was taken aback when my *Warkari* friend showed me extraordinary reverence and veneration, which is normally shown to saints. Knowing myself, I pulled him up, saying "What's happened to you? Why such queer behaviour ?" He said emotionally "You are a blessed man. I see Swami Samarth behind you. You have earned His grace and protection - How blessed you are !"

If we but take one step towards HIM, He will take nine steps towards us!

9. Dr. S. V. Marathe, Poona

I was a private medical practitioner. Though my practice was fairly good, I was on the look-out for government service, due to family problems. I started to pay visits to Swami Samarth Muth and one day, a lady suddenly called me and said that I would get a job in North West Poona.

Thereafter, even without submitting any application, I got a job as a Medical Officer in the Leprosy Hospital where I served for more than 16 years. It was by the grace of Sri Swami Samarth.

On 24th April 1974, a dreadful incident happened which was a turning point in my life. I was working in my office when all of sudden two patients rushed in and attacked me with a dagger and stabbed me in the abdomen. Blood gushed out and I felt giddy, even then I could gather enough strength to apprehend the assailant and hand him over to the police. My condition became very critical, yet I did not lose courage or hope and started reciting the name of Sri Swami Samarth and the 'Mantra' *Om Namah Shivay*.

Dr. Mrs. Mehta, the Chief Surgeon offered to perform the operation, although she was not on duty that day. I was operated upon successfully. I was, all the while, chanting the name of Sri Swami Samarth and my family Goddess. I was saved from the jaws of death by the grace of Sri Swami Samarth.

The reason for the attack on me was that I had discharged the two patients, as I found them to be fit and they no longer needed the services of the hospital. But they wanted to continue staying in the hospital for its several free services. Hence they came to kill me, but my protector Sri Samarth was with me.

Thereafter, upto the present day, I had a number of spiritual experiences which convinced me that I was and am under the constant protection of Sri Swami Samarth. The Goddess Shakti and Sri Swami Samarth are ever guarding me and my family.

I offer worship daily at the feet of Sri Swami Samarth. I have no anxiety or fear and am ever calm and unruffled, come what may.

(This gentleman has expired; even until the last moment he was uttering the Nama Japa Sri Swami Samarth.)

10. V. K. Phadke (Author of the Marathi biography of Sri Swami Samarth).

Since my early childhood, I have had experiences that some unknown power has been always protecting me.

One day I felt that I should get a deer skin for my meditation seat; but where to get it? A day or two later I casually went to the S. N. Bhat Muth to have Darshan of Swami Samarth Padukas and His photos. There Mr. Bhat without my asking or even mentioning it, gave me a deer skin, telling me it was a present, from him to me. I went home full of joy proudly carrying with me the deer skin, as if it was the Prasad of Sri Swami Samarth Himself.

Once I went to Akkalkot for the *Darshan* of Sri Swami Samarth. In the *Samadhi* Muth I offered my prayers and sat in meditation. On the left side there was the sacred cotton bed of' Swamiji, kept in a locked room. A desire arose in me, to have some token article sanctified by the touch of Sri Swami. How to get it? It seemed as if I could pick a little cotton from a tear in the beds, by stretching my hands through the bars of the door. I knew it was improper, nothing less than a theft. How could I think of such sacrilege in such a holy place? I restrained myself and was trying to suppress my desire, when a sparrow suddenly flew into the room, sat on the bed picked at some cotton and while it was flying back, Lo! a little cotton from its beak dropped in front of me. I got the token *Prasad* I longed for. Sri Swami Samarth does not disappoint any devotee. He is ever the wish-fulfilling tree - the *Kalpa-Vriksha*.

11. D. N. Zad, Tailor, Nagpur

I am a devotee of Sri Swami Samarth since the year 1961. I have passed through very critical times, often having to go without food because of poverty. A friend advised me to read *Guru Charitra* and as I took to reading it, my earnings improved and I was more comfortable financially.

One day a holy person and an old lady took shelter under the "Banyan" tree in my compound. I was working on my sewing machine when I saw them. I somehow felt Swami Samarth had come and I requested them to come into my house. They blessed me and left.

On 26 April 1964, I had a serious accident, wherein I was knocked unconscious and was removed to hospital. When I regained consciousness, I was convinced that I was saved only by the grace of Sri Swami Samarth. Again after some days, I heard a voice whispering that I was ever safe under the protection of Sri Swami Samarth.

What harm can befall those who have surrendered unto Him!

12. Dr. V. Gauri, Ph.D., Scientist, London (UK)

I first met Nana Paranjpe in June 1989. I was an agnostic and a former communist. I had no belief in God, let alone saints or miracles.

I felt very peaceful in the presence of Nana - peace, which was unusual and unique. Nana gave me a sacred cloth which I was to carry with me at all times. I kept this cloth in my handbag and did not remove it after returning to London.

Since then, I have escaped from various accidents and weather disasters, which would have killed any other person. At the end of 1989, the south east coast of U.K. was battered by hurricanes and storms, with winds of 138 mph. This was the most disastrous year for the British insurance industry with losses due to the storm, amounting to over Pounds Sterling 2,000 million! I was driving in the worst hit area of Kent and I saw 30 MT. (tonne) lorries toppling over. I personally saw dozens of vehicles being blown off the road and am unable to explain why I escaped unhurt. My car was shuddering and whining in the wind, but by the grace of Sri Swami Samarth, I escaped.

In March 1990, I was in the same car travelling to Liverpool on the M6 Motorway at 90 mph, when my car tyres burst and my car miraculously turned around and went into the central reservation and came to a halt there! The central space is not available throughout that motorway. I was lucky that my car tyres punctured at THAT spot - anywhere else and my car would have crashed into the crash barrier.

Two other things happened - (1) fortunately no other car was behind me; (2) one gentleman, at great risk to his own life, stopped his car and ran across the motorway, opened my door and pulled me out and escorted me to the safe side of the road. This was because in such accidents, there is always a chance of fire and explosion.

The police came and were amazed that I had escaped unharmed. Furthermore, my car had only sustained a bump, in one door.

After the police replaced the tyre, in spite of their advice, I drove off and reached Liverpool, only an hour late!

A week before I wrote this (1993), another miraculous event took place. While returning from Sheffield on the M1 motorway to London, my car's electrical system ceased functioning, while I was driving at 70 mph. My car has electronic fuel injection, which means that with electrical system failure the car comes to a halt within a short distance. This is dangerous because the speed drops suddenly and since the electric systems don't work, it is not possible to give hazard warning signals. Any car behind, thus, has no warning and at 70 mph that can undoubtedly cause accidents.

Strangely, my car went on for at least 5 miles, till I reached a service station. It was as if the car was under divine control, because it ran smoothly till it came to a parking lot where I entered and the car "froze" - I literally did not have to apply my brakes to stop! Throughout the whole experience, I was like a spectator. It was like watching a movie, where the Director is in total control and one just watches the events as they unfold.

The protection and love that Sri Swami Samarth has for his devotees and even for people like me, who until recently never used to pray, is incredible! I pray that by the grace of Maharaj, we may be guided; may He grant peace and love to all mankind!

13. Bhakta Bhringa, Thane

While I was travelling by train one evening, I was, chanting Strotras and Nama Japa of Gurudev Datta. Suddenly I uttered Sri Sadguru Swami Samarth spontaneously and this threw me into a trance, wherein I had the vision of Sri Swami Maharaj with His golden splendoured body. His celestial figure stepped forward and stood in front of me; a golden pot shining brilliantly was held in His hand. He started pouring new currency notes and golden coins from the pot and said "My dear boy, take as much of this wealth as you desire".

I stood bewildered and bewitched by His divine figure; the glitter of money had no attraction for me. My eyes were glued only to His sacred feet. I touched His feet and I had no desire to touch the money. Swami Samarth then blessed me and said "Well my dear boy, I am pleased with you; have no fear or worry". Saying thus, He disappeared. I came back to my earthly consciousness but the vision has remained indelible in my mind ever since. That is the power of *Nama Japa* "Sri Swami Samarth".

> "Jab Jankinath Kripa Kare
> Tab Kaun Kare Bigad".

When Jankinath *Sri Ram* showers His grace, who can cause any disturbance?

I firmly believe that it was due to the discipline and sense of detachment I had acquired, which bestowed on me the discretion to cling to His feet, rather than go for the money. When Swamiji gave me the vision, was it a test he put me to, for verifying the steadfastness of my faith? Anyway His grace saved me. I believe very much in the power of His name; may it be my constant armour and protection! I have also had the blessing and privilege of composing in Marathi a sonnet *Pancharati* in praise of the Glory of Sri Swami Samarth.

14. Mrs. Kamala Utgi, Poona

I have full faith in the power of Sri Swami Samarth. I used to go to His Muth located in Sadashiv Peth, daily for *Darshan* for over 8 years. After garlanding and offering prayers to Sri Swami I would return home. This always used to give me peace and solace, amidst all the turmoils of worldly life.

In *Samsara* insurmountable difficulties and calamities pour in. As a housewife, once I suffered from physical ailments and mental worries which became almost unbearable for me. I was disgusted with my life and with a view to ending it, I went to the river bank, got into the stream to drown myself. At that moment an unknown voice called out "Don't be stupid and foolish. Come back. I am there to protect you". Ah! Like a hypnotised person I walked back to the bank. I realised it was the voice of Sri Swami Samarth Himself. I sat down on the river bank. Meanwhile, someone from my house came searching for me, with a lamp in his hand and took me home.

Since then, I never despair, whatever be the trouble. HE assured me "Why fear when I am with you". I leave all my woes unto Him to take care and solve.

15. Gopal Karmarkar, Poona

I went to Ganagapur in 1921 for the *Darshan* of the

Nirgun Padukas of Sri Narasimha Saraswati. I wanted to offer worship to the *Padukas* with my own hand, but I was not allowed to do so and I felt disappointed. One day when I was sitting in a shop at Ganagapur, an old man approached me and directed me to go to Akkalkot where I would be able to fulfill my wish.

Accordingly I went to Akkalkot and got the *Darshan* of the *Padukas* in the *Vadakhalcha Muth*. I smeared *Asta Gandha* on the *Padukas*. Lo! I felt a thrilling sensation all over my body. I felt that they were the very *Nirguna Padukas*' of Sri Narasimha Saraswati which I was touching with my own hands! After all, Sri Swami Samarth was none other than Sri Narasimha Saraswati!

I felt thrilled with joy and after this experience my life entered into a new phase. Although not given to writing poetry before, I started composing poems and *Abhanga* in praise of Sri Swami Samarth. Every time, whenever I meditate on Swami and start writing, I forget myself and feel *Abhangas* flow spontaneously out of me.

16. Baba Jadhav, Sangli

I went to the confluence of the rivers *Bhima* and *Amraja* at Ganagapur and did penance. One day at 12 noon, a yogi wearing only a *Kaupin* (cod-piece) but radiating divine splendour approached me and asked me to go to the temple and take *Prasad*. Accordingly I went there and took *Prasad* and began to look for the yogi who had directed me. I could not find him anywhere. Suddenly, I saw a photo in the temple, a photo resembling the yogi exactly. When I asked whose photo it was, I was told it was of "Sri Swami Samarth"! After this event, I became a devotee of Akkalkot Swami.

17. R. S. Pujari, M. A., Poona

When once Swami Samarth draws one to His Lotus Feet, one is for ever secure under His protection. Mysterious are the ways of His Grace !

Until 1969, I never imagined I could write Sri Swami's biography. The leading magazine *Prasad*, invited authors to take up this work and I was inspired to take it up with the prayer "May He help me in this Himalayan task".

Swami Samarth showered His grace on me and the articles were published. They were very well received by readers and devotees.

Though I later wrote a book *Sarveshwar* on Swamiji, I had not visited Akkalkot till then. I had no urge, but Swamiji drew me to visit Akkalkot. Within a week of publication, I went there with a group of devotees. I had a strong desire to offer a copy of my book at the *Samadhi Mandir*. As it was late at night, I could not find anyone to guide me, but the difficulty was soon removed by Swamiji. A police constable came to guide me to the *Samadhi Mandir*.

I went inside while he waited, outside. I placed the book at the *Samadhi* dedicating it "unto His Lotus Feet".

On coming out, I wanted to give the constable something for his unusual kindness but he said "Swamiji ordered me to guide you. I cannot accept anything - it was His command I carried out".

An article on Sri Swami Samarth appeared on *Punyatithi* day. I longed to get a copy and contacted the author thrice for it, in vain. I was feeling very disappointed. One day, when I was brooding and desiring that I should get it, I received a re-print! I am not a regular visitor of any temple, but I am attracted to His Muth by some unknown force!

18. Gurunath, teacher, Bombay

Who can understand the love of an *Avatar*? Even if we are caught in the blinding veils of *Maya*, the *Avatar* who is God Incarnate, never lets us get too deeply enmeshed in as *Babaji* tells Lahiri Mahasaya (the Guru of Paramahamsa Yoganand's Guru, the *Paramguru*), "For more than three decades, I waited for you to return to me. You slipped away and disappeared into the tumultuous waves of life beyond death. The magic wand of your *Karma* touched you and you were gone. Though you lost sight of me, never did I lose sight of you ... ... Patiently, month after month, year after year, I have watched over you .... Now you are with me!"

Sri Swami Samarth also loves all of us, maybe the 'prodigals' more so!

I was very proud of my rational and logical mind. I would exhort my students constantly to be logical and lambasted them, if they dared to be irrational in their work. I was proud to be scientific and did not have any interest in the spiritual or religious world.

One day a friend of mine, who was also a rationalist asked me to collaborate with him on a scientific experiment - the purpose:- to expose those who in the guise of Sadhus, Mahatmas or Yogis, were fooling ordinary people. They were a disgrace to our country, keeping it backward and in ignorance.

I agreed and thus began our joint 'odyssey' into the world of the spirit and conversion from agnostics to complete devotees of Sri Sadguru Swami Samarth!

After having done controlled trials, involving prediction of the future, by half-a-dozen Yogis, Mahatmas (all of whom proved amazingly accurate), we were on the way to Kolhapur to meet and test another Yogi. We got a lift only upto Karad and from there, we were to proceed to Kolhapur in an acquaintance's car. This acquaintance decided to accompany us and after meeting the Yogi at Kolhapur (whose predictions also subsequently proved correct) started on the journey back to Karad the next day.

The acquaintance, in the hospitable manner one often sees outside cities and in semi-urban areas, insisted on our having lunch at his house. We reluctantly agreed and settled down in the living room, which was huge and full of hundreds of books. Being a book lover, I immediately started inspecting them and found them to be in Marathi. While I can read and write Marathi, I prefer reading books in English as my reading speed in English, was 100 times faster than in Marathi. So I sat back on the sofa thinking that there was no book for me. My two friends were busy talking about various Marathi authors and their books, and I was left out.

I seized the opportunity to relax and reflect on our trip. After some time I heard a voice telling me that there was a book for me and to search for it. I got up and started searching but after an avid search, I could not find any English book. I returned to my seat and wondered whether my imagination was playing up. After some time, the same voice, full of authority again told me "There is a book in English for you. Look over there" My head was made to turn, so that I saw a pile of books on a corner table. The voice continued "The book meant for you is at the bottom of that pile - search properly".

I was propelled out of my chair and guided to the pile in a jiffy and located the book meant for me, in next to no time. The book was the English biography of Sri Swami Samarth by Mr. Karandikar. I straightway asked to borrow it, which was agreed.

On returning to Bombay I started reading the miraculous manifestation of Maharaj. While reading, I happened to note that the publisher's address was very near where I stayed. One day I dropped in and met him - He was P. B. (Nana) Paranjpe, whose saintliness and love immediately captured my heart. There was a huge portrait of Sri Swami Samarth there and I felt very welcome and experienced tremendous love flowing from Maharaj.

On the next visit, as I sat before Maharaj, I felt so happy, I thought my heart would burst with the overflow of happiness. I felt so much love - love of a kind never available on earth - a mother's love, a wife's love, a close friend's love or indeed a lover's love were nothing compared to this Divine Love. Tears flowed copiously - they were tears of joy, which I could not stop regardless of my trying to do so. Nana noticed and asked Maharaj why I was crying. Maharaj told him my *chitta* was getting purified; so I could continue "crying". I should clarify that I was very happy and I had no negative emotions of any kind but the tears kept flowing. They stopped after about an hour, as automatically as they started. I felt thoroughly light and refreshed and my mind felt as if a great burden was gone.

While this was happening, Maharaj asked Nana to present me with a sacred saffron cloth. This cloth was saturated with His *Shakti* and this was a great honour for me. Since then I have felt the hand of Maharaj guiding me, saving me from danger, warning me if I was about to do something foolish etc. He has taken on my burden and through Nana is guiding me through the various pitfalls of living in *Kali Yuga*.

By His grace, I got a professor's job in a post-graduate institute. This institute had 5 yogis living *normally* as faculty, unknown to any other staff members. By His grace I could identify them and I could get the benefit of *Sat Sangh*. One would not expect to meet so many yogis in a post-graduate institute!

Once I had to lecture a very critical and hardened group of managers. They were very demanding and other faculty members were stretched to their limit by this class. When my turn came, I prayed to Swami Maharaj and dedicated my lecture to Him, before commencing my talk. I was guided by Maharaj throughout and "I" gave the most brilliant talk in my life, in fact I was the only person ever to get a standing ovation, leave alone a standing ovation for 5 minutes, in that institute!

By the grace of Maharaj and Nana I feel secure and protected. I find myself wondering where the sceptical rationalist has gone - the answer is I am still a rationalist, but I am no longer sceptical. I have witnessed innumerable miracles and seen some incredible things. I now realise that "science" is in its infancy - it has still a long way to go before it can find answers to spiritual healings and miracles. The laws governing miracles are explained by Paramahamsa Yogananda, in his wonderful book. What Isaac Newton said, about science and himself is still true of all mankind, whether scientist or otherwise. He said "I am standing on a beach with millions of particles of sand. All I have done in my life is to understand one of these particles".

It is only after we encounter Divinity in the *Avatars* and their chosen successors like Nana, that we BEGIN our journey of understanding life itself. The veils of *Maya* are caused by our ego - *Rajasaic* and *Tamasaic* inclinations. The only way to *Mukti* is by removing the veils of *Maya* which cloud our mind. We can't do this without the grace of a Guru or the blessings of an *Avatar* like Sri Swami Samarth. Therefore, by surrendering to Maharaj, we can rest assured that He will guide us on the path of Self-Realisation.

May Sri Swami Samarth, bless all of us and guide us away from spiritual darkness to light. May His grace eternally protect us in this dark and difficult *Kali Yuga*!

19. Dr. V. M. Bhat, M. B. B. S., Poona

With utter humility I cite my own experiences with Akkalkot Swami. The occasion was in November 1944, when He appeared in my dream one night - it was as if He was made up of beautiful solid light and lustre.

After this I had coronary thrombosis and recovered after 2 months. In 1952, due to frequent attacks I had to give up my practice and retire from active life, to Poona. Here came the surprise of my life.

Prof. Godbole Ph.D., Professor of Geology in the Engineering College, Poona, had been a lifelong devotee of the Swami of Akkalkot. Dr. Godbole goes into *Samadhi* occasionally and gets a message in that state. I chanced to meet him only once for a few minutes.

Some days after that, he came all of a sudden at noon, to see me and abruptly asked me whether I had heart disease. I replied "Yes". "Then he asked whether I was a follower of Akkalkot Swami. He was very much surprised when I said "No". He then wondered why Swamiji was so anxious about my health. After some hesitation, he joyfully exclaimed that the Swami had sent a message for me through him. He said "Dr. Bhat, believe it or not, but Swamiji appeared in my *Samadhi* state and asked me to go to you and tell you to read some verses daily, from *Lalita Sahasranama*. Though this book is out of print, we will obtain it easily. That is the message and I was ordered to convey it to you. I have done my duty, follow it if you like, it is your business."

I was overjoyed and amazed at the same time to hear this message. I told Prof. Godbole that I would willingly follow Swamiji's advice.

I asked my son to get me the recommended book, but he could not get it! I casually asked my priest and he said he would bring it. Having got it and reading it daily, I have had no heart trouble since then.

Still more surprising is the accidental confirmation I got from a person, I have never seen or known before. I was told by one of my friends that a person with *Siddhis* had come to Poona. We both went to see him. When we met him, he suddenly went into a trance and suddenly asked what relation I had with the Akkalkot Swami, I replied that I did not know anything about the Swami nor was I devoted to Him. He too, was puzzled by my reply. He then questioned me whether I or my forbears had received any gifts from a saint, I recalled that my grandfather had been a devotee of Vithal Swami[37] and he had been given two wooden sandals, one coconut and the *Guru-Charitra*.

He then said "Yes. Now the relationship is clearly established." I could not understand. He explained "Vithal Swami was a disciple of Swami Samarth. Since then for years, Swamiji has without your knowledge, been watching over you and protecting you."

I got unexpected and independent corroboration of Dr. Godbole's message and I was overwhelmed with feelings of joy and gratitude for Swamiji's solicitude for me.

I offer my sincere and profound apologies to Swamiji and beg to be excused for my ignorance. I hope that since He has already bestowed so much favour on me, I am already pardoned by Him.

20. Samarthdas, General Manager, Bombay

From my childhood I had a strong feeling that some great being was protecting me and liked me very much. I had no idea who it was. Whenever some crisis arose, I did suffer my *Karma*, but somehow when things seemed bleak or hopeless, miraculously things would get sorted out.

---

[37] See Chapter 7

I rose from salesman to General Manager in just 12¼ years! I knew there were many people as good or better than me and my background was lower middle class, but I could get a breakthrough into the highest ranks of management, by the grace of God. I realised much later, that it was Sadguru Sri Swami Samarth who had invisibly guided me and saved me in many crises. I will recount below only a few.

I was the Head of Commercial Department in one company. Since I was a bachelor, many of the unmarried female staff tried to attract me and seduce me. I had decided very early in my career, that I would treat my female colleagues as my sisters and stay away from any affairs of any kind.

One night I had a strange dream wherein one of the girls (who by the way was very attractive) entered my cabin came round the desk and held my head to her breasts. Then her female friend (also working in the same office) burst in and both started shouting at me, as if I was trying to sexually assault her. I woke up with a start. The dream was so vivid, I could remember her dress and whole sequence of events as if in a movie. I decided to be careful the next morning, taking the dream as a warning by some great soul.

I entered my cabin as usual, 15 minutes before office hours began and had a strong presentiment that my dream would come true. Just then the girl I had seen in my dream came in. I could not believe my eyes. She was wearing the same light brown sleeveless blouse and chiffon sari that I had seen her in, in my dream! Just as in my dream, she started to come round the desk. I stopped her, asked her rudely what she wanted and simultaneously, pointing to the chair, ordered her to sit down. By this time, I stood up making it impossible for her to hold my head to her bosom! Totally confused, she kept coming round the desk! I told her firmly to tell me whatever she wanted, from where she was and she halted. Just then her friend - also seen by me in my dream - burst into my cabin ! She was perplexed to see that their conspiracy had not gone according to plan and she just made a lame excuse and left. I then hinted to the girl that I knew what she was upto and that it wouldn't work. Thus, I was saved from being blackmailed into an unwilling marriage, to an unscrupulous girl!

The personnel manager (in the same company) used to stay opposite Nana Paranjpe and used to tell me about him. I disbelieved in saints and pooh-poohed all his conclusions!

I left that company and became General Manager in another company. My car driver was a Muslim, but on his own, he obtained a picture of Sri Sai Baba of Shirdi and stuck it on the car dashboard. Within 6 months I met three saints - 2 great disciples of Shirdi Sai Baba and Nana Paranjpe! I saw my life turn towards the spiritual.

In all 3 cases I was taken to these saints without any plan or preparation by me. I now realise on looking backward and reviewing my life that Sadguru Swami Maharaj has been invisibly protecting me and guiding me through life, till I was mature enough to meet the above-mentioned saints. Of late my earliest childhood memories (1 - 2 years of age) have been surfacing and they are as under:

When I was an infant, we had a servant called Govind who for some reasons loved me and would offer to look after me. My mother, a housewife with 4 children, plus assorted aunts and uncles to look after, would agree. At first he used to take me to nearby temples, (one of which has a portrait of Sri Swami Samarth) and talk to me about the various gods there. Later, when I was between 1 and 2 years of age, he started taking me to the famous Mahalakshmi temple and also the Swami Samarth Mandirs at Mahalakshmi, Girgaon and Dadar, in Bombay.

At 6 years of age, even though I was selected by 3 schools in Mazgaon, Dhobi Talao and Girgaon, my mother decided to enter me in the Girgaon school, obviously guided by Swami Samarth, despite the excellent reputation of the first two schools. Thus 11 years of my schooling, were spent literally in an area hallowed by 2 temples of Sri Swami Samarth and 2 direct disciples of His, - having lived there: Sant Thakurdas and Swami Soota. Of course, I was totally ignorant of all this at that time.

Since my meeting with Nana and Baba in 1984, my life has finally been channelled into the spiritual track.

Swami Samarth takes care of you whether or not you know about it!

May He bless us and may the world be peaceful and people be happy.

21. V.V. Dhotre, Furniture Contractor, Poona

Our family members have all been devoted to Akkalkot Maharaj, for the last three generations. Further, we have been fortunate to have had contact with and receive the blessings of Tat Maharaj and his disciple Balkrishna Maharaj.

I had the good fortune of knowing Sri Swami Rama. In 1965 he blessed me by visiting my firm. He recounted in the minutest detail the tragedy that befell me in July 1961, due to the floods caused by the bursting of the Panshet Dam: I was a helpless spectator of the destruction brought by the raging waters.

My place was totally submerged 25 feet deep. Every article, tables, desks, chairs were all washed away. I was panicky and distraught - not at the loss of all my property, but from the fear of losing the photo of Sadguru Swami Samarth, which was dearer to me than my own life.

I cried and prayed "Maharaj, I can suffer any loss, but cannot bear the loss of your photo". HE seemed to have heard my plaintive cry, the photo was found intact, hanging high above in a secluded corner without any support! I pressed the photo to my bosom and cried in joy and gratitude. He had saved what is most dear and precious to me, compared to which all my losses count for nothing. When Swami Samarth is there to bless one in person, what harm can ever befall one?

I prostrated at the feet of Swami Rama when he narrated this past episode. He assured me "Mr. Dhotre, you are under the supreme protection of Sri Swami Samarth, you have nothing to fear. HE is all-pervading, eternal, and immortal. Do continue your worship at the feet of your mighty master, His grace will be - your protection forever".

Mrs. Ellis, an American disciple of Swami Rama was thrilled by the narration and said "Unless His biography is available in English, how can we in the West, get to know the Swamiji and understand Him?"

Swami Rama closed His eyes and prying into the future exclaimed "Why not! His biography in English will appear and will be available to the English-speaking world! Wait and see, it will appear in German, French and other languages too!

About 115 years[*] have passed since Maharaj laid off His physical body. He is eternal and immortal. His presence is felt, His blessings are showered, His *Adesh* is heard by hundreds of His devotees even now. He appears in His physical body to His devotees even now. There are countless instances of this. I always pray to Him and prostrate at His feet. He is my sole

[*] in 1993

succour and protector and I always feel His invisible Divine presence.

22. Dr. J. D. Wadadekar, Trustee of Sri Swami Samarth Muth, Poona

I have been a humble devotee of Sri Swami Samarth since 1936. I have had a number of experiences and I receive directions from Him.

I have visited *Parvati* hill chanting the name of Sri Swami Samarth, regularly. One day a roaring sound started and it continued day after day for 24 hours, Being a doctor myself I tried all possible cures to no avail. This affected my peace of mind.

Then I surrendered completely at the feet of Maharaj. My prayers were answered and by His grace the resounding noise in my ears stopped once and for all.

I was employed in the Medical Council in Poona, as adviser and served for a number of years. One day, an agent from a medical firm, kept 3 boxes in our custody and went on tour.

When the agent returned from tour, he found one of the boxes empty and alleged that the contents had been stolen.

I was officer-in-charge and as I was regularly attending office, he openly held me responsible. 1 tried to convince my superior officer that 1 was innocent, but he was not convinced. This was a tense situation since my career and reputation were at stake.

I prayed to Swami Samarth at the Muth. "Swami Samarth! Save me please. You know I am innocent, let my innocence be proved by Your Grace."

Maharaj heard my prayers and a wonderful thing happened! One day the agent confessed his mistake to my boss, of his own accord. He had removed the medicines himself, but had forgotten to note in his diary. He begged pardon for the worry he had caused me.

My superior called me and told me I was innocent. With tears in my eyes I said "Sir, here is my resignation. I do not want to continue in this place." After resigning, with a relieved mind, I took a vow "I shall serve none else but my only Master - Sri Swami Samarth."

I started my own clinic and by His grace I am very happy. I am able to support my family fairly well. There were many difficulties and calamities I had to wade through, but I always felt His protection.

For the last 36 years there has been a *Bhajan* programme in my house on Thursdays and on every Saturday at the Muth, which I visit twice daily. As trustee-in-chief of the Muth, I have been discharging my duties and serving my Master to the best of my ability and with love and devotion. It is all by His Grace.

23. Madhusudan Bhide, Bombay

I have been worshipping Sri Swami Samarth since 1967. I often visit the Muth at Kandewadi (Girgaon) and other places hallowed by the memory of Swami Samarth.

On 12 January 1972, I felt that I was being directed to go on a lone bicycle journey. I thought it over for 2 - 3 days. Bangla Desh had just become free and I decided to cycle there.

Before proceeding on my journey, I visited the Muth at Chembur, prostrated at the feet of Swamiji's picture, worshipped His *Padukas* and prayed "Please protect me on my adventure."

The journey was to cover about 2000 miles beset with numerous risks and difficulties. On the way, there would be rivers, mountains, valleys; the weather changed from place to place and the food also varied.

I did not take any weapon with me, relying only on the grace of Swamiji for my safety. I covered 45 miles per day on my cycle. On the way I had encountered danger from wolves, monkeys, snakes and even tribals. I also met people who commended my effort and favoured me by giving shelter, food, fruits, etc..

I finally reached Bangla Desh and I met the then Prime Minister. The whole journey had lasted 53 days and by the grace and protection of Swami Samarth, I was able to complete it. An example is provided by the dacoit I met. Instead of doing me any harm he offered me hospitality. As he bid me good-bye he said "I have been in this forest for over 40 years, but I have never come across any person travelling singly. You seem to have God as your friend and guide. Do you want any help? I shall give money if you need it".

I visited Akkalkot in 1974. I joined a *Bhajan* party and sang continuously for 2 hours and was felicitated, which was entirely due to Swami's grace.

Nana Paranjpe is guiding me on my spiritual path. On Dassara day I was favoured with Samarth *Padukas* from the hands of Nana. I worship them daily. May the present crisis in India pass and may all the people have peace and prosperity by the grace of Sri Swami Samarth.

24. R. S. Sahasrabuddhe, Sub-editor & a Biographer of Swami Samarth, Poona

From my childhood, Sri Swami Samarth has held an appeal and attraction for me; I have cherished devotion for Him in my heart.

In later years, after retiring as Sub-editor of "Kesari" I regularly worshipped Swamiji. I got His *Darshan* in many forms and my devotion and love increased day by day. I also wrote His biography in Marathi.

I have always remained unruffled and unafraid in my difficulties by the grace of Maharaj; they all resolve themselves. The more we pray to Him with sincerity and devotion the more His Grace and Love are poured on us. He showers His blessings on His devotees lavishly. I am fully confident that Sri Swami Samarth is ever alive and is present everywhere. He gives His *Darshan* to His yearning devotees always.

25. L. N. Joshi, B. A., B. T., Bombay

I am a devotee of Sri Swami Samarth; my father too was His *Bhakta* and he took me to Akkalkot and initiated me into a life of devotion. Since then I have been regularly offering my prayers to Him.

My wife was once suffering from high fever accompanied by asthma and cough. She went into a coma as the fever would not subside. The doctors treating her had no hope of her survival, only God could help her in that state. I offered my earnest prayers at the feet of Sri Swami Samarth and my wife was saved. She recovered and the danger was averted.

My eldest son-in-law suffered from epilepsy. The doctors declared that the disease was incurable. Once more I offered my prayers at the feet of Sri Swami Samarth to save him. By His Grace, my son-in-law gradually recovered and finally became completely well.

As a high school teacher I had financial hardships. Every time I appealed to my saviour Sri Swami Samarth. He would come to my aid. After my retirement, I went to Lonavala and started coaching classes for students. As I had no pension, I had to work hard in my old age, but by the grace of Maharaj I could get job after job. Though I am 74, I am still working and pray to Swami that He may bless me and keep me fit and independent.

Once I felt tired of life and dejected. I was advised to read *Guru Leelamrit* by Dr. Deshmukh. He advised me "give up all medicines and only reading will cure you." I started reading it and I did get cured. I became hale and hearty.

I wondered how long I could toil for my livelihood. Here again Sri Swami came to my rescue. The Government passed a resolution in 1972, by which I started receiving a monthly pension. Further, Maharaj sent one gentleman, who came like an angel and prepared my pension papers.

Swami Samarth thus constantly showers His blessings, taking the whole responsibility for the welfare of His devotees. The assurance given by Him to His devotees, that He not only "provides their requirements, but also ensures their security," always holds good. I bow my head a thousand times at the feet of Sri Swami Samarth.

26. M. S. Parkhe (Industrialist), Poona

I belong to Akkalkot and our family house is near the Balappa Muth, with which we have been closely associated for the last 65 years. We feel that we are under the continuing and complete protection of Sri Swami Samarth and consider HIM to be our family deity, Guru and Protector.

I was born, brought up and educated at Akkalkot upto my 8th year and left for Poona for further studies. My faith in Swami Samarth continued to increase day by day.

One morning, I got a revelation - I saw the bright celestial figure of Swami and while looking the head of Swami got separated from His body and in the gap caused thereby there came a series of blue spots. These spots in turn transformed themselves into Gods and Goddesses. This emanation of deities lasted for quite some time and the head of Swami reappeared. To me this was a clear indication that Sri Swami Samarth is the embodiment of all Gods and Goddesses *"Sarva Devata Swarupa"*. This unforgettable vision has made my faith firm and unshakable that Sri Swami Samarth is none other than an incarnation of Lord Dattatraya. I began to feel his presence everywhere. I feel a great sense of confidence and fulfillment in life, with the umbrella of Sri Swami Samarth's grace over me, all the time. I had the good fortune of installing an idol of Sri Swami Samarth, near the *Vada Khalcha Muth*, in 1935.

Then, as if by providential arrangement, I got permanently associated with the Balappa Muth. Sri Gajanan Maharaj became related to me as brother-in-law. This family tie changed to spiritual bonds and now He is my Guru and Guide.

In my bungalow on Fergusson College road, *Satsanga* has been regularly going on every

Thursday, where *Japa* of Sri Swami Samarth is performed, followed by *Aarti.*

27. N. S. Karandikar (Biographer), Poona

After completing the biography of Akkalkot Maharaj, Mr. Dhotre and Nana Gadre of Poona, sanctified the copy of manuscript by keeping it at the feet of Swamiji, around which a silk shawl had been placed. After *Aarti* the shawl was given to me as *Prasad.* Later, I was asked by Mr. Dhotre, to narrate the divine experiences of devotees of Sri Swami Samarth.

The next night, Mr. Dhotre got a revelation that Sri Swami Samarth had also been present on the occasion. He sat on a deer skin in His characteristic pose and expressed His satisfaction by nodding His head and blessing me. Further He was wearing the shawl given to me. When Mr. Dhotre related his vision to me, I was overwhelmed with feelings of joy. On that very day I got *Darshan* of His *Padukas.*

28. D. S. Wadekar, Poona

My father was a staunch devotee of Swami Samarth and I imbibed and inherited the spirit of devotion and love from him. Even after his *Maha Niryan,* Sri Swami Samarth graced our house by His manifestations. Once He asked my mother to prepare food. He partook of it heartily and went away.

Once my father was on his death-bed and there was no hope of survival, Sri Swami Samarth came and averted his death. Before his death, my father foresaw it and said "Sri Swami Samarth has arrived here to take me with Him". With these last words, he bade good-bye with *Namaskar* (folded hands).

At the time of His departure, Sri Swami had given His trident, *Padukas*, *Atma-Linga* and *Kantha-Mani* to my father. These are worshipped in our house daily.

29. Dr. V. Raykar, Poona

I was born in a village near Chiplun. Prior to my birth, my parents were sad as none of their issues had survived. They had visited the Swami Samarth Muth at Chiplun, prostrated at His *Padukas* and prayed "Maharaj, May we be blessed with a boy and let him live long". They had a revelation the same day - "Yes, you will have a long-lived son, but you will have to dedicate the child to this Muth on the 12th day after birth".

In due course I was born and dedicated to the *Muth* with heavy hearts. My mother begged Gopalbuva#, to allow her to bring me up for some years, till I could look after myself. She was given permission, provided I was brought up as the child dedicated to Swami Samarth.

I lost my mother while still a child. My father married again and I was neglected. One day a relation of ours came with her son, to stay with us for some days. My father used to offer money to the family deity and

---

At the Chiplun Muth.

at the year-end, he would donate the accumulated money to Brahmins.

One day, he found some money stolen. My father suspected me and I was taken to task. As I had not stolen the money I remonstrated. My father became irrational and whipped and thrashed me mercilessly, after holding me upside down. All the neighbours gathered and chastised my father for beating me so inhumanely. Our guest's son meanwhile confessed that it was he who had stolen the money.

I was hardly 8 then and it was my great misfortune to receive such treatment from my father. I made up my mind to run away and went to Chiplun. I went to the Muth, prostrated at the *Padukas* of Sri Swami Samarth and prayed for His grace and went my way walking in an easterly direction, begging from place to place and seeking shelter wherever possible. I did so for 3 months! On the way I stayed among cowherds, shepherds, farmers, etc.. I came to Poona after 3 months. By chance I met Dr. Palsule and Dr. Hegdewar who paid for my studies, in Bombay.

Meanwhile, my father began searching for me and caught up with me in Bombay. There, he tried to persuade me to come home. I refused, as all attachment and affection for my home and family had vanished. In spite of the innumerable calamities and difficulties, by the grace of Akkalkot Maharaj, on whom I relied, I completed my medical studies.

Mahatma Gandhi advised me to go to the villages for practice. I selected the Konkan for setting up practice and came to Chiplun. I needed Rs. 100 for setting up my own dispensary. The banks offered to give me the money if I could get 2 sureties of Rs. 50 each. My father was not prepared to help and I did not know anybody. I waited and prayed. Suddenly there was an outbreak of cholera. I was offered half a rupee for each inoculation. I could save Rs. 100 at the end of three months, with which I set up my clinic.

My wife had liking for social work and set up a hostel for orphan girls. In the past 25 years, hundreds of girls have been brought up in the hostel, educated and married by us. My practice also thrived and I set aside Rs 1,00,000 for social and philanthropic work.

One day I got *Adesh* from Swami Samarth that my work at Chiplun was over and I should go to Poona. I have been running a colony known as *Shubham Karoti* Colony and started social work. Every moment I feel that I am the child of Sri Swami Samarth and that I am ever safe and secure in His Hands. How else could it happen that a neglected semi-orphan acquire position and status and serve the community socially, medically, and in several other spheres. Is it not the grace of Sri Swami Samarth alone?

30. S. Kulkarni. (Biographer), Poona

I have written the life sketch and memoirs of Akkalkot Maharaj in Marathi. While I was writing the book, I was beset by physical ailments, but by the Grace of Akkalkot Maharaj, I was able to complete and publish it. Another book of Devotional *Stotras* is also being prepared by me.

I firmly believe that Swami Samarth is guiding and blessing His devotees, removing their physical and mental worries.

I have visited almost all the Muths and Mandirs of Akkalkot Maharaj and everywhere I have felt the thrill of His live presence.

(Many more people have sent account of their experiences. If all of them were to be included, this book would be too voluminous.)

IN CONCLUSION

Like an iceberg, only a tiny portion of Sri Swami Samarth's manifestation is known. To try and describe His glory is like attempting to write the whole Encyclopedia on a grain of rice!

This biography may have captured, only an infinitesimal fraction of Sri Swami Samarth's true glory; It is hoped that like a few drops of holy *tirth* it will provide benefit to readers.

Sri Swami Samarth was Gurudev Datta in human form having come to give His divine message for the well being of all humanity. Let us recapitulate His message.

1. You reap what you have sown. You cannot shirk off your responsibility for your past Karma.

Nevertheless, Divine Grace can ward of some bad effects of your karma. Take to His name, chanting of His name (*japa*) can destroy all sins, it consumes them like fire. Surrender unto Him unreservedly, there is no greater succour for you in this *kaliyuga* than the name of the lord.

2. Cultivate *viveka* (discrimination) and try to recognise the reality i.e. God behind all pluralistic phenomena in the world. Just as the lotus blooms in the midst of mud and is unaffected by filth, so also we should live our life, using our discrimination and be unaffected by Maya.

3. Do not shirk work. Work is the means for both self sustenance and self perfection. Laziness destroys both the body and soul. Whatever *Swadharma* (work) has come to your lot, take it up in all sincerity, devotion and earnestness as worship unto Him. Within you, no *Swadharma* (work) is low. Efficiency and perfection in work is *Yoga*.

4. Only enunciation of principles or precepts will not help; it is sheer hypocrisy if they are not put into practice; what our *Dharma* requires is *Acharan* (practice or implementation) and not *Prachar* (talk or preaching).

5. Seek *satsang*, the company of the pious and saintly people - *darshan* of these holy people sanctifies one.

6. Cultivate selfless devotion. Cultivate humility and egolessness. God loves the humble and pure-

hearted. God is in all - see God in all. Do not forget that all are alike in the eyes of God - all are His children.

Maharaj has stated:

I am ever alive; I am everywhere, at all times. If you call my name, I shall certainly respond. All are dear to me. Call out Swami Samarth and I shall be with you instantly.

We have in Sri Swami Samarth the *kalpavriksha* - the wish-fulfilling tree. He is the ever-responding Almighty, which is experienced by thousands of devotees in the past, as well as today.

PRAVACHANA (DISCOURSE)

(Text of pravachana delivered by Paramapujya Nana Paranjpe, at Trimbakeshwar, near Nasik.)

OM SHRI GANESHAYA NAMAH

Vakra Tunda Mahakaaya
Sooryakoti Samaprabha
Nirvighnam Kurme Devo
Sarvakaryeshu Sarvada

Ode to Lord Ganesha
means:
Oh! You are equal to crores of suns,
You, who has a huge body and a twisted trunk,
Remove all the obstacles, Oh Lord of all activities.

Gurur brahma gurur vishnu
Gurur devo maheshwara
Gurur saakshaat parabramha
Tasmai shree guravenamah.

means:
Guru is Brahma, He is Vishnu, He is Lord Shiva,
He is verily the Supreme Lord
I bow to that Guru

AUM.......AUM..... AUM..... Maharaaj Swami Samarth.

We have gathered here today, by the grace of our gurus, on this auspicious occasion of Khojagiri poornima (Full Moon). On this auspicious day let us decide that we shall practice:

Ananyas chintoyanto
mama ye janaah paryupaste;
Tesham nityam bhi yukhtanam
Yogakshema Vahamyaham.

God assumes responsibility for the welfare and protection of His devotees.........of those devotees who always take complete *sharan* (refuge), body and soul in Him.

It is not enough only to seek refuge, but we must take His name all the time and remember Him. If we do this, then the Lord will look after us.

We have taken birth in this *mrutyu loka* (the world of death), where the eternal cycle of Birth and Death is constantly taking place.

Punarapi jananam, punarapi maranam..........

In this *mrutyu loka*, so many saints have come, so many avataars like Krishna have come, Parmeshwar Ram has come, but all of them had to depart from this world. Everybody who comes to this earth has to die, after having done their duties and various actions for which they took birth.

We too have to depart from this world. If we wish to escape the cycle of birth and death, we have to take refuge in GOD. Only seeking refuge is not enough, our "chitta" should be purified. This purification is possible only by good and positive samsakaras - pure thoughts, words and deeds.

God does not take responsibility for our actions - God says "As you sow, so shall you reap". Our actions are in our control. Actions will be pure only if our *chitta* is pure. If we have impure thoughts, our actions will also be impure, so that, instead of using this birth to attain *mukti*, we shall have to undergo rebirth.

Nothing is intrinsically bad in this world, everything is pure, auspicious and personification of *ananda*. If you perceive me as a bad person, some other person may perceive me as a good human being. This *bheda* (differentiation) is because of our outlook and orientation. Remember, nothing is bad in this world,
everything is pervaded by *ananda* - God.

If a black cat crosses our path, some say, "It is inauspicious, now we shall fail in our task". They forget that the cat has as much right to walk on the road as humans have, since all are created by God. Parameshwara is *anandaswaroopa* (God has created everything out of joy). Where there is joy, *namasmaran*, love , nurturing relationships and other positive qualities, there God definitely resides.

On the other hand, where there is argument, hatred, criticism, jealousy and other negative qualities, there God will definitely not reside.

Therefore, if we wish to liberate ourselves, on waking up we should pray to GOD every morning "I have awakened today, only by your grace. Even a blade of grass cannot move without your will. Give me grace so that throughout the day, my thoughts, words and deeds will be pure and positive." If we take HIS name and pray in this fashion every morning, then God shall definitely take care of us. We must do our duty and carry out our responsibilities throughout the day. Even Lord Krishna worked everyday and performed HIS duties. He used to take cows to pasture, guided other cowherd boys, fought Kamsa and defeated him, protected innocent and pure people etc.. Like Sri Krishna, Sri Ram also did his duty. When these great Avatars did their duties and cheerfully bore their responsibilities, what should we say of us ordinary mortals!!

How should we perform our actions?

Karamanye vadikarassye na phaleshu Kadachana ...

We have only the right to perform actions, but not the right to the fruits of the action.

Bhaajile beeja kadhi naa ugavale....... if we take any seed and roast it or boil it, it will never sprout again. Similarly, if we perform all actions in God's name and dedicate all the fruits to HIM, we shall begin to acquire freedom from rebirth.

When we say *Krishnaarpanamastu, Bramharpanamastu* or *Guru Dattatreyarpanamastu*; it means that I dedicate the fruits of my actions to you; Krishna, Brahma or Sri Gurudevadutta [literally: lay the fruits of our actions at GOD'S feet]. If we were not to do this, the results of our actions would rebound on us, leading to our sinking in the mire of our Karma even more.

If a mother brings up her child with the selfish expectation, that, the child will look after her in her old age, the mother lays herself open to being hurt, if the child were not to do so. Her unselfish actions alone can avoid creation of fresh karma. If she had performed her actions as her duty and dedicated their fruits to God, she would have been free even in this life.

Thus, we have only the right to action and not to the fruit of our actions - If GOD wishes HE will see that you are looked after. As Sri Jnaneshwar said, "if your lifespan is long, even if you meet a murderous dacoit in a jungle, if God's Grace is on you, he will not kill you. Not only that but he will offer you food[#]. On the other hand, if your lifespan is short and GOD's grace is not on you, your death is certain."

GOD is everywhere, from a minuscule ant to Lord Bramha, the whole universe is pervaded by Parameshwara. If we realise this and incorporate this realisation in our behaviour, then we shall never do harm to anybody by thought, word or deed. We shall not be jealous of anybody, nor will we argue, fight or criticise anybody. We shall have equipoise and not differentiate between people.

Sri Jnaneshwar said, "The whole world is my home. All the people in this world are mine --------- I belong to them and they belong to me." He did not differentiate between anybody whether men or

---

[#] See the experience of Mr. Bhide, Chapter 10.

women, by class or by occupation. He treated them all alike, without differentiation.

Parameshwara has given every being the right to *moksha*. This right is not restricted to Bramhins, but is open to all. It is also wrong to think that only human beings can have moksha. We read in the Puranas, that when an elephant was trapped by a giant crocodile, it called out to Lord Vishnu and He gave salvation. The belief that one has to be born in high caste families to attain moksha is wrong. Everybody can attain moksha. If we buy sugar, it will taste sweet, regardless of which shop we buy it in. It will not taste bitter, if you buy it from one shop and salty if you buy it from another shop. So long as it is sugar, it will taste sweet.

Thus, all beings are the same and have equal chances of salvation. Everybody has *Parameshwara* in their hearts. We should learn to recognise this. To attain GOD we needn't go far and wide, to temples, holy places. If we do lots of hustle and bustle, we will not see GOD, we should do our duty in the right way. If we do not perform our duty correctly, GOD does not like it and we shall have failed.

The duties and responsibilities of people at different stages of life, at various places are all different. The duties and responsibilities of a child, an adult and and old man are all different. If we perform these properly, then we shall always be happy and our mind will be at rest.

If we earn our money by right means and spend it on good causes then the happiness we have, will be great. On the other hand, if we spend it by wrong means and with evil purpose, then the end of life of such a person is so bad, it is beyond description.

To attain GOD, we should have good thoughts, words and deeds. If we are without bad habits and we don't hate anybody, we have a helpful nature, then we can attain GOD.

It is most important that we must do our duties effectively. We must bring up our children well, look after our families, look after the welfare of our wives or husbands, behave well with our neighbours, do our duty to the town or region and our country, effectively.

This is our Dharma and if we do not do our Dharma, we shall not enjoy *ananda*. GOD will remain far from us. *Parameshwara* is *ananda swaroop*. If there is jealousy, hatred, arguments, then the atmosphere gets vitiated and GOD will not reside in such a house.

When this happens, we cannot have happiness or any understanding of GOD. In order to be happy, we should enshrine GOD in our hearts and go deep into meditation on Him. *Parameshwara* is one - Rama, Krishna, Vishnu, Mahesh, avataars, all are one. If we follow this philosophy we shall soon enjoy peace of mind and happiness.

As opposed to this, if we devote ourselves to one god, one day and another god the next, our energies will be wasted and we shall not be able to attain GOD, which is our goal. Therefore focus your mind only on one GOD and/or saint and pour all your devotion there.

In this kali yuga in the name of Dharma, a lot of wrong things are being done. Through wrong guidance, lots of families have broken up, people have fallen into difficulties due to taking advice from all kinds of buvas (fake gurus).

It is said that, without a guru one cannot progress spiritually. However one has to meet the *right* guru. As Jnaneshwar said, "You will not benefit by putting any stone around your neck, assuming it to be the philosopher's stone (*Pareez*). Only a genuine guru can be of value."

Nowadays, with the high cost of living, it is not possible for an average person to carry out the rituals, do various ceremonies and poojas, go on teerthyaatras, recommended in our scriptures. Rather, it is better to stay home and improve our behaviour, give proper guidance to our children and uphold our Dharma.

In these difficult times many people desire a guru, they feel that they will not make any spiritual progress without one. THERE IS NO NEED TO SEARCH FOR A GURU. THERE IS NO GUARANTEE THAT EVEN IF ONE SEARCHES FOR ONE, A GURU WILL BE FOUND. IF ONE WERE TO BE FOUND, HE/SHE MAY NOT BE THE RIGHT ONE, OR THEY MAY NOT BE GOOD. So long as mangoes (on a mango tree) are raw, no birds or insects are attracted to them. But once they ripen, birds and insects from miles around are attracted and flock to the sweet mangoes. Similarly, so long as the *sadhak* is not spiritually mature, he/she will not meet his/her guru. If they carry out their sadhana properly, in time their guru will turn up at their doorstep.

Until then, what should we ordinary people do? All saints have, said that they are to be found in their books.˙ Samartha Ramdas said that he could be found in "Das Bodh". This book is a guru-shishya dialogue and gives direction to the *sadhak*. Similarly "Jnaneshwari", a commentary on the Bhagvad-Geeta, ·by the great saint Jnaneshwar, was written over 700 years ago, but is still. as powerful in guiding sadhaks now, as in the past.

Tukaram also said that he could be found in his (Tukaram's) Gatha. Thus all the great saints have left us their written works and told us that we should select the works of any saint we like and study it thoroughly. We should reflect upon what we read, steadfastly. We must make it a point to read a little, everyday. Our behaviour, thoughts, and actions should be parallel to our reading. Only talk and scholarship but no practice, has no value. One should practise what one says. Jnaneshwar says that one who does exactly what one says is worth acclaim, nay, a veritable saint.

Saints do not ask anything from anybody, on the contrary they are givers. Tukaram was desperately poor for over 18 years, yet he never asked for anything from anybody. Shivaji sent gold and jewellery, as a token of respect to Tukaram. Tukaram's wife begged him to accept the gift in view of their dire poverty, but Tukaram refused the gift, saying that gold and jewels were an *updadi*, i.e. an obstacle to spiritual progress.

Another story of Tukaram: Tukaram often used to roam around Dehu, most of the time on Bhandara Hill, lost to the world, for days on end, repeating "Vitthal, Vitthal" to himself. His wife and children were hungry more often than not. They did not have clothes to cover themselves.

One day, while he was away, one lady came to their neighbourhood. This lady had a *pareez* stone, which could convert metal into gold . Tukaram's wife begged the lady to loan this stone to her for a few days, so that she could atleast feed her children. The lady took pity on her and gave her the stone. Tukaram's wife converted whatever metal she could find to gold, using it to buy foodstuffs, clothes, jewellery and refurbished their house.

When Tukaram returned, he was surprised to see the changes and asked his wife about it. When he was told about the *pareez*, he asked to see it. Upon being shown the stone, Tukaram took it and breaking it into two, threw the pieces into the river. Tukaram's wife started crying and asked him what should she tell the lady when she returns to claim the *pareez*. When the lady came, Tukaram met her and asked her to come to the river bank. He jumped into the water and brought out five stones. He told the lady to select any stone she wanted. Whichever stone she picked, turned out to be a *pareez*! She took one and departed. Tukaram's wife asked for one of them. Tukaram threw all the stones back in the water and said, "One should suffer one's *prarabdha*, patiently and gracefully."

There are people who acquire *siddhis* in the process of spiritual development. These *siddhis* divert the sadhak from spiritual progress.. The raj hansa can separate milk from the mixture of milk and water. Similarly, the sadhak should discriminate and avoid *siddhis* like filth.

Sant Jnaneshwar possessed all the *siddhis* - He made the buffalo recite the Veda. He, with his brothers and sister, flew on a brick wall. He let his back be used like a *tava* (frying pan) to enable his sister to make chappaties, etc., In spite of possessing all these *siddhis*, he never once misused them. He and his brothers and sister suffered horrific injustice at the hands of his relatives and townsfolk, but he never used the powers that he had, against them. He was *poorna Bramha* (i.e. He could create anything), but he bore his *prarabdha karma* patiently and never once hit back, at their tormentors.

Nowadays, there are a lot of buvas and yogis who have acquired some powers, who are on the prowl. Like fisherman catching fish in his net, these people too are expert at "fishing" out people in trouble or wanting something desperately, like a child or a promotion, or a house, etc.

These people produce rings or ash and ask for money. They may produce small objects to induce faith in a person, before beginning to cheat them. These are not true miracles, they are hypnotically produced - Some may tell the past, others may tell secrets known only to you, etc. These are misuse of *siddhi* powers and of no lasting value. If you wish to use this birth to progress spiritually, then you should stay away from siddhis.

Various, so called guru may say, "give me Rs 5000, I shall give you a ring to protect you". Or they may ask for gold saying that they will give an amulet (taveez) in exchange. Wherever money is asked, or where guradakshina (donation for the guru) is asked for, take for granted that these people are not genuine. The guru of all the gurus is Lord Dattatreya. Datta means to give - HE does not ask for anything. Therefore, anybody who asks for money or gift or any articles, cannot be your guru.

If by giving money one could obtain anything and fulfill ones desires, then rich people could have created havoc. Many rich people come to me; their wealth is in crores of rupees, but not one has been able to change his destiny. Their lives are full of misery and frustration. They have no happiness. Do not think that money is everything and don't chase money. Chase GOD and try to find HIM. Do not get frightened by obstacles. Never fail to do your duties and responsibilities.

God is always testing us. A small boy in school has a test - it is quite simple; in upper classes it is a little more difficult; the college tests more difficult and M.A., the toughest of all. Similarly a *sadhak* who is a beginner, has few problems; as he /she progresses, the problems become more and more difficult. If people lose their jobs or their child is ill, they will often say, "What good has God done to me?" God does not ask you to worship Him, you get the fruits of your own actions. If you sow a mango seed, you will get a sweet mango fruit; If you plant a tamarind seed, you get tangy tamarind. AS YOU SOW, SO YOU REAP. Whatever joys or sorrows we have, we should realise that it is due to our own past actions i.e. our prarabdha (cumulative fruits of our actions in our past lives.)

Some couples do not get children; some get them, but they may not survive, some may have them but they may be physically paralysed or mentally subnormal etc., somebody's husband leaves them, couples split up - Why do all these things happen? These are the result of our own action in past lives.

Two children are born at the same time - yet one may be in a slum and the other in mansion. One may have no clothes to wear, no proper food or shelter, whilst the other may be having food in gold and silver plates. Both were born at the same time, yet they have different *bhoga* i.e. enjoyment. This is due to their different *prarabdha* they carry over, from their past lives.

Having understood this, at least in this life we can try to keep our slate clean. We understand what is right action and what is wrong action; we know our duties and our responsibilities, therefore we can try to rectify our behaviour and carry forward positive karma, if not neutralise some of our past karma.

In the course of life, from infancy through adulthood to old age, we spend more than half our life in sleeping, one third in working and the rest in social activity. Most people think that whatever *paapa* (wrong actions) they have done is so small, as to be accommodated on the tip of a needle. They think they have done a great deal of *punnya* (good actions) and have great expectations of good results.

We have to learn to recognise GOD - we cannot see GOD through human eyes; we have to see GOD through spiritual eyes. Many people say, "I have prayed steadfastly for years, yet I have not found GOD or seen HIM." One has to learn to see GOD through day to day experiences - when we smell a rose we cannot see the perfume, yet we know it exists, similarly we should see GOD in our day to day experiences.

The person who acts as she/he says and has a pure mind; who does pure acts and deeds, can be identified by the radiance their faces display - their eyes mirror their pure soul. These are saintly people and GOD is to be found in them. Lord Krishna said, "I am everywhere. My special places of residence are: The sun, the moon, the stars, the banyan tree. In animals like lion, tiger and elephant, I am found wherever there is *teja* (spiritual radiance) e.g. in the presence of saints or yogis".

Thus, one can find GOD. It is necessary to read holy books. The books printed nowadays are valueless, they may be found within seven days, in waste paper heaps. On the other hand the *"Jnaneshwari"* which was written 700 years ago is still read extensively and is worth its weight in gold. *"Tukaram Gatha"*, Samartha Ramdas' *"Dasbodh"* are also read avidly and treasured and are rarely to be found on sale through footpath vendors.

If you wish to progress on the spiritual path, you should treat these books, written by saints as light houses. Just as a light house guides the sailor through treacherous waters, so these books guide sadhakas through the shoals of life. These books reveal the lessons learnt by the saints through experience, and give solace as well as give courage to face life's kicks and jolts. Reading these books is as good as being in the saints' presence and GOD can be found in them. To sum up, where can we find GOD?

GOD can be found in the sunlight , food, water - there is not a single place where GOD is not. GOD is *sakshi* - the eternal witness. There is no thought or act which is not witnessed by GOD. If you think you can hide your acts from GOD, by doing them in the dark, you are only fooling yourself. As you behave, so the world will behave with you. If you make a sour face in front of a mirror, you will see only your sour face.

Therefore, if you want to realise GOD, keep your actions and thoughts pure. Do not be crazy about money and try to acquire it by impure means. Whatever money you get by the dint of your hard work, be satisfied that, that is your real wealth. Lots of people accumulate black money. Such money does not give positive results; such people rarely have happiness, their families are full of discord and hatred, their children turn into alcoholics or drug addicts, their health or that of their partner is bad etc.

Do "Sat" dharma, give donations to charity, to the poor, earn your wealth by positive means, don't take or give bribes. Live your life with good thought, words and deeds, only then will you attain GOD. Have affection for everybody.

GOD is in all of us and is called *prana* or *linga deha*. Our *prana* or *linga deha* can exit from our body at any time, given the large number of exit points in our body, but it does not do so. It exits only when the time for death arrives. In the *bhakti* marg (the path of devotion) some people say that some devi (goddess) or some godlike Khandoba is speaking through them or possesses their body. They speak in strange voices, or they dance and sing. This is not *bhakti* born out of knowledge, rather it is *bhakti* arising out of *bhavana* or imagination. When has God come? When has God gone? Where has God gone?

If the devotees realise this, then they will not sing or dance or shout loudly. GOD does not require us to shout loudly, in order to hear us. Even if we whisper softly or just think of GOD, HE hears us. Great saints like Tukaram or Jnaneshwar never said that GOD had possessed them or left them. I do not want to criticise anybody, I am trying to show the true path to GOD. This dancing or shouting and singing causes damage to the body, hands and feet ache at the very least. The people witnessing this may criticise or denigrate these displays of excessive *bhakti*. Some will say these displays are fake, others may believe them. All these divisions will end in taking people away from GOD. If the devotee decides that this should not happen, it will not happen.

Let me tell you about my own experience; While meditating, I used to go into samadhi. I used to hear the primal sound very loudly (i.e. the primal sound AUM). I sometimes used to dance. I requested Maharaj to stop this; I told Him it was not necessary to have outer display of devotion. So many people left in disbelief or doubt, that such external displays were giving negative results. Sri Swami Samartha acceded to my request and I never did this again. Therefore devotees should do *bhakti* without getting trapped in *bhavana*.

You have to behave truly, carry out your duties and responsibilities correctly. If you behave crookedly, you may fool people for some time, but ultimately you will be exposed. Money earned through wrong means causes immense damage to self and family.

Bad thoughts cause wrong actions and can cause children to grow up delinquent and destroy the family. Bad company can cause damage to the body. Good actions and good thoughts are GOD.

There is no need to sacrifice family welfare and to spend a lot of money for worshipping GOD. Money is better spent in bringing up children and educating them properly. Living harmoniously with relatives and neighbours, assisting them in times of need, is true service to GOD. GOD is not found only in temples or places of pilgrimages; GOD is everywhere. Learn to see GOD and desire to be with GOD at all times. There is no point in blaming GOD for our troubles and misfortunes. A knife can be used by a surgeon to operate and heal; while a murderer uses a knife to kill. The instrument is the same; but the motives are different. Our body is the instrument; it too can be used for good or bad purposes. Think about it.

Patram pushpam phalam toyam;
Yo me bhaksha prayesyati.

(In this verse, Sri Krishna says that even a leaf, or flower or fruit or drops of water, is acceptable to HIM.)

GOD does not want baskets of fruits, nor big rose garlands. GOD does not want expensive clothes or perfume bottles. What GOD wants is pure love, *bhakti* and *bhava*, arising from the heart, untainted by selfish desires. If you can do this, then you will find GOD.

298

Punarapi jananam, punarapi maranam - If you wish to escape from this cycle, then do introspection and *nama smaran*, along with prayer.

Lord Krishna has said that the person who dies while doing *nama smaran*, alone gets *mukti*. It is only possible if we have lived our life, in the manner recommended above. If we do not make a habit of prayer and *nama smaran*, then we shall not be able to think of GOD, at our last moment and will not attain *sadgati*.

After death, the *linga deha*, embodying the unsatisfied desires remains behind. These desires may be for food or clothes or wealth etc. Sometimes if a person dies leaving behind huge wealth, the *linga deha* will remain behind and take birth as grand child or nephew, so that it can continue to enjoy the wealth. (Our ancestors left us *dharmic vidhis* i.e. rituals to be performed after death, in order to assist the departed one toward mukti).

If we want *mukti*, we have to destroy our *vasanas* (i.e. desires). We can destroy our desires only if we devote ourselves to God and pray steadfastly. We should control our *indriyas** (senses: taste, touch, seeing, and hearing).

Drinking alcohol destroys the control of our *indriyas*. Many people get drunk and roll in gutter; dogs also roll in the gutter, is there any difference between a

---

*By practice of fasting or by the practice of pratyahara, dharana and dhyaana (part of asthang Yoga) regularly.

drunk and an animal? This happens because of bad company, bad friends and bad thoughts. That is why it is necessary to have good associates. Do sat sang and you will find it easier to control your thoughts and actions. Reduce or stop alcohol completely. Keep your mind calm. Sit in a quiet place and do *nama smaran*. If you will practise all these, you will attain GOD.

The person who faces difficulties bravely, who is not afraid of destiny can be considered to have won. People who have conquered fear, are on the true path spiritually.

Lots of people ask me whether they are on the right path; they ask if I read these books, if I do these charities whether I will attain GOD. The answer is clear; How do you behave in your office? How do you behave with children? How much improvement has taken place in your practice of spiritual life ? Are your thoughts and actions purer? You can measure these yourself and see whether you have progressed. We may fool people but, it is impossible to fool God who resides in our heart.

Guru Maharaj guru jai jai parabrahma sad guru;
Mukam Karoti vachalam
Pangalam langhayate girim
Yat Kripa tamaham vande
Parmananda Madhavam.

(The dumb will speak, the lame will climb hills, if there be the grace of Krishna, or the sadguru).

In the light of the above shloka, therefore , what should we ask of GOD ? Do not ask for petty things, do not ask for drugs or liquor! If *guru krupa* (grace of guru) be there, even if you take sand, it will convert to gold; but if you do not have *guru krupa*, even gold will turn to sand.

The devotee who has the grace of Swami Samarth will have no need to fear anybody. However the person who does not have grace, will be perpetually in trouble; she/he will always be subject to harassment, always subjected to criticism and troubled by other people. Therefore take refuge under the umbrella of Sri Samarth and be safe.

GOD is every where and in everything. The shivalinga is made from a similar stone as the idol of goddess or Hanuman. The stones are from the same area but the "roopa" (appearance) is different. These differences are Maya. Different *bhaktas* do different rituals and *upasnas*, according to their orientations. God rewards each according to their intensity of devotion. Take a mirror ; if you twist your face, the mirror will reflect a twisted face! As you behave with the world, so does the world behave with you.

Learn to see GOD everywhere and in everything. Make use of this birth to attain realisation and become immortal. Sri Ram and Krishna and great saints have left their bodies, but they have left behind their words, thoughts and actions to guide us.

Krishna's Dwarka is gone; Rama's Ayoddhya is gone; their big empires and kingdoms have vanished; but their valour and brayery have remainéd to inspire us. In the same way, one should try to become immortal, by brave deeds and noble actions.

Realise God and attain salvation. May GOD help you and protect you.

Aum shanti, shanti, shantih.

APPENDIX I

HOW TO IDENTIFY A REAL "SAT PURUSH" OR POTENTIAL GURU

"Sat Purusha" are saintly people who are the personification of absolute truth. That Truth is God is verified in their presence. In their presence one feels:

(A) Intense Peace (Shanti)

As they are fixed in the divine at all times, nothing can disturb a "Sat Purushas" equilibrium. They generate positive vibrations, so that devotees feel peaceful and their mental turmoil automatically subsides. The questions which torment them cease and the devotee is left mentally cleansed.

(B) Happiness (Santosha)

The only motivation a 'Sat Purush" 'has is to make devotees happy. Their grace includes everybody and the devotees' welfare is their only objective.

(C) Love (Prema)

Their love is universal extending to all living beings. They see God in everybody and everything. Devotees feel intense love and compassion flowing from a "Sat Purusha."

Other characteristics of a "Sat Purush"

(1) Desirelessness

They have no desire for money, food or clothing. If any demands are made from devotees, then that person cannot be a "Sat Purush".

(2) Ananda (Happiness)

The "Sat Purusha" always exhibits "Ananda". There is divine laughter in their eyes, even though their face may be serious. They often display a keen sense of humour.

(3) Abheda (Vision of unity)

They do not differentiate by sex, age, caste or creed. They treat everyone with equal respect and love.

(4) Ahimsa (Non-violence)

They see God in everyone including those who may attack them physically or verbally by insults or innuendo. They rarely criticise anybody. Their 'Chitta" is unsullied and pure.

(5) They help or assist anybody without considerations of family, friends, or relations intervening.

NO NEED TO SEARCH FOR A GURU

God loves everybody. Guru is nothing but God in human form. However, Guru can come in forms other than human too. God often guides His devotees through books - These can be accepted as "Grantha Guru". Nana has advised that "Das Bodh" by Swami Ramdas Samarth or "Jnaneswari" by the great Maharashtrian Saint Jnaneshwar can be accepted as "Grantha Gurus." One should read these steadfastly and reflect on their inner meaning. Upon doing this, one's 'Chitta" will slowly get purified and one becomes spiritually "ripe". It is only then, that the Guru may appear. The Guru may come in human form or appear in dreams or visions. The devotee must not think that the 'dream' Guru is any less, than a 'visible' Guru in human form.

In fact great saints often give "Diksha" (initiation) in a dream or vision. Time and again, when the devotees present themselves before their Guru in human form, they are told that there was no need for them to have come at all, as they were initiated in a vision or dream.

There is thus no need to search for a Guru. The Guru Himself or Herself will come to you at the right time. In the meantime one should purify oneself by steadfast practice of "Astanga Yoga" or by reading of scriptures.

APPENDIX II

PILGRIMAGE PLACES OF THE DATTA SAMPRADAYA

1) GANAGAPUR: Near Sholapur

This place is believed to be *Dattasthan* - the place where Lord Dattatraya resides eternally, There are many who have been blessed by the *Darshan* of Lord Dattatraya here. Ganagapur was the place where the *Dattavatar* Sri Narasimha Saraswati stayed for 24 years and His *Nirguna Padukas* are enshrined in a temple here. In the temple is an idol of the God *Chintamani*, installed by Sri Narasimha Saraswati. His *Danda* is also in this temple.

Ganagapur is a great spiritual centre and large number of devotees regularly come there seeking spiritual succour. The *Nirguna Padukas* are very powerful and responsive and devotees find fulfillment of their desires, relief from their afflictions and cures of their physical ailments.

It is on the banks of the river Bhima and it is believed that the Bhima river has in it the water of 8 *Tirthas* from all over India. There is also the holy hillock of Vibhuti (holy ash) from which, for centuries, devotees have taken some, as (Prasad) - Yet the hillock has not got depleted.

At the *Sangam* of the 2 rivers Bhima and Amraja, there is the temple of Sangameshwar. It is said that Sri Narasimha Saraswati used to come here from Ganagapur (2 miles away) daily for a bath. There is a grove (on the banks) of *Aswatha* trees and He used to sit in meditation under one of these trees. *Sadhakas* find this place most congenial for meditation.

There are 13 small rooms provided for devotees' meditation and *Sadhana*. Tembe Swami got the *Darshan* of Sri Narasimha Saraswati here, near the *Papa Vinashi Tirth*. Although devotees flock here all through the year, it is virtually flooded during *Datta Jayanti* and *Dassera*.

2) NARSOBA# WADI: District Kolhapur.

This place is also associated with Sri Narasimha Saraswati. HE did *Tapasya* here for 12 years, under the *Audumbar* tree here. This place abounds with natural beauty and is vibrant with spiritual sublimity. Many saints chose this place for their penance among them being Tembe Swami, Narayan Swami, Kashikar Swami, etc.

Near the temple, the river Panchganga flows gracefully. During the rains, the river waters rise and submerge the temple, as if washing the holy *Padukas* which are enshrined there.

This place is located 19 miles from Jayasingpur, a railway station located on the Miraj-Kolhapur line. Buses ply regularly from both Sangli and Kolhapur to this place.

In rural Marathi the appendage "ba" is often affectionately added after altering the name. Thus Narasimha Wadi becomes Narsoba Wadi. Shivaji is often referred to as Shivba and the god Pandurang as Pandoba, to cite some examples.

3) AUDUMBAR, District Sangli

This is another great *Dattasthan* on the banks of the holy Krishna river. There is a temple where *Dattatraya Padukas* were installed by Sri Narasimha Saraswati.

There is an ancient *Tirth* known as *Koti Tirth*. On the other side of the river, there is the temple of Goddess Bhuvaneshwari. An account of the prowess of this deity is given in the *Guru Charitra*.

Celebrations of holy festivals take place in a big way. The atmosphere is sublime, so that people who come here get spiritually uplifted.

4) GIRNAR: Saurashtra

It is commonly believed that the chief abode and eternal home of Lord Dattatraya is Girnar. On the highest peak is a small temple, wherein are enshrined the Datta Padukas. This is known as Guru Datta Sikhar. It is about 12 miles from the Junagadh station.

This has been 'the' pilgrimage place all through the ages. Bharatrihari, Goraknath, Kisornath, Niranjan, Rang Avdhut of ancient times were all said to have made their pilgrimages to Girnar. Saints of recent times too, have vouched to their having had visions of Gurudev Datta, on this holy peak.

About 10,000 steps have to be climbed to reach Guru Datta Sikhar. Devotees do not feel that the climb is arduous, even though the steps are steep. Miracles have been witnessed here. An old

asthmatic lady of 60 climbed all the way to the top
and she got rid of her asthma by the grace of Lord
Dattatreya.

5) MAHURGAR: Vidarbha, Maharashtra

Mahur is situated near Wani and Hinganghat. Buses
run from Nagpur, Akola and Pusad to Mahur.

This is the "Matapur" described in the *Guru Charitra*. It
is believed to be the resting place of Lord Dattatraya
at night. It is also one of the *Shakti Pithas* in
Maharashtra. Renuka Mata, the mother of Lord
Parashurama and wife of the great sage Jamadagni,
is the presiding Goddess here.

The Datta Mandir Renuka Devi Mandir and the
Anusuya Mata Mandir are all situated on the peaks of
Mahurgarh.

6) LAD - KARANJA : Akola District

Karanja was the birth place of Datta Avatar Sri
Narasimha Saraswati. It is near Akola which is a
railway station on the Bombay-Nagpur line.

It is believed that this place derives its name from
Karanja Muni who is said to have performed severe
penance here and made it holy. Several great Rishis
were also said to have chosen this place for their
Tapasya. Thus, it was a great *Tapobhumi* even in
ancient times.

Tembe Swami used to pay regular visits here and was blessed with the vision of Sri Narasimha Saraswati here. There is a Guru Mandir here in which is enshrined the idol of Sri Narasimha Saraswati and also His *Nirgun Padukas*.

This is revered as a place of extraordinary spiritual power and earnest devotees reap spiritual benefit here.

7) NARESHWAR: Gujarat State

This was a densely forested area previously. The disciple of Tembe Swami - Ranga Avadhut - did *Tapasya* here and attained enlightenment. He was directed to this place by Gurudev Datta, Himself.

In the *Ashram* built by Ranga Avadhut here, the idol of Dattatraya and his *Padukas* are installed. The idol is in a seated posture. The *Ashram* has great spiritual appeal and is enhanced by natural beauty all around. This is situated on the Baroda-Miyagam line of the Western Railway. .The station is named Nareshwar Road.

8) GARUDESHWAR: Baroda (Gujarat)

It is a beautiful place situated on the banks of the river Narmada. The Shulpani forest begins here. It is here that *Garuda* killed the demon *Gajasur* at the instance of Lord Vishnu, in very ancient times. A temple consecrated to *Garuda Bhagwan* is situated on the hill.

This is also the place where Tembe Swami attained *Samadhi* in 1914. This place is hallowed by the stay of Tembe Swami. A beautiful idol of Guru Dattatraya is installed in the *Ashram*.

Buses are available from Baroda and Rajpipla to Garudeshwar.

Other Places

There are other places of pilgrimage of importance, as under:

a) BHATGAON in Nepal is considered by some as the birthplace of Lord Dattatraya.

b) NASIK: A single faced idol of Lord Dattatraya is installed in Datta Mandir, which, is considered a second Ganagapur.

Datta Mandirs are also located at Asti, Brahmanath, Tembhurni, Vijapur, Chikurdi, Dattanagar, Digraj, Ranjangaon, Kagal, Loni Bhapkar, Dhom, Khamgaon, Bhor, Devgiri Fort, Bale Kundri, Pune, Sakhali Goa, Kurvapur, Khandari etc.

In fact, the whole *Bharat Varsha* (India) is Datta *Bhoomi* - The land of Dattratraya.

APPENDIX III

IMPORTANT MUTHS OF AKKALKOT MAHARAJ

1) AKKALKOT

There are 5 Muths here and all of them have great emotional and sentimental appeal for devotees and are regularly visited by thousands of people from far and near.

(a) Samadhi Muth

This Muth is in the residence of Cholappa and is the place where the body of Maharaj was interred. An idol of Swami Samarth is installed there, as are Swamiji's *Padukas*. An idol of Lord Ganesh manifested itself (*Swayambhuva*) and was found in the ground near the Muth on 4th August 1964. This is installed quite close by.

The Muth is in the care and custody of Cholappa's descendants who conduct all services there. A sublime atmosphere pervades the Samarth Muth and His presence is felt and experienced by devotees.

(b) Vadakhalcha Muth

This Muth was built under the shade of a huge banyan tree and is located in the heart of the city. The banyan tree used to be the favourite place of Sri Swami Samarth. He used to sit under it for hours.

Once while Swamiji was resting there, one of His devotees Jyotiba went to fetch water from a distant well, as the water from the well near the tree was brackish and unsuitable for drinking. Swami asked him why he was going so far, when the well water near the banyan tree was good.

Jyotiba had to obey the Swami's command and grumbling at His eccentric ways he took water from the nearby well. Lo! The water had become very 'sweet' - Swami's word is infallible! Till this day this well water continues to be sweet and the well never gets dry.

It is in this place that Maharaj laid down His body. The beautiful surroundings and the serene atmosphere provide a spiritually uplifting presence for the devotees; in fact, the devotees feel the live presence of the Swami even now:

(c) Balappa Muth

Balappa Maharaj erected this Muth which has the *Atma Linga Padukas, Chaati, Danda, Rudraksha Mala* presented by Akkalkot Swami. Many come here and find themselves greatly benefitted. They find great solace and peace.

(d) Joshi Buva Muth

Chintopant Tol used to reside at this place. He always worshipped Swamiji's feet in his mind; he was so devoted to His feet, that one day when the Swami visited his house he prayed earnestly to Swamiji to leave His Foot Prints to him for daily worship. Sri Swami Samarth stood for a while on a wooden seat and Lo! the impression of His feet got engraved on the seat, as if they had been engraved by an artisan.

This seat with the Foot Prints of Sri Swami Samarth is now enshrined in the Muth.

(e) Raje Rayan Muth

The story of Raje Rayan is recounted in Chapter 8. This Muth was built by him in compliance with the Swami's directive, at the then huge cost of Rs.10,000. The holy *Padukas* of Swami Samarth are enshrined here and receive regular daily worship.

2) BOMBAY

(a) Sri Swami Samarth Muth, Kandewadi (Girgaon)

This Muth was established by Swami Soot, at the instance of Sri Swami Samarth. It is visited by a large number of devotees. The *Padukas* of Sri Swami Samarth here are amazingly life-like.

(b) Sri Swami Samarth Muth, D. L. Vaidya Road, Dadar

This Muth was established by Balkrishna Maharaj. A very large and life-like picture of Sri Swami Samarth which responds to the devotees' pleas for help, is placed in the *Garba Ghar*. The *Atma Linga Padukas* of Sri Swami Samarth are also enshrined there.

At least one pure and blessed devotee has seen the physical manifestation of Balkrishna Maharaj here, telling him that "The Avatar of Sri Swami Samarth is here even now. Call to Him and He will respond and be with you". There are original photographs of Sri Tat Maharaj and Balkrishna Maharaj. Our Akkalkot Maharaj's presence is intensely felt here and a sincere devotee's pleas are answered without fail.

(c) Mahalakshmi, Bombay

The *Atma Linga Padukas* of Sri Swami Samarth are enshrined here. They were sent by Him to Vinayak Rao Vasudev, which incident is told in Chapter 5.

These *Padukas* are tiny and of an unknown metal. They were produced by Swamiji from His mouth as a manifestation of His grace. Even though they are tiny, they have intricate signs and symbols of divinity visible, as if they were engraved.

Many lucky people have been blessed, by the physical manifestation of Sri Swami Samarth to give *Darshan* to them, even in recent times.

One artist to whom Swamiji revealed Himself painted the experience of His *Darshan* in 1989. Swamiji physically manifested Himself to satisfy the yearning of another devotee in December 1990.

This temple is not visible from the main road. It is located at the end of a lane, on the side of Mafatlal Park, on Bhulabai Desai Road. It is a beautiful setting by the sea with the famous Mahalakshmi temple visible on its right side.

d) Thakurdwar Muth, Bombay

Thakurdas was a great devotee of Sri Swami Samarth. His story is recounted in Chapter 8. He installed the *Samarth Padukas* near the Raghunath Mandir, at Thakurdwar, in Girgaon.

(e) Akkalkot Maharaj Muth, Chembur

This Muth was the one set up by Siddhbai, the daughter of Swami Soot, shifting from the original one at Kamathipura.

The Swami Samarth (Padukas) presented to Swami Soot, are enshrined here.

Nana Paranjpe used to reside here, until he shifted to "Suman Nagar" in Chembur. (He shifted to Lonavala and lives there since 1985).

3. SRI SWAMI SAMARTH VISHWA KALYAN KENDRA, Apta Phata (Road), Panvel

The main mover and architect for setting up the Muth and a charitable Trust for "Vishwa Kalyan" - the welfare of the people all over the world - is Nana Paranjpe.

The temple with Sri Swami Samarth's life-size idol, is located at a very picturesque place, on the banks of the river Patalganga. The whole area comprising the temple and the planned library and meditation complex, together with rooms for devotees to stay, are permeated with the intense spiritual presence of Datta Avatar Sri Swami Samarth.

The Muth also has smaller temples dedicated to *Hanuman*, Sri *Siddeshwar Shiva Linga* and a temple wherein the *Padukas* of Sri Krishna Saraswati, the foremost disciple of Akkalkot Swami are enshrined.

During holy festivals and auspicious occasions, mass feeding of devotees and tribals residing nearby is carried out. People come from all over Maharashtra state to this Muth. It is planned to provide medical aid, primary education, economic assistance to the poor by "adopting" orphans and poor children and providing for clothing, food and education. Of course, the larger welfare, the spiritual well-being - is also catered to, by spreading the teachings and ideals of the *Datta Sampradaya*. Nana has visited the U.K. and U.S.A. carrying the banner of Sri Swami Samarth and to improve the spiritual well-being of the people there.

A visit to this Muth will prove rewarding to a sincere devotee, as the grace and blessings of Swami Samarth Akkalkot Maharaj are showered upon those who come here.

4. POONA

(a) Muth near Srinath Talkies, Budhwar Peth

The leather sandals, *Padukas*, of Sri Swami Samarth are enshrined here. HE had graced this place by a visit and blessed it saying that His presence would ever be felt there. Datta *Padukas* are installed under the *Audambar* tree and an idol of Swamiji in marble is enshrined in the *Garba garh* of the Muth. The idol is standing with arms akimbo, and is reputed to give different impressions to devotees at different times. A holy and sublime atmosphere permeates the Muth.

(b) Muth at Sadashiv Peth

This Muth was established by Mr. S. N. Bhat. The beautiful surroundings of the Muth, the majestic life-like pictures of Sri Swami Samarth in the Muth, contribute greatly to the sublime atmosphere of this Muth.

5. MUTHS AT OTHER PLACES

(a) Tathavade, near Poona

A disciple of Balkrishna Maharaj, installed Swami Samarth *Padukas* in this village near Poona.

(b) Maindargi, near Akkalkot

The leather sandals, *Padukas*, given by Swamiji to the Muslim constable, vide Chapter 7, are enshrined here.

(c) Jalna, near Aurangabad

This Muth was established by Sri Balappa Maharaj in 1900.

(d) Baroda

A beautiful marble idol of Sri Akkalkot Maharaj is installed in a temple near Sursagar.

e) Surat

Sri Balkrishna Maharaj established the Swami Samarth Muth in 1911.

f) Vengurla, Ratnagiri District

Sri Anandnath Maharaj was a great disciple of Sri Swami Samarth. He set up this Muth. The *Atma Linga Padukas* presented to him by Swamiji are installed at a Muth in Dhavade. He also set up Muths at Yewala and Hodawade near Sawantwadi.

(g) Devalgram and Rajpur

These Muths were installed before Sri Swami Samarth settled down at Akkalkot and are thus very sacred.

(h) Ahmednagar, (Poona District)

Nana Joshi was presented *Atma Linga Padukas* by Sri Swami Samarth which are installed in the Muth here.

(i) Nakhare, Ratnagiri

The *Padukas* given to Nana Sohoni personally by Sri Swami Samarth, are installed in a Muth here.

(j) Chiplun

Gopal Buva built a Swami Samarth Muth here, vide Chapter 7.

(k) Shivadav, (Ratnagiri)

(l) Other places in India:

Murtijapur, Umred (near Bilaspur), Kej, Bijapur, Thana, Bassein, Dehu, Saval, Vere (Goa), Phaltan, Churchan, Umrale, etc.

It is possible that there are Muths all over Gujarat and Maharashtra apart from some in Karwar, Bengal, Bihar, Orissa, Rajasthan, Madhya Pradesh and Uttar Pradesh as Sri Balappa Maharaj had gone all over India with Swami Samarth Padukas.

(m) Abroad

I. Leicester (U.K.)

The marble Padukas of Sri Swami Samarth were installed by Nana Paranjpe, in the temple run by Abaji Panshikar.

II. New York (U.S.A.)

Here too, Nana has installed the marble Padukas of Sri Swami Samarth for the spiritual well-being of people.

Sri Swami Samarth is present everywhere and protects us and looks after our welfare at all times.

APPENDIX IV

SHAKTI PAAT - TRANSMISSION OP SPIRITUAL POWER

In Indian tradition, the ultimate reality cannot be attained by one's efforts, but only through *Guru Kripa*, the grace of the Guru. Thus, by His mere touch Ramakrishna Paramahamsa transformed the agnostic Narendra to a spiritual master, the glorious Vivekananda.

The following are the principal methods of induction of spiritual power.

1. Sparsha Diksha: Initiation by touch; as a bird sits on eggs to hatch them.

2. Drik Diksha: Initiation by sight. This resembles the action of the fish, which needs only to look at its eggs.

3. Vedh Diksha: Initiation by thought, as a tortoise nourishes its young by thinking of them.

This is also the initiation by "Silence" that Ramanna Maharshi practised.

4. Shabda Diksha: Initiation through speech - *Mantra* or other oral instruction.

Initiation by *Sankalpa* or *sparsha* is quite rare. The commonest method is by *shabda* or *drik diksha*.

Ramanna Maharshi said "Realisation is the result of the Guru's grace more than of teachings, lectures, meditations, etc. These are only secondary, but (Grace) is the primary and essential cause".

If by the grace of the Guru, the Kundalini is aroused, all practices become superfluous. Steadfast devotion to the Guru, faith in one's own self and equilibrium of mind, disciplined and pure life and sincerity of effort - these will lead one onwards.

The recipient of grace, may exhibit some signs, like loss of body consciousness, tremors, ecstasy, horripilation, perspiration, thrilling sensations, etc. The aspirant may have mystic experiences like seeing lights, visions, hearing the *Anahaat Naad* (the "Pranava" - "Om" - the sound not audible to ordinary people), levitation, etc.

Earnest disciples will not fail to find one's master. At the right time the Guru comes even without the disciple seeking Him. A spiritual destiny operates in these matters.

APPENDIX V

SIDDHIS

On steadfast practice of *Astanga* Yoga, certain spiritual powers arise unknowingly in the aspirant or *Sadhaka*. These are called *Siddhis* in Yoga parlance.

These *Siddhis* are to *Yoga* what temperature is to a fever - an accompaniment. As will be seen, immature and foolish people can get seriously obsessed with the *Siddhis* which they acquire willy-nilly and block their progress to Self-Realisation. All great saints and *Avatars* have warned against aspiring for or being enamoured by *Siddhis*. Therein lies the Importance of starting all yogic practice with the traditional eight principles, firmly kept in mind. The first two are the most important.

1) YAMA - comprising of

a) *Satya*; adherence to truth, in thoughts and words.

b) *Ahimsa*; non-violence.

c) *Asteya*; non-stealing e.g. not plagiarising others' (written) work.

d) *Brahmacharya*; literally living with Brahman, i.e. remembrance of God in every action that we do.

e) *Aparigraha*; non-covetousness - controlling desire for property of others.

(2) NIYAMA - comprising of

a) *Soucha*; cleanliness of mind and body.

b) *Santosh*; contentment - always being happy with what God has given.

c) *Tapa*; discipline and sacrifice or austerity. This alone is conducive to control of senses which are the root of almost all problems.

d) *Swadhyaya*; study of scriptures like the *Bhagwad Geeta* or *Upanishads*, accompanied by study of oneself.

e) *Ishwar Pranidhan*; surrender to God.

The extent to which, a *Sadhaka* succeeds in the correct and effective practice of *Yama* and *Niyama*, depends on their spiritual evolution. It may take years. However, the grace of Guru can reduce the period required, to master the first 2 steps of Yoga.

The importance of taking *Yama and Niyama* seriously must be re-emphasised, as even "ripe egos" have fallen back into lower states, due to their lack of self-control in one or more of the above-mentioned areas.

There are 23 *Siddhis* which are classed into 3 grades: great, medium, and small. The small *Siddhis* are 5 in number and they are acquired by one whose heart is purified, *Chitta Shudhi*, by devotion (*Bhakti*) or Yoga. They are:

1. *Trikaala Jnatvam* - The knowledge of past, present and future.

2. *A-Dvandvam* - Beyond dualities of life e.g. cold-heat, pleasure-pain etc.

3. *Para Chitta Adyabhijnataa* - To know the mind of other.

4. *Pratisthambah* - Control of the effect of winds, fire, weapons, poison, water and the sun.

5. *A-Paraajayah* - Victorious; cannot be defeated by anybody.

The medium *Siddhis* are 10 in number and the one with divine qualities gets them. They are:

1. *An-Oormimattvam* - The body cannot be affected by the *Oormis* - The 6 modifications of being, namely, hunger, thirst, grief or sorrow, infatuation or stupefaction, delusion or confusion, old age or death.

2. *Doora-Shravan* - To be able to hear at will, speech from a distant place.

3. *Doora-Darshana* - To be able to see at will, events and things, in all the 3 worlds.

4. *Mano Java* - To travel to any place, bodily, instantly if one desires.

5. *Kaama Roopa* - To assume at once any form one desires.

6. *Parakaaya - Pravesh* - To enter into another's body (dead or alive) leaving one's own body temporarily, e.g. Adi Shankara.

7. *Swachanda - Mrutyu* - To die at a place and time of one's choosing. Death has no control.

8. *Saha - Kridanu - Darshanam* - To see the sports of Gods (in heaven) and have prowess and capacity to participate in them.

9. *Yatha - Sankalpa - Samsiddhi* - To attain whatever is desired.

10. *Ajnaa - Pratihataa - Gatih* - Whereby one's commands and movement have no obstruction.

The great *Siddhis* are 8 in number and are seen only in one who is established in the Self and has no body consciousness, i.e. one who has lost the sense of 'I' and 'mine.' Such great souls will naturally attain them; they cannot be acquired. They are:

1. *Anima* - The power to reduce one's form to the Size of an atom, - assume subtle or invisible states.

2. *Garima* or *Mahima* - To make body heavy or weighty, so that even, 100 people cannot lift it. Also the power to expand or enlarge the body to any size or extent e.g. Hanuman.

3. *Laghima* - The capacity to make the body light as a feather. By the use of *Laghima*, great yogis can levitate even 25 feet above ground!

4. *Prapti* - Power to reach or touch any object however far, whether Jupiter, Uranus or the stars.

5. *Prakamya* - Power to fulfill wishes and materialise objects by mere *Sankalpa.*

6. *Ishitva* - Power to control all earthly objects.

7. *Vasishva* - Power to control all living beings.

8. *Yathaa - Mastada - Vasyati* - This power leads to the state of highest bliss, through ending all desires.

Even a cursory reading of the different types of *Siddhis*, shows us how sometimes even highly spiritually evolved people can "fall" into their trap. The lure of *Siddhis* is a trap and obstruction, as well as distraction, on onward progress. Remember what Sri Swami Samarth said to Vithal Swami about his use of *Siddhis* (See Chapter 7). One should not forget one's destination or swerve from the ultimate goal. The goal of Yoga is beyond mere acquisition of *Siddhis*. The only goal of Yoga is union or absorption in *Brahman*, the merger of the individual soul with the Supreme spirit.

All these *Siddhis* were often seen in Sri Swami Samarth. They were self-manifest *Swayam Bhuva* in Him - they were part of His Divinity. They were His very nature, they were not "acquired".

BIBLIOGRAPHY

1. "Biography of Sri Swami Samarth Akkalkot Maharaj" by N. S. Karandikar, published by P. B. Paranjpe, Bombay, 1977.

2. "Sri Akkalkot Maharaj" by V. K. Phadke. Ramyakatha Prakashan, Poona, 1976 (In Marathi).

3. "Sri Swami Samarth" edited by R. C. Dhere, Anmol Prakashan, Poona, 1975 (In Marathi).

4. "Sri Namdeo Maharaj" (Biography) by Nana Gadre, published by Sri Swami Samarth Vishwa Kalyan Kendra, Apta Road, Panvel (In Marathi).

5. "The Autobiography of a Yogi" by Yogananda Paramahamsa, Jaico 1982.

6. "Ramanna Maharshi" by Arthur Osborne, Jaico 1982, 4th reprint.

7. "Teachings of Sri Ramakrishna". Advaita Ashrama, Calcutta, 1985, 10th reprint.

8. "Sai Baba of Shirdi" by K. V. Kamath and V.B.Kher, Jaico 1991.

9. "Yogic Powers and God Realisation" by V.M.Bhat, Bharatiya Vidya Bhavan, Bombay, 1975, 3rd Reprint.

10. "The Science of Yoga" by I. K. Taimni, The Theosophical Publishing House, 1986, 7th Reprint.

329

11. "Patanjali Yoga Sootras" by Swami Prabhavananda, Sri Ramakrishna Muth, 3rd Ed. 1953.

12. "Sahasra Namavali," Sri Swami Samarth Vishwa Kalyan Kendra, 1985.

13. "A Guide for the Perplexed" by E. F. Schumacher. Jonathan Cape Ltd., 1977.

14. "Sai Baba, the Master" by E. Bharadwaja, Shree Guru Paduka Publications, Ongole, 1993.

15. "Avadhuta Gita of Dattatreya," Translated by Swami Chetananda, Advaita Ashrama, 1988.